rethinking
possible

a memoir
of resilience

REBECCA FAYE SMITH GALLI

SHE WRITES PRESS

Published 2017
Printed in the United States of America
Print ISBN: 978-1-63152-220-8
E-ISBN: 978-1-63152-221-5
Library of Congress Control Number: 2017934839

For information, address:
She Writes Press
1563 Solano Ave #546
Berkeley, CA 94707

Cover design © Julie Metz, Ltd./metzdesign.com
Interior design by Tabitha Lahr

She Writes Press is a division of SparkPoint Studio, LLC.

Portions of this work have previously been published in *The Baltimore Sun, The Towson Times, North County News, AutismAfter16.com, NanaHood.com,* and *The Herald-Dispatch.*

Names and identifying characteristics have been changed to protect the privacy of certain individuals.

To my father, who taught me that no experience is ever wasted unless you let it be. I wrote this book to answer one question: What do I want to teach my children about what life has taught me? And so this book is for my children, Brittany, Matthew, Madison, and Peter. I love you deeply—always and forever.

Contents

What's Planned Is Possible

*All the love we come to know in life springs
from the love we knew as children.*
—Unknown

WE WERE FIVE, until we weren't. Our world was orderly and predictable, until it wasn't. We knew so much about love, laughter, and the joy of being family, until we didn't. I remember one Friday night meal so well. Especially my prayer, the one that still haunts me.

It was summertime and we'd been preparing for weeks. In 1964, I was six years old and I thought I knew everything. I was the rule-follower and vigilant enforcer, "in charge" (or so I thought) of my four-year-old brother, Forest, and my baby sister, Rachel, who was three.

After each trip to the grocery store, we would watch Mom set aside one or two items for the "beach box," a sturdy cardboard box she tucked beside the refrigerator, far out of our reach. Saltines, Peter Pan peanut butter, Mt. Olive dill pickles, and two boxes of Life cereal filled the front, while the special treats, Lance cheese crackers and Little Debbie oatmeal pies, were mostly hidden near the back.

Our plan was to head out before daybreak the next morning for our annual two-week trip to Myrtle Beach. My siblings and I colored as we waited in the den for Dad to get home. It was almost time for dinner, a family staple you could set your watch by. Six o'clock was the usual magic hour when all outside distractions were turned off, put up, or otherwise silenced so we could share an uninterrupted family meal together. We knew no other way to dine.

That night was a special dinner, a "clean out the refrigerator" breakfast-for-dinner meal—eggs, bacon, grits, and gravy. I watched Mom's shadow dart back and forth between the stove, refrigerator, and sink. Then I heard a pop. "Canned biscuits tonight, guys," I whispered. "Don't say anything, Ray." I shot a look at my sister, her blonde pigtails swinging back and forth with each stroke of her crayon as she hummed, "Oh My Darling, Clementine." She stopped coloring and returned my look, a slight smile curling at one side of her mouth.

"She won't." Forest interrupted our standoff and moved in front of our sassy sister to see if he could get those mischievous green eyes to lock onto his soft blue ones. "Will you, Ray?"

"But homemade biscuits are better." She peered beyond Forest to rest her impish eyes on me. "And I don't like canned biscuits." And the battle of the sisters, another family staple began.

"Yes, you do," I said.

"No, I don't."

"Yes, you do, Ray. You eat them all the time."

"No, I *don't!*" She pounded her fist on the coloring book. "Homemade biscuits are better and you know it, Becky," she fired back, far too loudly as she jutted out her chin and crossed her arms, jamming her fists into her armpits, her posture of defiance I knew too well.

"Shh," I hissed. "Mom's going to hear you."

True to our Southern roots, canned biscuits were the exception in our household. But this fight wasn't about biscuits.

"Your mom makes a mean biscuit," Dad said each night when a fresh hot homemade batch was passed around the table. Canned biscuits were a rarity. But if served, we were never supposed to mention it. "Mom works hard to get that dinner on the table. Let's be grateful, not critical," Dad would remind us. Apparently, Rachel hadn't learned that lesson, so of course I had to set her straight. She could hurt Mom's feelings if she complained. Maybe even ruin dinner.

"Everything alright in *there?*" Mom's voice cut through our bickering. It wasn't her "chocolate voice," the one that was anything but sweet—that rich dark growl let us know we were in trouble for sure. This time it was only her warning voice, louder than normal to drown out the iron skillet's sizzle, but still sharp and melodic with the last syllable emphasized for attention-getting effect.

"No unpleasant*ness*," she crooned, her shadow darting faster. "You kids know bet*ter*. Your father will be home *soon*."

"See?" I whispered, jutting out my chin in my own defiant posture. Dad called Rachel "little bit" because she was the youngest and small for her age, but there was nothing little about her ability to stir things up; we could count on her for that.

"Remember, Ray, we are going to the beach tomorrow, the beach!" Forest gave her shoulder a gentle squeeze, and then widened his eyes. "So we should eat what we have. They may not be the best, but they're still good, right?" Ever the peacemaker, Forest had presented his case.

Rachel looked down at her scribbling and studied it. "Well, okay," she sighed, unfolding her arms so she could start coloring again.

Forest smiled at me and I grinned back in approval. "Hey Ray, you smell that bacon?" I said, trying to lighten the mood and unify the troops. We love bacon, don't we?" Forest and I both nodded encouragement to her.

"Yes, we do!" she replied and finally smiled, beginning to hum again.

We'd done it. Forest had helped her focus on the good while I reminded her of what we all loved and could look forward to. Together, we'd ganged up on our sister to get her to behave, a dynamic we would continue—until we were no longer three and we couldn't.

"Dinner!" Mom called, motioning us in as she primped her hair and pulled her bright red lipstick from her apron pocket. "Your father's coming up the back steps." She touched up her lips and quickly blotted them with a tissue, stashing both back into the pocket before running her tongue across her front teeth and checking her smile in a knife blade's reflection. Then she looked at the three of us, searching our faces. "Is everyone hap*py?*"

"Yes, Mom," we said in unison. That's what mattered. Happiness was a premium commodity in our household, right up there with family time, gratitude, and planning. And Mom was the master of happy—she looked it, lived it, believed in it, and faithfully promoted it. But happiness took work. We each had to do our part, whether preparing the dinner table or settling our differences. I shot Rachel another look, trying to raise one eyebrow like Mom did when she meant business. Then Dad burst through the back door into the kitchen and announced, "I'm home!"

"Dad-deeee!" we squealed and jumped on his neck, his Old Spice aftershave lingering despite the end-of-day stubble. His jet-black hair hadn't moved—slicked back into place with that little dab of Brylcreem. He kissed Mom hello while we still clung to his neck.

Old Spice and Brylcreem—the smells of the sixties, of safety, of my larger-than-life father, the anchor of our family. At six foot three, my lanky blue-eyed minister father towered over all of us in both presence and charisma. He had a flair for the dramatic—both at home and at work from the pulpit—well, actually anywhere he went. With little effort, he commanded the room with his booming voice, broad smile, and eyes that seemed to look into your very soul.

"Are we ready for dinn-nahh?" he asked, his deep refined tone playfully mocking the hodgepodge menu—even though it was a family tradition. Any meal can be a special family time with the right attitude, and Dad always knew exactly how to spin it to make it special. We each took our place at the table, immediately holding hands. Thank goodness the biscuits were beside Dad and the bacon was beside Rachel.

"Becky, I believe it's your turn to pray," my father said, nodding and shooting me a quick look, one of his signature pulpit moves he used to direct the service. Mom concurred with her approving smile and matching nod. No one could take a bite before we said amen. It was important to be thankful, even for canned biscuits.

I started my standard, "God is great, God is good . . ." But just before my "amen" and our customary hand squeeze, I took a short breath and added, "And please, God, let nobody die during the next two weeks."

"Becky!" my parents exclaimed, both forgetting the hand squeeze. Rachel's and Forest's eyes popped open, their jaws dropping in shock, so surprised they were that I'd apparently done something wrong.

"Well, isn't that a good prayer?" I asked, raising my voice a little higher and thinner, hoping for an angelic tone. "I just want folks to stay real healthy for the next two weeks. If someone dies, it'll ruin our vacation. Dad will have to come back to do the funeral."

Although I don't recall the exact response, I'm sure I received a lengthy lecture on the purpose of prayer. Even so, I thought I'd hit the right mix: I'd blessed the food and let God know what was on my mind—just in case he forgot. Regardless, I still hated funerals. They messed up my plans.

Funerals were the kind of thing I worried about as a PK—a

nickname for preacher's kid that I didn't like much but accepted. PK's, like doctors' kids, have to deal with being on call, emergencies, and the reality that other people's problems become our own in a split second. Although I grew up in a household of faith, where flexibility was a requirement, I didn't like the three D's—death, divorce, and disease—intruding on our family plans. These life-changing events were just a side effect of my father's job, a routine yet necessary nuisance.

I cringe now at the thought of that foreboding conversation, the selfishness, the shallowness, the way I discounted others' tragedies. But then I remember that I was only six years old. And it *was* a gutsy prayer. At least I was honest.

Later that evening, all five of us gathered for the pre-packing meeting. Dad rattled off each item on the checklist and the kids took turns hollering, "Check!" as mom looked on.

"Great job, guys!" Dad said, kneeling down to give us each a hug. "Faye, I believe your children have their ducks in a row."

"We do, Daddy," I said and turned to my siblings. "What do we say, guys? What does Daddy always say?"

"What's planned is possible!" we said, just as we had rehearsed. And we knew this plan by heart.

We knew next would come packing time, Dad's artful but systematic way of stuffing every nook and cranny of the large trunk of the Ford LTD. "Lay it all out," he would soon instruct so he could size up the load. "Luggage here. Beach chairs and sand toys there. Books over here." And we would litter the driveway with our memories-in-waiting.

We knew the alarm would be set for 5 A.M. the next morning, but that Rachel would already be up by then. We knew she would wake Forest and me—like she did every morning, but this time we wouldn't mind since the earlier we left, the sooner we would get there.

We knew Dad's "study time" would fill every morning while we played on the beach with Mom. We knew around noon we'd meet Dad back at the house for lunch. We knew he'd come down to the beach for twenty minutes about midafternoon. "I don't really like the beach," we knew he'd say when we begged him to stay longer. "It doesn't like me," he'd say since he burned so easily. "But I love it because you love it." Then he'd kiss us each on top of our heads and go back to the house.

We knew Mom would cook every night except for Thursday when we would go to Calabash for seafood. We knew we'd have to come in early from the beach that day to avoid the "gosh-darn beach traffic" and "the cotton-pickin' long lines" outside the restaurants—although that was precisely how we judged the "good ones." We knew we each would have a vote in what restaurant we finally selected, although Dad could be mighty persuasive if one struck his fancy or he had the "inside scoop" from one of his friends. We knew we would be seated in whatever restaurant we picked no later than 5 P.M. After all, that was the plan.

We knew Mom would get the flounder and Dad would get the two-choice combo platter, "shrimp and oysters, please." We knew Forest and I would get just shrimp, no slaw, but with extra hush puppies. And we knew Rachel would get a cheeseburger, plain, no mayo, mustard, or pickles since the juice ruined the taste of the cheese. But before we would even get in line, we would have checked the menu posted in the window to make sure they served cheeseburgers, since, well it *was* a seafood restaurant.

We knew Forest would order iced tea without ice. We knew the confused waitress would say, "Excuse me, sir. Did your son say iced tea with no ice?" We knew Dad would explain that Forest thought that ice diluted the flavor of the tea. Then Dad would joke that Forest must have ancestors from London, "Who else do you know orders iced tea without ice?" Then he'd rub the top of Forest's shoulders and tell him, "That's alright, son, the Brits are a fine lot," and pull him closer to say, "It's okay to march to the beat of a different drummer."

We knew if Rachel were in a precocious mood, she'd complain, "Why does he order tea that way? It takes too long!" Then add, cutting her eyes at me, "That's *stupid*." Then I would tell her that she was the one with the stupid order. Who gets a cheeseburger at a seafood restaurant anyway? (Even though secretly that burger looked pretty good, especially since I really didn't like shrimp; I only ordered it to please Dad—and be like Forest.)

And then Dad would say, "Now girls," with his deep stern voice and I knew that she'd done it again—got me in trouble when she's the one who'd erred. Then Mom would lift one brow and say softly in her public scolding voice that we had been unkind to one an*other*, un-lady*like*, and "plain." And we would get up right then, in the middle of restaurant, to apologize and hug one another as instructed.

But squabble or not, we knew when the order of iceless tea came, Dad would ponder the tea bag and its life of extremes— how we boil it to get it hot, and then ice it to cool it down. How we make it sweet with sugar, and then make it sour with lemon. Forest and I would listen intently—even though we heard the story each time we went out to a restaurant. And Rachel, predictably, would roll her eyes.

But before the food came, we knew Forest would beg at least once, "Dad, tell one of your jokes." Dad had so many we thought he should number them so we would only have to call out the number. But instead, he'd give us a few options and then usually tell them all. We'd all laugh hard and long, but we knew Forest and Mom would laugh until they couldn't breathe and sometimes cry. Most of all, we knew we would have a great time, a highly anticipated expectation we exceeded every summer for fourteen years.

Until we couldn't.

"What's planned is possible," my father taught us at an early age.

"Got to get my ducks in a row," Mom said at least daily as

she showed us how to plan your work and work your plan. Set goals, focus, and achieve them, I learned. Our family, individually so different, was united by lessons and traditions that were meant to last a lifetime.

But sometimes, the best-laid plans simply aren't possible.

Chapter 1

The Accident

We are shaped and fashioned by what we love.
—Johann Wolfgang von Goethe

FOURTEEN YEARS LATER, Sunday September 3, 1978.

The grill was still hot, smoking after the third batch of burgers for our Labor Day celebration. The smell of freshly baked brownies had lured some of us inside. I knew some of the kids, but had been invited by a friend of a friend to an off-campus apartment I'd never visited before. I was twenty years old and had just begun my junior year at the University of North Carolina at Chapel Hill. I was looking forward to that sweet-spot year, comfortable with college expectations without the senior year pressures of figuring out what's next.

The phone rang, interrupting the banter of our casual reunion.

"Hey, Becky," my friend hollered from the back of the kitchen. "It's your dad."

"That's weird," I mumbled as I excused myself from the group, leaving a lone brownie perched on the side of my paper plate. "I wonder how he found me." I was at an obscure off-campus apartment. It was 1978, so there was no call-forwarding, custom greetings, or leaving messages. An uneasy tightness started twisting my stomach before I even said hello.

"Dad?"

"BB," Dad began, using his pet name for me, "There's been an accident," he said and then swallowed hard. "Your brother's been hurt."

"What?" I whispered, sucking in air and information as my knees bent and I slumped to the floor.

"He was waterskiing on Lake Hickory and hit the edge of the pier," Dad continued in a steady tone. "He hit his head . . . we are moving him to Winston-Salem . . . he's unconscious." His voice trailed on with information that I heard but could not process. The words stalled outside my ears, unable to break through the disbelief. Forest. An accident. Waterskiing. Hit his head. Unconscious. Going to another hospital in Winston-Salem, an hour and a half away.

"But he's going to be okay, right Dad? He's going to be okay?" I stammered back to my father. Forest had just come to visit. I just gave him a haircut. I just borrowed his leather-trimmed jeans. We wore the same size.

"He's stable, BB, but this is serious." Stable, but not okay. Coded words. Dad was so solemn. Usually he was optimistic, hopeful. He could find the good in any situation. But this time I could not get one positive word out of my father.

More words and questions pulsed across the wire. We pieced together a plan. I called my boyfriend and he agreed to drive me from Chapel Hill to the hospital in Winston-Salem. Mom, Dad, and Rachel would meet us there. I drove back to my apartment, threw a few clothes in a bag, and waited on the steps for his arrival. I'd never heard Dad's voice so grim, so unwavering, so haunting. I squirmed on the brick step and traced my finger along its edge, letting its rough but firm pattern attempt to stabilize my spinning mind. But it was no use. All I could think about was my precious family.

WE WERE MORE than a family of five—we were five RFS's, we were proud to point out:

Robert Forest Smith Jr. (RF)
Ruby Faye Smith (Faye)
Rebecca Faye Smith (Becky)
Robert Forest Smith, III (Forest)
Rachel Fern Smith (Rachel)

The Smith Family

Dad would kid us that it took him quite a while to find a woman with just the right initials. After two years of marriage and a miscarriage, I was born. Two and a half years later, Forest was born, with Rachel joining us only seventeen months later. At one point, Mom had three kids under the age of four. We had a busy, active household.

As a family, we shared more than our initials. Sit-down breakfasts and six o'clock Southern suppers punctuated our daily routine. Mealtime conversations focused on our schedules, school happenings, current events, and opinion swapping about everything from the latest movies to the current congressional race.

My siblings and I were well-schooled in all aspects of family life, void of the typical gender limitations assumed at that time. Rachel and I knew how to wash a car, mow the lawn, and check the oil in our cars. We could spiral a football, sink a free throw, and hit at least a double on the softball field. I wasn't much of an athlete, but I was still a competitor. In another dinnertime blessing, I prayed for my team to beat Rachel's in basketball.

Again, Dad tried to help me with that "purpose of prayer" conversation.

"BB, you should have prayed for the best team to win."

"But Rachel has the best team," I said matter-of-factly. "And I want to win!"

Forest, a three-sport athlete with exemplary sportsmanship, knew how to fry a pork chop, set the table, and thread a needle. We all knew how to make "hospital corners" with our bed linens, clean a toilet, and jumpstart a car battery.

My father's grandfather, Papa Benfield, was a minister, as was my father's Uncle Knolan. When Dad "felt the call" to the ministry, both men gave Dad the same advice: "Make sure to spend time with your family. The needs of the pastorate can be all-consuming." They were right about that, as my childhood prayer attested.

Dad took their advice. As soon as they were married, my

parents decided that sundown Friday to sundown Saturday would be reserved for the family. Once they had children, Friday night was date night and Saturday was reserved for the family— picnics, sports, cookouts, and special outings with each child. I loved spending time with my family. My parents were bright, funny, and always in motion, learning and teaching. When I turned thirteen, when all my other friends were complaining about their parents, I remember secretly wondering what I was supposed to rebel against.

Our family was close by design.

MY STOMACH STILL churned as I tried to reconcile Dad's strange voice with what lay ahead. I glanced at my watch and decided to go back into my apartment to grab a few packs of Lance cheese crackers and a couple of Cokes, staples I always had on hand. I sat back down on the step, opened a pack, and took a bite. It was an odd but reliable comfort food, helping me get through more than one all-nighter—and a few hangovers. That familiar crunch and nutty taste reminded me of those Saturdays long ago when Dad would take me to the Esso filling station where his buddy, Rex, would fill up our car with the weekly allowance for gas. Dad would buy a pack of Lance and a Coke for me for a quarter. It seemed so extravagant at the time. I would munch on my crackers and sip on my Coke, enjoying the salty sweetness, while I listened to Dad "shoot the breeze" with Rex. Dad would ask him about his service station business, his family, and then tell him a few jokes.

Dad could talk to anyone about anything, it seemed. Whether in the pulpit, at a gas station, or hanging out in my college dorm room, he peppered his conversations with timeless stories as well as knee-slapping jokes. My friends loved him. "Glad you got to see me, girls!" he would boom to my college buddies before he heel-clicked and saluted good-bye, leaving them perplexed. He nicknamed everyone, often to help him remember names, which was so important for a minister. "How are you today, Miss Sarah-with-an-h?" he would ask. "How's it going, June bug?" he'd quip. "Good morning, Pa-trish-aa!" he would announce, as if he were at a horse race and she were the winner. And to really throw them off balance, he'd ask, "How are you prognosticating?" with the face of a straight man waiting for a punch-line response, which again, was usually another puzzled look.

"Your dad is a hoot, the funniest minister I've ever met," my friends would tell me. Occasionally someone would try to cash in on Dad's heavenly "connections," and ask, "Can you help us out with the man upstairs and arrange for some good weather for tomorrow's football game?"

"Sorry," he'd reply without blinking, "I'm in sales, not management."

I thought about that role as I took one last bite of my cracker while my boyfriend pulled up. I threw my bag in the backseat, jumped in the car, buckling up my seat belt.

And then I wished with all my heart that Dad was in management.

❦

MY BOYFRIEND, CARTER, lost himself in his "tunes," as he liked to call them, singing along to "Hotel California." Our bumpy two-year relationship was at a good place, for the moment. Carter was a scholarship athlete, one of the captains for UNC's wrestling team. We'd met our freshman year. When I told him about Forest's accident, he borrowed a friend's car to drive me to the hospital.

I don't remember talking, only thinking. Detailed thoughts.

Distracting thoughts. Untouched by hardship, neither one of us had much to offer one another. At age twenty, how could you possibly know what to say to help? We were in foreign territory, so I let the radio's blare fill in the chasm for the ninety-minute trip to the hospital.

The sharp edge of Dad's voice still rattled me. Then I thought about Mom, his perfect companion. I was sure she was right by his side, as usual. I cut my eyes to glance at Carter. Perfect companion? Not so sure. I wondered if Mom and Dad had any bumps in their college days. Maybe we only heard the storybook version. Mom, Ruby Faye, was the oldest of four, her other siblings similarly named: John Ray, Robert Clay, and Pearl May. Her mother called the girls, Ruby and Pearl, her little "jewels." Mom's father died, leaving his wife with four children ages eight, seven, six, and five. Because of the "financial situation," as Mom used to explain, the children moved to an orphanage in Kinston where Mom stayed until she received a scholarship to attend Wake Forest University—in Winston-Salem. There, she met my father.

I flipped the visor down and adjusted my sunglasses. The glare of the open road hurt my eyes—and my heart. Winston-Salem. Mom and Dad met there. I was supposed to go to school there. And now Forest is in the hospital there. The city that held so many memories, so much promise, now terrified me.

⚘

I LET THE shaded warmth of the sun slip my mind into more reflections about my family. My childhood seemed distant, yet present every day. *What made us so close?* Although love and laughter ruled in our home, expectations were high. We were the first family of the church, with five pastorates that had ranged in size from five hundred to two thousand. I couldn't remember a time when I didn't feel like we lived it a glass bowl. It wasn't uncomfortable—just a fact of life. We were often tutored on what to say, when to say it, and exactly how to say it, from how to answer the phone to what kind of information to give out about our family.

As for discipline, Dad was the tough parent, in charge at all times. He would "give us to the count of three" to "straighten up and fly right," or else. He rarely got to three.

Forest at age three

Mom was less stringent, but focused on kindness and manners. "Pretty is as pretty does," she'd say. "If you can't say something nice, then don't say it at all." In fact, there were limits on the words we were allowed to use. We did not lie. We "told stories." Nothing was ever stolen. It was "misplaced." Mom even had trouble with the word, stink. Things did not stink. They "smelled badly."

Yet they were a team. Saturday nights were a prelude for the Sunday service. Mom painted nails and pin-curled hair. She made sure each child had picked out a complete Sunday outfit— lacy socks and gloves for the girls, a bow tie and vest for Forest.

Even in our teens, we spent Saturday evenings together as a family. All five of us would hang out, playing basketball in the backyard or washing our cars. Dad would grill steaks, while Mom made salad, baked potatoes, and Forest's favorite dessert, a cherry cream-cheese pie with a homemade graham-cracker crust. We often ate in the dining room using the good china and cloth napkins so we could practice our table manners. Then Dad would retire to the study for one final rehearsal of the sermon he would deliver the next day.

Then I remembered it was Sunday. Had they had that meal last night? What if it was—what if? The unknown was scrambling my thinking, jumbling the past and the future with the present that made no sense. Forest had to be okay. Had to be! And I took off my sunglasses and buried my wet eyes into my hands.

⚘

WINSTON-SALEM, TWENTY-five miles, the sign read when I finally looked up. I slipped my sandals off, tucked my feet under me, and shut my eyes to block out the haunting what-if's for just a little longer and focus on Forest, on what I knew. I must stay positive.

Winston-Salem was the home of the Wake Forest Demon Deacons. Hadn't Forest just finished his application for early admission? I knew he was working on the essay. He would be a shoo-in, no question. Student Council President. Youth Council leadership at church. Sports. Mission work. Music. Hadn't he just been elected president of a regional council, too?

Leadership came so naturally for him. Like Dad, others seemed to be drawn to him for guidance. Yet, like Mom, he was a sensitive soul. Patience and understanding permeated all of his relationships. He even managed to puzzle Dad a couple of times, I smiled. That's hard to do.

"Sometimes you got to 'get mean,' son." Dad would say after a loss in a football or basketball game.

And I'd watch Forest listen, but then discount the advice. "You don't have to be mean to win, Dad," I can hear him saying.

In elementary school, Forest was bullied one time and came home to tell the family. Dad thought it was the perfect time to educate him about the "fight or flight" response and encouraged him to stand up for himself and fight.

"But Dad," Forest said, "There is another option. I can make him my friend."

I marveled at my younger brother and his offbeat but on-target insight. He never felt like my "little" brother in that stereotypical annoying way. There was nothing little about him—his thoughts, plans, laughter, or presence. In fact, I don't think I ever called him my little brother, just, my brother. Sandwiched between two sisters, Forest liked his unique role, often signing his notes to Mom or Dad, "Your only begotten son."

He was preparing to do what I had wanted to—attend WFU, like Mom and Dad. Those were my plans, too. Until that letter came.

⤳⧔⤶

I THOUGHT I'D blown it. That final interview was terrible. I'd told the scholarship selection panel about my high school accomplishments, my well-rehearsed future plans, and then skated through all the sensitive political questions about Watergate, the pardon, and the stumbling Gerald Ford, having pored over the latest issues of *Newsweek*, *BusinessWeek*, and *Time*. One stately gentleman whose three-piece suit was garnished with initialed cufflinks and a Carolina-blue striped tie asked me something about the aid programs for the OPEC countries. I had no answer. I remember staring at his gold cufflinks and thinking it was over.

"I don't know," I'd said. Like Forest, I was never very good at BS. One lady looked down at her notes and scribbled furiously. The three-piece suit guy cleared his throat and shifted in his seat. "I'm sorry," was all I could think of to say. "But I have to be honest. I really don't know." And I held the tears until I got back home.

It's not your first choice anyway, I kept telling myself. I'd only applied to UNC because I'd been nominated for a Morehead (now Morehead-Cain) scholarship. We were Demon Deacon fans to the core, especially when pulling against the always nationally ranked UNC Tar Heels during basketball season. Ugh, could I really go *there?* Mom and Dad met at WFU. Dad had served on their board of trustees. We even named our German shepherd "Deacon."

"What's in this envelope could change your life," Dad said, waving it high above his head. And it did. The letter offered a four-year scholarship that included tuition, books, paid internships, and a stipend. It was a lot to consider, especially given Dad's minister salary. I was the first of three who would need college tuition. I accepted. But Dad always enjoyed telling folks, "Yes, she chose UNC, but they had to pay her to go there!"

That was the Dad I knew. Finding just the right spin, even in disappointment. Please, oh please, let Dad be the Dad I knew and find something positive to say.

⁂

CARTER'S VOICE SNAPPED me out of my thoughts. He was singing again, Fleetwood Mac this time. "Don't stop, thinking about tomorrow, don't stop, it'll soon be here, it'll be, better than before, yesterday's gone, yesterday's gone. Don't you look back . . ." But somehow that's all I could do. I kept replaying Dad's words. When I thought about it, he didn't mention Rachel when he called. That was odd. She and Forest usually skied together. They had become close after I left for college. I didn't miss the squabbles and drama, but I envied the way they tag-teamed high school. They worked at the same dry cleaners, had the same friends, and both loved to water-ski.

I wonder if she was with Forest when he hit the pier. Oh my, I wonder if... if... if she saw it! I sat up straight, wide-eyed as a cold shudder froze my spine. I shook my head hard, trying to erase that horrific thought. I couldn't bear it.

⚬§⚬

WE PASSED THE exit for Wake Forest campus as we approached the hospital. Keep thinking of the future, the plans, I reminded myself. Forest would go there, I was sure of it. He'd earned it. Like Dad, he was unafraid to be front and center, and comfortable in the spotlight. Although I teased him about wearing his three-piece Sunday best to run his Student Council meetings, I secretly admired his guts. Even though I could handle the spotlight, I preferred a behind-the-scenes brand of leadership—networking, negotiating, problem-solving to gain consensus. Forest, on the other hand, came alive onstage.

His dreams were huge, far larger than mine. Although we both had plans to pursue a law degree, Forest carried a United States Senate Seal on his key ring, vowing that one day he would be there and give the same seal to his supporters as a senator had given to him. Wake Forest was his next step; Winston-Salem his next stop.

But not like this.

We arrived at the hospital. Carter parked the car while I rushed in to find my family in the intensive care waiting area. Rachel was balled up at the end of a faded green couch, her knees tucked into her chest, her arms crossed, fists up into her armpits. There was no

1978 Forest dressed for student council meeting

defiance this time—she rocked herself softy, with no words. She glanced at me and then returned her stare to the floor.

Mom sat at the other end of the couch, perched on its edge with her shoulders slumped, hands clasped, and head bowed. She looked as if she were in a deep prayer as her lips were moving but no sound was made.

Dad was pacing, his hands shoved deep into his pockets as his wingtips tapped softly on the polished floor. He heard me and spun around to greet me. "BB, honey," was all he said before he hugged me tight. I could feel him swallow hard as he held me. No words from him—again. When he finally released me, I looked up into a face that matched the unknown voice I'd heard on the phone only hours earlier. Mom and Rachel moved awkwardly to join us, lumbering as if they were sleepwalking.

Mom's face was pale, her bright red lipstick now a faint shade of crimson. Rachel barely looked up before we all hugged, but I could tell she was clutching something in one hand. We held each other for a while and then settled around a table in a nearby waiting room.

"What happened?" I said.

"It's my fault," Rachel said, her voice low and robotic. "I should have been there with him. He said just one more round. That Dad said it was okay. He told me he would meet me back at the house and threw me his wallet." She unclutched her hand to release the smooth brown wallet that thudded onto the center of the table. We all stared at it as if it held the key to Forest's life, his next planned moment.

"No, no, honey," Dad said as he got up to hug her. "This is not your fault, not at all. It was an accident, honey. An accident." Forest had called home earlier in the afternoon to ask Dad if he could stay out a bit longer. They had planned to hit some golf balls, but Dad relented, letting his nearly eighteen-year-old son have a little more time in the sun with his friend. Rachel, then sixteen, was with them for a while, but had left before his last run in the cove. Apparently he was waving to some friends on the shore and skied too close to the pier, hitting it with his leg and head. He landed face down in the water.

Forest's friend and some bystanders helped pull him from the water and onto the pier where he tried to stand up and speak, but then collapsed. The rescue squad rushed him to the local hospital where he was first examined, then transferred to North Carolina Baptist Hospital and Wake Forest's Bowman Gray's School of Medicine, some seventy miles away from Hickory.

We sat in the small room, with small talk, and small Styrofoam cups of terrible coffee, each of us praying for Forest to wake up. For Forest to be okay. For Forest to be Forest and come through this. Somewhere in all the hubbub, Carter came in, comforted us as well as he could and then left. He had to return his friend's car and get back to school for practice. Our numbed family of four settled into the rhythm of receiving reports from doctors and saying prayers with ministers and friends. We greeted each with a hopeful smile. But the reports weren't good. Forest was not improving.

Although I wanted to see my brother, at the same time, I didn't. Maybe if I didn't see him, the accident wouldn't be real. I hovered outside his door and finally I slipped into his room, staring at the floor's cream tiles, flecked with shades of gray. I exhaled, dabbed my eyes and then raised them slowly to look at my brother.

He was quietly sleeping it seemed, his long lean body resting comfortably on his hospital bed.

Except for the tubes. And the pumps. And the beeping.

I moved closer, trying to reconcile what I saw and what I knew. Though Forest and I were almost three years apart; we could pass for twins. We shared brown hair, blue eyes, and a matching long-legged build. I touched his brown hair, the exact same shade as mine. I'd just cut it. The trimmings went everywhere. I'd never cut anyone's hair before. "Not too short," he said gently. "You can do it, Beck."

I wanted him to open his eyes, to see my eyes in his. I tried to talk to him. About his hair. About our plans for me to visit him at WFU. "Hey, Buddy, you got to get better here." I took his hand in mine. When we were kids, Dad would take our hands and entwine our fingers, covering our wrists. Then he'd ask Mom or Rachel to pick out which fingers belonged to whom. I loved playing that game. I so wished we were twins. Still, we were more than siblings; we were the best of friends. We confided in one another, debated political issues, and probed deep philosophical questions about the meaning of life. We also could laugh until we cried at a good joke. "Remember, bud. We have more dancing to do. More contests to win."

Was it only eleven months ago that he'd call me to ask if I could make it home for the Sock Hop at school? "I'd like you to be my partner," he said. So I brought back the latest Chapel Hill dance steps and we shagged, hustled, and bopped our way through the night while Wild Cherry's, "Play That Funky Music" and other '70s hits blasted from the speakers. "Pretzel One," he called out, and I grabbed his hand behind his back to begin the twisting shag move. "Pretzel Two," he called again, and I reached behind my back to offer him my hand for the reversal. "Double Pretzel," he whispered for the double-twisting grand-finale move.

"And the first place winners for the 1977 Hickory High Sock Hop dance contest are—Becky and Forest Smith. Come up and get your trophy!" The crowd cheered as Forest kissed my cheek and hugged me, holding my hand as we made our way to the stage.

I rubbed his hand, so warm yet still. "Wake up, Forest, wake up," I whispered to my brother. But the sleep was too deep.

Becky and Forest Summer 1978

Chapter 2

Forest

Her absence is like the sky, spread over everything.
—C. S. Lewis

I KEPT WATCHING Dad, looking for that confident optimism that so permeated his ministry and our family life at home. He was the great fixer of broken spirits, yet he took the time to teach us the small stuff that mattered—how to fix the disposal with a slot-headed screwdriver, stop the bleeding of a razor nick with a spit wad, and in my grade school years, how to perform "surgery" on Peter Rabbit, my favorite stuffed animal.

"He won't play, Daddy. He's broken again," I would say, padding into his bedroom in my footy-pajamas with my bunny in hand.

"No problem, pumpkin," he'd reply. "Did you bring the flashlight? Get the needle from your mother?"

"Yes, Daddy." The six-foot giant would fold himself up on the edge of the bed, repositioning the nightstand's light between us. He'd take my button-eyed Peter Rabbit and gently cut open his side with his marble-handled pocket knife. Then he'd remove the music box and use the knife again to pry open its lid.

"Can you give me some more light there, pumpkin?" I'd shine the flashlight into the inner workings of the music-making device. The metal teeth were stuck, hung up by small threads that had somehow worked their way into the box and twisted around the barrel, preventing the turning motion that created the music. "Let me have the needle now." And one by one, my father removed each thread until it would play again.

"You fixed it Daddy! You fixed my Peter Rabbit!" I'd always squeal, and squeeze his neck hard. Then he'd close the lid on the box, put it back in Peter Rabbit, and sew him back up.

"You're welcome, pumpkin. Now run along to bed. Hug him tight tonight."

"Okay, Daddy. Thank you! You are the best. You can fix anything!"

Well into our early-adult years, life had been a willing participant in our plans. But as the hours stretched into days, and a week had passed, we were faced with an unimaginable decision about my brother.

⚮

"WE'LL NEED A miracle," the chief of neurosurgery told us. "We'll need several miracles to pull Forest through this. He has fifty or sixty bruises all over his brain. Quite frankly, his brain looks like the scan of a person who did not survive. A doctor viewing this scan, and not knowing the situation, would conclude he was looking at the report of an autopsy."

I don't remember what happened next. I know we were sitting together when we received this report. I know there were tears, hugs, and not many words.

Eventually, Dad pulled me to the side. "BB, this is not good, honey. I am so sorry," he said. And then he hugged me, pressing his cheek near my ear. "Daddy's not going to be able to fix this," he whispered. We turned to stare at Forest's open hospital room door as I clasped his draped hand in both of mine. His class ring from Wake Forest felt cold. It was huge, far larger than most. And real gold, fourteen karat with a large onyx stone. He'd chipped the stone once and had it replaced immediately. He always took his rings off to preach. "They get in my way," he said. He used his hands and arms to illustrate his points, his large robed stature always impressive. But with silent Holy Communion, he directed the entire service cueing the deacons with only his eyes, a few nods, and his lower lip that reached up to overlap the upper one. I squeezed his hand and searched his face for guidance of what was to come.

I found none.

He was a man of strength, of pageantry and preparedness. His sermons, the result of twenty hours of study and research, were full manuscripts before they became notes; his pastoral prayers were scripted and timed. Both were rehearsed at least twice before delivery.

Now he had no script. No cues. No rehearsals. No plans.

The machines beeped on.

"How long could this go on?" I asked him.

"I don't know," he said. It was the answer we both kept getting in response to most of our questions. But with the doctor's help, it finally hit us—we were prolonging Forest's death instead of his life. We gave permission to let nature run its course. I don't remember Dad or Mom signing any papers, but I do remember each of us telling Forest good-bye.

He was "too sick to live," Mom said. So he died. On September 12, 1978, my brother died.

THE NEXT DAY Rachel came into my room in our family home and sat on the bed beside me. It was time to get dressed for the visitation to be held at the funeral home. We had just left Mom and Dad's bedroom where we made the family decision not to have the casket open. Forest's head was shaved, they told us, and he didn't look like himself. So instead we would display photos and a portrait. "You won't believe it, Becky," Rachel said, lowering her voice to a whisper. "Right after Forest died, Dad put God in the Black Chair. Yelled at him for ten minutes."

"What? Are you sure?"

"Well, I wasn't there, but one of the youth pastors told me. Dad dropped to his knees and told God off. Even cried."

"Dad yelled at God in front of all those people?"

"Yeah, he said it was 'powerful.' But kind of scary if you ask me." The Black Chair was Dad's creation, a response to a question from the three of us. When I was twelve, Forest ten, and Rachel nine, we decided it was time to address an equity issue that had been brewing for some time. The three of us marched into the bathroom, our chosen private room, and closed the door to craft our game plan. I sat on the toilet's edge while Rachel and Forest perched on the side of the bathtub, facing me. For once, we were all on the same side.

"It's not fair," Rachel whispered.

"Yeah," added Forest, "we never get a turn."

After more discussion we crafted a plan. I would speak on everyone's behalf. We filed silently into our parents' bedroom. Dad sat in his black leather chair while Mom stretched out on the bed; both were reading the newspaper. I wasted no time. With my brother and sister flanking each side, I boldly addressed our father. "Dad," I began, "who do we tell off when we get mad?"

Dad paused and looked at the three of us, studying our faces. "What do you mean?"

"Well, when you and Mom get mad, you tell us off. So, who do we tell off when we get mad?"

"Me . . . your mother . . . both of us."

"No way," I shot back, but then added quickly, "sir." Rachel and Forest nodded appropriately. Gladys Knight may have had the Pips, but I had my brother and sister for backup. "We don't dare tell you off when we get mad. You'd punish us!" The Pips uttered affirmations.

Dad was silent, and then put his hands together, fingertips touching, pressing in and out. He licked his lips, cleared his throat. We braced ourselves. "All right," he began. "Anytime I'm sitting in this black chair, you can tell me off. You can say anything you have on your mind." Mom raised both eyebrows, and then nodded in agreement.

"But you'll get mad and punish us," I reminded him.

Dad paused, considering the point. He leaned forward, elbows on knees, his blue eyes steady and focused. "Tell you what I'm going to do, kids. I can't promise I will not get mad, but I do promise I won't hold anything you say against you. I will not punish you for what you say."

We were stunned—wide-eyed and openmouthed. But I rallied quickly. "When can we get started?"

"Now," Dad said. And we were off. We let them have it for almost an hour. We recalled every injustice we could remember, naming date and time, chapter and verse. It was great! We could tell them anything and we didn't get punished. In the years to come, the Black Chair became the code name for a safe place to talk. The kitchen table chair was the Black Chair when one of us shared about our first beer. The living room lounger became the Black Chair when another shared the confession of a sleepover at a friend's house—that wasn't. And the back-porch rocker became the Black Chair when a heart-broken sixteen-year-old wondered aloud if she would ever be asked out on that first date.

And now I'd learned that Dad had used it—on God!

"What did Dad say?" I asked Rachel.

"He said stuff like how senseless Forest's death was, how wasted his life. Asked how God could let this happen. Doubted his power to do anything about it. Said he'd already given his life's work to God so why did he have to take his son," she paused, her own tears beginning to well. "It was a big deal, Becky. I hope Dad is alright."

"Yeah, me too." We sat there for a minute. "Did you know Forest read his Bible every night?" I asked her.

"Yeah. I think he would ask Dad to read it if he was too tired."

"Yes, he told me that, too. Do you, Ray? Do you read your Bible every night?"

"Nope," she said. "Do you?"

"Nope. And I don't think I'll start anytime soon."

God hadn't answered our prayers. He wasn't listening to me or my pastor father. Why bother talking to him?

⚬⧜⚬

THEY CLOSED THE high school the day of Forest's funeral. The church overflowed with thirteen hundred people and that deep abiding sadness of untimely death. I wanted to wear black that day, but I had no black dress. My college roommate, Joy, let me borrow hers. I was in a life that wasn't my own. Didn't even have the wardrobe for it.

Before we entered the sanctuary, a physician friend offered Mom medication. "These will keep you from crying, Faye," he softly told her.

She looked at him tenderly, eyes brimming. "But I want tears," she said simply, and gave him a hug. For twenty years, I had watched Mom take great pride in her role as the pastor's wife, the master of happy, the instructor and enforcer of appropriate behavior. And now I watched her want the tears. So public she was with her private pain. I studied her. So raw. So open. So different.

And then my own pain sucked me back into myself and I focused on the deep-red nubby carpet under my moving feet that was leading me into the pew. I felt a strange gratitude for the carpet, for its unwavering path that led to a pew, to a reserved place, and to a finite period of time that was orchestrated and oddly safe. I was so weary of the unknown.

⤙⥾⤚

THE PEWS WERE packed. Family and friends jammed in tight as we huddled for strength and comfort at the 2 P.M. service. As preacher's kids, we were used to crowded pews. Forest, Rachel, and I would routinely sit with Mom and our friends during Sunday worship. Not that we were angels all the time. In our younger days, we would often use our watches' second hand to time Dad's pastoral prayers. Or count the number of "a's," "an's" and "the's" as he spoke. Or practice sign language.

Dad was always in the pulpit, in front of the four of us. But that day, Dad was not in front of us. He was beside us. Forest was in front of us. And we sat there, the four of us—the *wrong* four of us, bewildered and misplaced. Who was this man in the pew beside me? Away from the spotlight. In a suit, not a robe. Seated. Speechless. Maybe he was broken. Maybe he had said too much to God.

Although Dad designed the funeral service, it was delivered by four other ministers. My father bowed his head with rounded shoulders while Randall Lolley, his former seminary classmate and a longtime family friend, read part of Forest's admission essay for Wake Forest, completed the day before his accident. "The last sentence of Forest's essay looms largest," Dr. Lolley said. "After describing himself, his life, his dreams, his hopes for the future, and his close and appreciated relationship with his family, he wrote, 'I would change nothing.' These were his last written words."

I would change nothing.

Dad slumped a little more. Mom sat erect, looking straight at Dr. Lolley as the tears ran freely down the sides of her cheeks, her unused tissues resting on her lap. Rachel folded her arms tighter across her stomach and bent forward, like she was going to be sick.

I, too, bowed my head—but not in reverence. I focused on the wet wad of tissue in my hands, my cheeks burning with confused rage as Dr. Lolley droned on. The simple words delivered a sharp twisted message of comfort in knowing that Forest was content with his life, yet a raw fury because I would have changed so many things about the day we lost him. What if he had come home on time? What if he had not made that last round of skiing? What if he had missed the pier?

I would change nothing.

What were you doing? Where were you looking? Why didn't you pay attention? I am angry at you—for being careless, for being thoughtless, and yes, for leaving me here to miss you for the rest of my life! How dare you die on me! I crammed tissues into the tears that weren't what they seemed. I was supposed to be sad and yet I was hurt and angry—and then ashamed for feeling that way.

What is wrong with me? What is wrong with all of us? Dad sat in the pew, speechless. Mom's face was streaked with unchecked tears—her guarded private self blatantly visible for all to see. Rachel had balled herself up so tightly that I could barely see her, like she was trying to disappear into the pew. This, from the flamboyant one who made molecules dance, rooms brighten, and knew exactly what button to push to get attention. And Forest. My precious brother. My "twin." My inspiration.

I would change nothing.

This from *that* kid, the one with all the supersized dreams. And plans. And God-given talents to deliver. How could that possibly be the last thing he wrote? Who are we now? Where is my family? What is happening to us?

For a family who knew so much—whose faith was so deep, love so abiding, and minds filled with mottos designed to keep us focused on the possibilities that were surely ahead—we knew nothing that could have prepared us for that kind of loss.

Chapter 3

A Family Shattered

The journey through grief is as unique as our fingerprints.
—Rebecca Faye Smith Galli

WE WERE SHATTERED. Forest's death tore our family apart. Gone were the playful lessons and humor of those self-serving prayers in our dinnertime routine. The gaping hole in our tightly woven fivesome was too large for us to mend for each other. So we splintered, each taking a different path to heal.

I almost dropped out of UNC. My mind was a sieve, so riddled it was with pain. I'd read a textbook passage and it would evaporate. I went to class but my notes made no sense. I spoke to my professors, but for the life of me I couldn't recall a word they said once I set foot outside their doors. My brain felt like it went dark. Dormant. Hibernating. No matter what I tried, I couldn't get it to wake up and perform. A thick fog of inertia began to settle in. I lost my initiative, my drive, my competitive nature—I simply did not care.

Then the doubts started. Why bother with it all anyway

when it could be taken away in an instant? Why plan? Why set goals? Why dream? I felt so different, so changed, so disconnected from the gal I used to be.

But my college buddies would not leave me. They'd met Forest and Rachel, and adored my parents. We'd been through two years of college together so they knew the Becky I'd been. I guess in their own way, they reminded me of who I was. We didn't talk about it much, but they must have instinctively known I needed them. Even though I shared an apartment with only one roommate, Joy, the three girls next door, Sharon, Cynthia, and Donna, popped in nonstop. We carpooled to campus. Shopped. Cooked. Ate most of our meals together. And then one night they got me back on the dance floor, something I was sure I'd never do again. I may have even smiled that night as I let the music wake up a part of me that I was sure had died along with Forest.

Only a few days before Forest's accident, I'd pledged a sorority, Phi Mu. It was unusual to pledge as a junior, but something I wanted to do to add another dimension to college life. My first meal with my "sisters" was the day after the funeral. I was uneasy, but somehow comforted by these young women, so kind and accepting. With events planned through Christmas, these new friends brought a fresh energy, a forward momentum I didn't even know I needed.

I was never alone. Because of these friends, old and new, I decided to stay in school. Their friendship and the structured campus life moved me through grief in a way I could have never done alone.

⚶

RACHEL'S PATH WAS far different than mine. I almost lost her, too. "Hey Ray!" I spouted, using the most upbeat voice I could muster. "I've been looking for you, girl!" I'd finally found her at a best friend's home. I was heading into finals, three months after Forest's death. "I tried to reach you at least five times at the house," I exaggerated, "but you were never there. You okay, kiddo?"

"Yeah, I guess."

"Are you living with the Snipes now?" I half-teased her.

"Not yet, but I might next year," she said, pausing and then mumbled on. "Mom's not home much. She joined a couple of support groups for parents who've lost kids and now she's leading one of them."

"Really?" I didn't say anything, but it surprised me. That's the last thing that would have comforted me, listening to others talk about kids dying too young. I was sad enough. Besides, I thought Mom would have been home more, grieving in private. But what did I know? Everyone was so different now.

"Yeah. Dad is busy settling in Huntington. Mom and I are supposed to go see him every other weekend." Her voice trailed off. "I like seeing Dad, but I hate being away from my friends."

That I understood.

Only weeks after Forest's death, Dad was asked to consider a new pastorate in Huntington, West Virginia, five hours away from Hickory. Our family was accustomed to moving, part of the PK package, much like the Army-brat life. We'd moved four times in nineteen years in North Carolina, each move strengthening our family bond as we faced the adjustments together.

But not this time. There was no family packing. No family move. No family of five moving through the transition together. We were only four now. And we were anything but unified. Grief wasn't the only thing tearing us apart.

After an intense interview process that included a "trial sermon" in a "neutral pulpit," a Baptist tradition that provides the search committee a chance to hear and see the candidate in a church besides their own, Dad was offered the senior minister position. Mom, Rachel, and I attended the trial sermon and liked the search committee representative, Mike Queen, and his description of the church and community. After more discussion within our small family, a few prayers, and some creative planning, Dad accepted. He would move to an apartment in Huntington for six months while Mom stayed with Rachel in Hickory so she could finish her junior year of high school. I would remain in Chapel Hill, three hours away from Mom and Rachel, six hours away from Dad.

Our family time and conversations, already limited by the landlines of the '70s, were suddenly stretched even more with geography.

"Dad calls every day at least twice. They talk," Rachel said. "Mom cries a lot. She tries to hide it from me." She stopped, and then blurted out, "I'd rather hang out with my friends."

"I hear you, Ray."

"But it's hard for them to come to the house—too many memories around. So we come here, to the Snipes, where they're more comfortable."

"Oh, okay. That makes sense. How are you holding up?"

"Not good." Her voice thickened. "I miss Forest so," she whispered. "And it's all my fault, Becky. I shouldn't have left the boat. I could have warned him. I should have been there. It would have never happened. It's my fault!" she sobbed, her words sliding into one another.

"No, Ray! We've talked about this. You couldn't have stopped it. Forest wasn't paying attention. It was an accident." I tried comforting her as best I could, but I was struggling, too.

"I want to be with him."

"No, Ray! Don't think like that. Please, don't think like that. Don't say that ever again!"

But she did. And she said it often enough to alarm Mom and Dad, who decided to get her professional help. I, apparently, was adjusting just fine. Attention was flying around everywhere, except in my direction, or at least that's how it felt. I was grateful for my girlfriends.

⁓⧰⁓

FOUR MONTHS AFTER Forest's funeral, January 14, 1979, Dad preached his first sermon in Huntington. Snow prevented Mom and Rachel from traveling to Huntington. I was at UNC beginning my second semester. Once more, Dad was in the pulpit, sharing his message. But this time there was no family to be found.

Dad mailed me a cassette tape of his sermon. I pressed play on my Sony Walkman and snuggled down into my bed covers one Sunday morning to listen. "Why stand I here?" he thundered to the congregation. "Because it feels right, yes, it feels right. Even with the obvious strains and drawbacks I'm going to be under, it still feels right." He paused and I could hear the drama build in the silence. "With me in Huntington and my daughters and wife in North Carolina and our only son in heaven, it still feels right."

I winced and paused the recording, his words opening up fresh pain. We were so scattered, so different, so not who we used to be. I couldn't bear to hear it. I took the headphones off and gently wrapped its cord around the player, tucking my father's words and message into my nightstand drawer.

Dad. How did he do it? That "feeling right" must have sustained him, even energized him. He jumped into the new congregational life, preaching, teaching, and dining out often three times a day to meet his new parishioners. Then, shockingly, he accepted a new role as the chaplain of the football team at Marshall University, whose program was still rebuilding after the horrific airplane crash of 1970 that killed all seventy-five people on board.

"I was honored to be asked," Dad told me. But it was so unlike him. Not only did he make this decision with little if any family discussion, he violated his own "rules." The games were on Saturday, a day he'd always dedicated to relaxation, family, sermon rehearsals, and in the last two years, weekly phone chats with me at college. Now he even traveled with the team some weekends, against what I thought was his hard-and-fast rule about no out-of-town Saturday weddings, since those "wore him out," leaving him less prepared for the rigors of his Sunday schedule. Plus, he regularly found time to meet with the players and coaching staff during the week. His supply of energy and availability seemed endless for others.

True to form, he coined a term for it, "reinvesting your love," one of his strategies for getting through grief that he talked about, preached about, and later included in his book about Forest's death. But, as his daughter still in deep grief, I didn't see it that way at all. In fact, his reinvestment deepened my loss. His laser focus on others distanced us even more. Gone were the frequent phone calls and playful betting on football games. Who cared if Wake Forest was playing UNC when he was on the sidelines of the Thundering Herd? He seemed distracted, almost obsessed with his new role and his new "sons" he'd discovered on the football field.

Despite the distance and changes, we stayed connected. Dad sent me the weekly bulletin that included his "Pastor's Perspective," a food-for-thought column that kept me current on his latest ponderings—when I read them. Once a month, he made sure I received cassette tapes of his sermons. And after moving our weekly phone calls to Sunday afternoon, we began to chat regularly again.

Sometimes the conversations were still awkward. He'd tell me about his "motivational talks," the pregame stories he shared with the football team. "BB, I told them the one about how we are all small pebbles who have the potential for making big ripples. I gave them each a small pebble and the quarterback put it in his uniform pocket! Plays with it in his pocket every game," he boomed. "My stories seem to get them fired up, BB," he'd say after each story.

And I'd want to remind him that I could use some of that "firing up" myself. And that not all ripples, especially those of his beloved team, are positive. Some ripples push others away.

But I didn't say anything. I was just a college kid with a busted family trying to keep moving forward despite all the changes. I didn't need to pick any fights; we were fragile enough. So I kept quiet and turned to my college friends and studied hard, but began to party harder.

⁓⅄⅄⤳

AFTER RACHEL FINISHED her junior year of high school, Mom moved to Huntington in the summer of 1979 where she and Dad bought a new home. They let Rachel stay in Hickory and live with the Snipe family since she desperately wanted to finish her senior year with her friends. I moved to DC for a summer internship program provided by the Morehead scholarship.

In Huntington, Mom busied herself with redecorating, entertaining, and the demands of being the new pastor's wife. During the summer, she faithfully wrote me each week, including a stick of gum, Juicy Fruit, our favorite, and at least two stamps to encourage me to write home. But when football season rolled around, she was swept up with Dad's enthusiasm, becoming a pom-pom waving fixture in the stands. And now she had another new title—the chaplain's wife.

Huntington this. Football team that. Rachel here. Mom and Dad there. In their new life together, Wake Forest's gold and black were overlaid with the Thundering Herd's green and white. Meanwhile, I dug my Carolina blue roots in deep at Chapel Hill that fall, only coming home for Thanksgiving and Christmas.

Our shattered family mended, separately, submerged in whatever world we could find to ease our pain. Dad continued his healing in a public way, preaching and writing on the lessons his grief was teaching him at the moment. He started a monthly column, "Looking Homeward," in a Hickory newspaper to keep him connected to that community. Within months, he became a noted lecturer on grief. "There is life for you after their death," he would tell parents who had lost children. "At first, you're not sure you will ever live again. You are certain you will never laugh again. But you will. You will always walk with a limp, but you will walk again."

You will always walk with a limp. What a perfect way to describe this pain! So public. So permanent. I wished I could find a way to express my pain. It seemed so easy for Dad. Was it his training? His education? His calling? His gift? I could barely say Forest's name without a meltdown of tears and a lasting funk. It wasn't worth speaking about it, so I tucked it down deep in my heart and let silence ice away the pain, or so I thought.

Yet Dad's words were not only revealing and accurate, they were helpful. People flocked to him for guidance and support. "You're not supposed to bury your children," he said in another sermon. "There is a word for those who lose their spouse—a widow or widower. There's a word for those who lose their parents—orphan. But there is no word for those who lose their children."

And, I wanted to add, there is also no word for those who lose a sibling.

As I watched my parents move through their grief, I wanted to ask them one simple, but never-spoken question: *What about me?* I did not die. I am still here. I am your child, too.

What about me? Can I not still bring you joy? Forest is gone, but I am still here.

What about me? I need you, but you are elsewhere, tending to your own pain, reinvesting your love. I have pain, too. Remember?

I knew I'd lost my brother, but had I lost my parents, too?

"Table of four?" a waitress would ask when we dined out during one of my rare visits home. And each of our taut facades would melt a little and we would shoot each other that knowing look. *Were we really only four now?*

Our close-knit family of five had been reduced to an awkward and foreign configuration of four. The numbers did not lie. Yet, for me, five was more than a number. It was a feeling—a comfortable feeling of effortless belonging. Bound by traditions and rituals and stories and laughter, we were solid. We each had our place.

Until we lost Forest. Our bond was forever broken. And I wondered, would I ever find that special family feeling again? Was it possible?

Chapter 4

A Marriage of Winners

To accomplish great things, we must not only act,
but also dream; not only plan, but also believe.
—Anatole France

MARCH 1980

THE PHONE WAS on its third ring. I dove across my double bed, snagged the princess handset off my nightstand, and lifted the cradle. "Hello?"

"Hey, Beck, it's Joe."

"Joe? You're back? Already?" I propped up on my elbows and pressed the phone into my ear. The line crackled and I strained to hear him.

"No, I'm still out here. We won't be back for a couple more days."

"Wait, you're calling me from Oregon?"

"Yeah, I wanted to check in with you about the project. I know it's due before I get back."

"Oh, wow. Well, how did it go? Did you win?"

"No. I'm out. Lost two matches. I'm done."

"I'm sorry." The line went silent. I'd watched Joe wrestle for four years, but I still didn't know what to say when he lost. Or when any of the wrestlers lost, even though I'd been hanging out with them since my freshman year. And now, as a senior, there would be no next time for Joe. I let the moment hang a little more then tried, "So, are you okay?"

"Yeah, I'm fine. Ready to move on." He paused to clear his throat, and then picked up the pace. "So how's the project?"

I updated him on the meeting he'd missed. I was team leader for our group in one of the business classes we were taking together, Organizational Behavior. I led the meetings, decided how to present our work to the class, and also had the awkward task of giving each team member participation points that counted as part of our grade.

"So, how's it going on campus?" he asked once we finished discussing the classwork.

"Crazy. It's the most beautiful day we've had all spring, and of course the season is over so all your buddy wrestlers who didn't qualify for nationals are partying their butts off with the lacrosse players. I know you've only been gone a week, but it's wild here. Your old roommate is giving me gray hair again. One day we're dating, the next day we're not. I think there's another cheerleader in the picture. I wish they'd stick to football players," I joked.

Joe laughed. "We'll catch up when I get back."

"Sure. Thanks for checking in," I let the smile show in my voice. "I see a high participation mark in your future," I teased him.

"Thanks, Beck. Take care. See you soon."

I hung up the phone and held it in both hands for a minute. Joe was a great listener. And he'd had a lot to listen to lately. I met him my freshman year and now we were heading into the home stretch of our senior year. Relationships were exploding, including mine with Carter. I sat up in bed to look out the window when I heard the apartment door open.

"Hey B, it's me," a voice called from the kitchen.

"Come on back, Bing." Sharon lived next door, part of the popping-in threesome who'd help me survive those torturous first twelve months of "firsts," after Forest's death. I'd shortened her last name, Bingham, to "Bing," and it stuck. She came back to my bedroom, plopped down on the bed beside me, and looked at the phone in my lap. "Who was that?"

"Joe. He's in Oregon. The NCAA's [the National Collegiate Athletic Association] are out there and he just finished."

"Wait, he called you from Oregon? Whoa, is something going on here, B?" She smiled.

"Oh, no," I said quickly, but letting the thought sink in. "He called about this project for class. I think he just wanted to make sure to get all ten participation points."

"Right. So he says." She smiled again. "How did he do out there?"

"He lost. I think that's the end of his wrestling career," I said. "He sounded sad, but still strong. He wants to get together when he gets back."

"Uh-huh. I hear you," she said, giving me a sly smile. "You know he thinks you hung the moon, don't you?"

"What? No way."

"I heard him talking to his parents after the last wrestling match about you, bragging about your Morehead, how smart you are, how great your family is."

"Really? He did?"

Joe was from New Kensington, a small blue-collar town just outside of Pittsburgh where he grew up next door to his father's junkyard. He spoke with pride about his parents, both first-generation Italian immigrants. His father dropped out of school in eighth grade when his own father was killed in a coal-mining accident. He started a junkyard business and worked six days a week, sometimes seven. In grade school, Joe's friends learned quickly not to play "junkyard" with him or else their matchbox cars would be smashed and stacked like the multicolored layers of crushed cars lining his father's auto-wrecker yard. Joe's mom was a pistol, with nonstop high energy just like Joe. She had him try swimming and gymnastics, but discovered wrestling was more suited to her son's small but wiry frame. She drove him to wrestling tournaments all over the country so he could improve his skills.

"He's a catch, B. Not dating anyone now either. And he's going places, you know," Bing pointed out, her eyes wistful as she glanced out my opened window. She'd heard all about my on-again/off-again romance and probably knew more than I did about cheerleaders and other intruders in that fragile relationship.

Joe was whip smart, everyone knew it. He could ace a test after only reading the textbook. And he had this natural business savvy, was a quick study of the complex world of coins, his favorite hobby, and had an incredible knowledge of stocks, bonds, and investment strategies that impressed all of us.

And, he wrestled.

"Well he's certainly changed in the last few years. Remember how small he was when we first met him? Did you know he grew four inches his freshman year?" I babbled on, mostly to myself. "I can't believe he wrestled at ninety-nine pounds as a high school senior. And now wrestles at 142. I think he went up five weight classes in four years and still started every year. He said Coach was not happy about that since he was recruited as a 118 pounder. But Coach was plenty happy he won the ACC's [the Atlantic Coast Conference] and earned a spot to go to NCAA's!"

Sharon laughed at my gushing and opened her pretty brown eyes a little wider. "Sounds like we may have a mutual admiration society here, B."

"Oh, really? I'm not so sure about that, Bing. But I must admit, his work ethic is impressive. He's so driven and focused. But, he's just a good friend. Fun to hang out with and a good study partner. That's all."

"Okay, so enough about that. What's on for tonight? It's Thursday so that's happy hour. Is it a date night or girls' night?"

"Girls' night! I think the friggin' cheerleaders are after my man, again, Bing. This on-and-off crap is getting old."

⁓⚭⁓

MOST OF THE wrestlers I'd gotten to know at UNC were from out of state, "damn-Yankees" my father called them, noting it wasn't derogatory if used as one long word. The guys seemed to be charmed by us "Southern belles," as they liked to tease us. After a few matches and late nights at our favorite disco, Mayo's, I started dating one, Carter. Joe was his roommate and teammate.

Joe and I became great friends, often leaning on each other for relationship advice, especially during the bumpy patches. He met Forest a few times during his UNC visits and was around my brother long enough to nickname him "Forest-fire." Joe admired Forest's passion for leadership. "That kid's a ball of fire." After Forest's death, Joe and I grew closer. He, too, had lost a brother, who died only three days after birth.

Joe UNC 1980

After his return from the NCAA's, Joe and I helped each other with résumé and interview preparation. We were both ready to move on from the craziness of college life and determined to find good jobs. Late one Friday afternoon before our final spring break, he called from the campus career service office.

"Hey Beck, guess what? Someone scratched off their name from the IBM interview schedule. Want me to write you in?"

"Yes!" I practically shrieked. It was my dream company at my dream location—Charlotte, North Carolina. I'd been so disappointed to miss that interview posting, but had back-to-back classes. I even asked if I could put my name on the waiting list but was told it was pointless since no one ever canceled from IBM's schedule. I couldn't believe Joe happened to be in the placement office and took the time to check that list for me. After that interview and two more, IBM offered me an entry-level position as a junior recruiter. I accepted and became part of a large hiring team responsible for staffing the new plant/lab facility.

I was over the moon with excitement. Beyond their leadership in technology, IBM was known for their full employment policies—no layoffs, ever, a recruiter's dream. They hired from campus, and promoted and developed their people from within. The training and education offerings were considered graduate-school caliber; the two-year sales training program, an MBA equivalent. And their management development programs at the time were peerless. Charlotte, slated to manufacture the circuit board used in the soon-to-be announced IBM PC, was about two hours from the Blue Ridge Mountains, and two hours from the Carolina beaches. As a recruiter, I would be selling both IBM and Charlotte—what a piece of cake! And, my starting salary was unbelievable—even higher than Joe's. They even paid for my moving expenses.

Joe, too, was hired from a campus interview. The Black and Decker Corporation offered him a sales position—in Charlotte. Again, we couldn't believe the coincidence. We scoped out the

new town, shopped for apartments, and rented two-bedroom
units next door to one another.

I would have a roommate; he would have an office, vaulted
ceiling, and fireplace, we decided. Bing moved in with me and
began to look for a job while Joe and I attacked our jobs that
summer of 1980, often working sixteen-hour days.

❧

"BING, I'M HEADING over to Joe's tonight," I called out to
her from my bedroom.

"Again?"

"He's working late and I need to, too. I hate to keep you up."

"Right, B," she said, giving me her sly smile. "Have fun!"

"Does this look like fun, Bing?" I showed her my over-
stuffed briefcase and box of applicant files that I would soon
lug all of fifteen feet to Joe's front door. Our summer work pace
spilled into September. I worked in Joe's apartment often past
midnight, reading my job applicant files while he prepared for
his sales calls. Coffee and a crackling fire kept us going through
the chill of fall.

"What's that?" I asked one night as he opened a new jar of
multicolored pushpins.

"For my plans. Come see." He led me into his office. Tacked
on one wall was a gigantic map of North Carolina. "I'm plotting
my routes. Each pin color denotes an account size."

Planning. I loved it! Most reps made four to five calls per
day. Joe made ten to twelve, a tribute to his careful mapping and
a precision sales pitch. His boss called him "Smokin' Joe" for
his ambitious sales routes and rapid-fire presentations. Within
weeks, he topped the sales charts, building the fastest-growing
sales territory in the United States.

Meanwhile, IBM was inundated with applications—programmers, engineers, technicians, as well as administrative staff and a college co-op program. Sometimes I would read several hundred per day. I was often in the office before 6 A.M. and sometimes didn't leave until after 7 P.M., toting a stack of work with me.

"What are you doing in there?" Bing asked one Sunday night when I was digging around in my closet. I'd already laid out my clothes for the next day on my dresser—suit, blouse, shoes, and handbag with a matching necklace, earrings, and a bangle bracelet.

"Trying to save some more time," I said, pulling my sleeping bag out from under my sweaters. "I want to make my bed, like my mama taught me," I laughed, "but I don't have the time." I unrolled my sleeping bag and laid it on top of the bed. "This will help."

"You are going to sleep in your sleeping bag?"

"Yep. I'll hop in, sleep, wake up, scoot out of the bag, roll it into a neat ball, and stuff it into my closet. Tada! My perfectly made bed will be ready to bid me good morning as well as welcome me home."

"You know you're nuts, B, right?"

"Yeah, I know, I know. But I do have a favor to ask of you."

"What's that?"

"This layered look is taking way too long to do every morning. Can you French braid my hair so I don't have to blow it dry tomorrow?"

"Sure, B." she said. "Grab your hairbrush and we'll do it now." She started the plait at my right temple. "You know, I'm actually glad you are hanging out with Joe so much. He's the only one who can get you to take a break."

"Hmm. I guess you're right," I said, and looked at our reflection in the bathroom mirror. "I guess I haven't been a very good roommate, have I? We're just so busy, hiring nonstop."

"Oh, I know. Don't worry about me. I'm fine. I'm just worried about you. You are working so much. You need the breaks."

My "breaks" with Joe consisted of tennis, an occasional movie, or a fierce game of racquetball where he'd spot me ten points to keep it competitive—for both of us. By Christmas, we'd begun to date.

"I knew it!" Bing said when I told her I thought Joe and I could be more than friends. "Did I call that or what, B?" she teased me. "You guys are great for each other."

⁓≬⁓

WITH FOUR YEARS of college history, our relationship developed quickly. When Joe was promoted to a position in Atlanta after only thirteen months, he asked me to marry him. "We were friends for four years first," I told new friends. "We knew so much about each other before we even started dating."

We had the same dreams. He came from a family of four that had once been five. So did I. He was a hard-charging first-born out to prove himself to anyone watching. So was I. We both had a fighting spirit, unafraid to challenge limits and a steadfast persistence that fueled a deep-seeded need to excel.

My father used to joke about his own demanding nature when people would remind him that Rome wasn't built in a day. "But I wasn't the superintendent on that job," he'd quip. Joe and I laughed at the comment. But, as they say, we resembled that remark.

Our roots were deep; our vision for the future strong. We talked about and admired the Kennedy clan, not so much for their politics as for their loyalty to one another and the way they instilled in the children a sense that they could achieve any-thing—as his parents had done for him and my parents had done for me—at least in the early years.

We were raised to be winners. And I was determined to create the loving family I knew as a child—before we lost For-est. We were two Type A's ready to join forces to see what we could accomplish. Together. Forever. That was the plan, anyway. Surely it was possible.

Joe asked Dad for his blessing prior to popping the question to me. Although he had a hard time sitting still through an entire sermon—"I'm just not much of a spectator, Beck"—Joe admired my father's dramatic style and his commanding presence as well as his love of history and illustrative stories. He also paid close attention to Dad's tremendous preparation, especially the number of rehearsals.

Dad liked Joe and saw what I loved about him—his spirit, his drive, and the way we connected. "He's one smart cookie, BB. You'll need that, sweetie. And he seems to really respect you, both who you are and your potential." Mom agreed. They both were excited about our marriage and our future plans.

However, when I told them our proposed wedding date, Dad questioned the timing. "BB, we have a home football game that weekend."

I'm not sure how I replied, or if I was too taken aback to reply at all. Did being around those football players, that "reinvestment of his love" really trump my wedding? The words stung, even though he eventually agreed to the date.

So on November 7, 1981, Dad presided over our wedding ceremony. "Yes-sir-ee, I walked her down the aisle and then turned around and married her," Dad quipped when asked how he managed both roles as my father and my minister.

As for his team chaplain role, he was presented with the winning game ball, inscribed with my wedding date—and the game score. Oh great, I remember thinking when he gave it to me—as if it were some kind of trophy. Just what I need. A lasting reminder of a conversation I wanted to forget.

So much had changed. Graduation. A career. And now I was married. It was hard to believe that in three short years, Forest had missed so much.

JOE AND I returned from our honeymoon to a new apartment in Atlanta where he promptly left the next day for a ten-day business trip, spreading his magic to those who now worked for him.

I was home alone with the boxes. I knew no one.

Although I was grateful that IBM had transferred me to their Atlanta sales office, the move changed my work life dramatically. My sixteen-hour-a-day pace disappeared as I began a lengthy program of self-study and classroom instruction for my new role as a Systems Engineer trainee. I spent hours in a small cubicle at an IBM Learning Center library, five minutes from our apartment.

To fill the extra time, I joined a gym and found a jazzercise class, suiting up with neon leotards and matching leg warmers per Jane Fonda's *Workout Book* instructions. I visited local churches and considered getting a cat.

Joe called each night, no matter where he was or what time. We swapped details of accomplishments and the next day's plans. When he was home, we researched buying our first home and began training for a 10K, Atlanta's annual Peachtree Road Race. After two races and six months in our new home, Joe was promoted again, this time to Baltimore. Even though I'd just finished the eighteen-month training program, IBM again transferred me into another new role—a sales and marketing rep position.

Joe had the proverbial rocket on his rear end, and I was doing well myself, borrowing Mom's mantra, "Bloom where you are planted." In Baltimore, I was the regional Rookie of the Year. I won other local and national awards, the most prestigious of which was IBM's coveted Golden Circle Award. I enjoyed the work, the pace, and the people.

We lived at warp speed through our midtwenties, both

working long hours and weekends, developing our careers and our finances. As our thirties approached, our thoughts turned to starting a family. Since we both had families of four that once were five, we envisioned a large family of our own—at least four children. My goal was to give birth before I turned thirty, which would also give Joe time to finish his MBA.

What's planned is possible, we both believed.

~ ❧ ~

Chapter 5

Family Again

As for the future, your task is not to foresee it, but to enable it.
—Antoine de Saint Exupery

I THOUGHT I was pregnant, but the voice on the other end of the phone said the test was negative. I was crushed. Joe and I were twenty-eight and right on schedule with our family plan. I had tracked my ovulation to the day with the help of a basal body thermometer and some graph paper. Our timing had been perfect; I had the chart to prove it.

Devastated, I called Joe to give him the sad news and then plunged back into the rest of the workday, hosting a going-away party for an IBM colleague that night and leaving three days later for a weeklong conference in San Jose. On the way back to Baltimore, I made a side trip through North Carolina, meeting Mom and Rachel in Durham where Dad had been invited to preach the homecoming sermon.

"Any news to share?" Dad asked me after the service, knowing we had plans to start our family soon. "From the pulpit, you looked pregnant, BB."

Stunned at his timing, I told him I had no news. But I wondered if he could be right. I hadn't gotten my period and my basal body temp (yes, I was still charting) was still high, indicating a possible pregnancy. I raced in to the doctor's office Monday morning and dropped off another sample only to discover they were out of the pregnancy testing kits. The medical assistant said to call at 4 P.M. I called, but the results weren't ready so she offered to call me at home.

At 10:15 P.M. the phone rang. "Congratulations, Mrs. Galli. You're pregnant!"

I shrieked my thanks, quickly hanging up to call Joe. I hadn't told him I was going to be retested. One disappointment was enough. I dialed Joe's number, taking a deep breath to hold in my excitement. "Are you coming home soon?"

"It may be a while, Beck. Still practicing this pitch. It's for a new customer."

"Got it. Well, give me a call before you leave." He agreed. We hung up. And I sighed. "Nuts," I whispered out loud. I didn't want to tell him on the phone. I wanted to see his face. Still in my sweats and my Coke-bottle-lensed glasses that I never wore in public, I grabbed his favorite candy bar and drove to his office, hoping I could find him.

"Hi, Mrs. Galli," the guard said. "How are you this evening?"

"I'm well, thanks. I'm trying to find Joe to bring him a snack. He's working late. But that's nothing new, right?"

The guard smiled back at me.

"Any idea where he may be? Said he was rehearsing in a new conference room?"

"Oh, that's Building C," he said, directing me there.

I snuck in the back of the room and watched my husband in action. Alone, Joe owned the front of the room as if it were a stage in front of hundreds. He strode back and forth, clicking the slides as he spoke, their images flashing behind him, his hands waving—authentic to his heritage. His voice was strong, spitting out facts and figures with an enthusiasm-laced urgency that drew you in to each detail for fear you might miss something important. The smell of fresh coffee wafted my way, courtesy of the projector's soft fan. I smiled, my heart warm with joy—my husband was in his glory and I was about to make him even happier.

Then he missed a beat. "Ahh, crap!" he barked, punching the air and turning around to glare at the screen. He raked his fingers through his dark thick hair and then rewound his words—to the syllable—and went at it again. He nailed it that time. When he came to a pause, I whispered, "Surprise!"

"Oh hey, Beck," he said. "What are you doing here? Everything okay?" And he put the clicker down and came over to give me a kiss.

"Oh, just thought I'd drop in and bring you a snack." I handed him a Twix bar. "I know you don't indulge much, but thought you could use a sugar surge. How's it going?"

"Great! Still a lot to do. I'm trying to advance the slide and talk about the next one without looking at it."

"Oh, memorizing the transitions?"

"Yep. It's hard, but I want to get it right."

"You will." I paused and took his hands in mine. "Well, I have news," I smiled and looked into those lively dark eyes. "I'm pregnant!"

"What? Really?" He squeezed my hands and raised them in the air, stepping back to look at me as if I should already be showing. "But wait, I thought the test was negative."

"It was, but I went back this morning for another test. They just called me. It's positive!"

"Oh, this is awesome. The best!" he said, pulling me into him and almost suffocating me with a wrestling bear hug. We chatted a bit longer and then looked at our calendars to mark the due date, June 5.

When I got home, I called Joe's parents, Rachel, and Mom and Dad.

"Where's that soon-to-be father? Put him on the line. Let me talk to the boy!" Dad said.

"Yes, we want to congratulate him," Mom said. "Give him a big hug right through the phone!"

"Oh, he's still rehearsing. You know how that goes, right, Dad? Really, really busy. I'm not sure when he'll be home."

"Oh, okay," Dad said.

"Give him our love," Mom chimed in.

⚜

ON THURSDAY, JUNE 18, 1987, I was thirteen days past my due date in one of the hottest summers on record. I'd stopped work a month earlier, but seemed to find relief from the triple-digit heat only with ice-cream sandwiches and sweet tea. I felt like the stereotypical beached whale, but also probably looked like it since I'd gained more than fifty pounds. I was miserable, but hoped I could hang on for just one more day. I was scheduled to be induced on Friday.

Joe and I were up early, 6:15 A.M. I couldn't sleep and Joe wanted to get in one more rehearsal before going in to the office. For the first time in his career, he was invited to present to the Board of Directors. For weeks, he'd been rehearsing for this day. I just needed our little one to hold off a few more hours.

Around 8:30 A.M., I went to the bathroom and noticed a small gush of fluid. "Not sure if this is anything, Sweedle, but I'm calling Dr. B," I told Joe, still practicing his slides in the study.

"Probably not your water breaking, but come in through admitting and I'll check you since you're so late, Dr. B said. "But be prepared. We may send you back home." I listened to more instructions and then hung up and went into the study where Joe was packing up.

"Should I come?" Joe asked.

"No, Dr. B wants to check me, but I could be sent back home. I'm not even having contractions. Besides, we have our backup plan, remember? " I hugged him as hard as I could with my extended belly, and then gave him a kiss. "Good luck, Sweedle."

My girlfriend arrived shortly after Joe left and took me to the hospital to wait for the verdict.

"Looks like you have a small tear in the sac," Dr. B said. "But you're here so let's induce you today."

"Wow, okay," I said, recalculating. This was really happening. Today. I wasn't going home. "Should Joe come now?"

"No, you are probably in for a long night."

I was only dilated one centimeter and had no contractions—that I knew of anyway. "What time should Joe be here? Noon? One o'clock?"

"Oh, let's say 1:45. Really, no rush here."

I updated my friend so she could leave, and then called Joe with the plan. "I'm fine, Joe. This will take a while, they are telling me. Just focus on your pitch," I told him. "Good luck. I love you."

A large gray strap across my belly monitored the contractions, capturing the activity on a wide-ribboned tape that puddled beside my bed. My belly tightened, hard as a basketball, as if I were doing a slow controlled sit-up. From 11:30 to 1:30, I made phone calls and watched TV. The "sit-ups" were evenly spaced, making lovely mountains on the tape. Still, no pain.

"This is your first, right, hon?" the nurse said when she came in to get my vitals. "Hon," such a Baltimore thing, had always put me at ease.

"Yes."

"And where did you say your husband was?"

"In a meeting," I smiled nervously at her sharp look. "A board of directors meeting. It's really important. I told him to focus," I babbled on, mostly convincing myself as I felt her judging eyes flush my cheeks. "He's worked so hard. And I, I'll be fine, right?"

"Yes, hon," she said with a bit of a smirk and some kind of grunt. "You'll be fine." I certainly didn't feel like her "hon." I felt more like her dartboard.

A few minutes later, Dr. B examined me. I was 100 percent effaced, two centimeters dilated, but my water had not broken. He inserted a small hook, breaking the sac. I felt the warm fluid between my legs and watched Dr. B's face register a look I'd never seen from him: alarm.

"What's wrong?" I whispered, clutching the paper on each side of my hips.

"There's quite a bit of meconium, the baby's bowel movement within the uterus. That can indicate distress," he said, his eyes were still fixed on the wet paper beneath me. "I need to put a fetal monitor on the baby's head."

I held my breath as he moved swiftly, wincing as he inserted it and then exhaling with relief as I watched his face relax. The heart rate was 140, "excellent," he said as he left the room. It was 1:35. Joe would arrive soon.

Suddenly, alarms filled the room. Dr. B rushed back in, frantically adjusting the fetal monitor. An anesthesiologist ran in and began checking my IV while two more doctors came in with two more nurses. I peeked out the door and spied Joe, but Dr. B pulled him out of the room to explain. The heart rate had dropped to 60, which was dangerously low. Our condition was considered critical with the potential for an emergency C-section.

Nurse "Hon" shoved blue scrubs in Joe's hands, ordering him to get ready. He came over to my side, holding my hand while the doctors sorted out their roles. The anesthesiologist said she may not have time to do a spinal. If she has five minutes, she can do it. If not, she will have to put me under general anesthesia.

Dr. B turned me on my left side and gave me an oxygen mask, instructing me on how to breathe. I was petrified. Unable to speak with the mask pressing in on my face, I could not stop shaking. Joe smoothed my forehead and tried to calm me but we both were out of our minds with fright.

The medical team hovered, waiting for Dr. B's "go" signal, but he chose to wait and see if the oxygen would work. Within a few minutes the heart rate was back up to 140.

"Okay," Dr. B ordered. "Let's have a baby."

They started Pitocin, a labor-inducing drug and soon-to-be source of horrific pain. Joe could see the contractions on the tape before I felt them. "Beck, one is coming. In just a few seconds. Are you ready? Here it comes!" and I would tense up as he squeezed my hand tighter. "Oh no, another one is coming. It's bigger. Yes, much bigger. Look out!" and he would squeeze my hand even tighter, raising his voice in pitch and intensity, his play-by-play crescendo foreshadowing mine.

"Sweedle, you're not helping!" I gasped between the waves. "You're supposed to help me relax, remember?"

Finally, Dr. B gave me a shot of Demerol. Although it dulled the pain, it also made me ill. I threw up all over the bed, the floor, and the wall.

Nurse "Hon" was not amused.

Only an hour after the pain meds, I felt the sudden urge to bear down, like I had to go to the bathroom. Eight pushes later and Brittany Leigh Galli was born. She was beautiful.

The timing was perfect, just as planned. Joe graduated in May 1987. Brittany was born in June. I was twenty-nine.

⚶

JOE AND I had the "world by the tail," my IBM manager told me. Joe was poised for his next promotion, his MBA complete. I had just received my Golden Circle marketing award. And our firstborn was a beautiful, vibrant, healthy baby girl.

At first we thought she had no hair so I looked for more

creative ways besides dressing her in pink to show she was a girl. I bought a few elastic headbands, but then realized the issue. She wasn't bald; she was blonde.

"Oh my, Joe. Brittany has Rachel's blonde hair! I sure hope she doesn't have her mischievous nature, too." I finally found Velcro bows that would latch on to the flaxen hair, at least long enough for her three-month-old Olan Mills portrait.

Four months after her birth, I went back to work. I would get up with Brittany, feed her, dress her, get ready for work, put her in the car with me to go pick up the nanny, bring them both back to the house, and be at work—a forty-minute commute— by 7 A.M.

Inspired by the warm memories of our family dinners, I tried to be home before six o'clock so I could take the nanny back and get dinner together before Joe arrived. I used some of Mom's tricks—preplanning the menu and setting the table the night before. But inevitably, Brittany would get hungry early and Joe would be home late.

When Brittany was fifteen months old, IBM offered me a promotion.

"You should go for it," Joe said, when I told him about it after a rare dinner together. He'd brought his mug filled with hot coffee to sit down beside me on the couch where I was folding laundry.

"The job is in DC, Joe," I said, pushing the laundry basket out of his way with my foot and turning to face him. "That's a two-hour commute." I folded Brittany's sundress and ruffled diaper cover, placing them on top of his undershirts.

"But don't you need that regional step before you can get into management?" He sipped his coffee, cupping the mug with both hands as he leaned forward, those brown eyes serious, unwavering.

"Yes, you're right."

"You'd be a great manager, Beck. DC's not that far. People do it all the time," he said, scooting to the edge of the couch.

"You are already a high-potential candidate; they've already told you. It's a great opportunity. Go for it!" he repeated, standing up and spreading his arms wide almost spilling his coffee.

I grinned at his theatrics, his unbridled encouragement. I stood up and gave him a quick hug. "Thanks, Sweedle. I've got some thinking to do." I grabbed the laundry basket, leaving Joe to entertain Brittany. I could tell by his sneaky half smile that he was going to surprise her from behind. He loved to play-wrestle with Brittany, where he'd take her down and tickle her or sometimes do push-ups with her on his back.

I headed upstairs, turning my thoughts over with each step. I wanted to be his star, I did. But I was managing about all I could at the moment. I had only been back to work for a year. He couldn't pick the sitter up or take her home. One time I asked him, just to make sure, but he said, no, just like I knew he would. Before we married, I knew his career would eventually matter more than mine—even though I made more money than he did our first years out of college—ha! I smiled at that thought. But, the truth was that we both knew he had CEO potential and that was the priority—for both of us.

"Oops," I said out loud as one of Brittany's lacy socks fell out of the basket on the last step. I leaned back against the bannister, picked it up with my toes, and tossed it up and in one of her opened drawers. "She scores!" I roared to myself in my pretend announcer voice and then began putting away her other clothes.

I'd thought I may be able to have a career, but I also wanted kids, and had no idea if I could do both. No one in our families had done it. And neither family was nearby to help. My parents were eight hours away, still entrenched full-time in their church work and community projects. Joe's were six hours away. Although Mom had come in to help me for two weeks after Brittany's birth, and Joe's mom followed with another week after that, I had to manufacture a local support system. And with only one child, it was already a juggling act of guilt—at home feeling guilty for not being at work and at work feeling guilty for not being at home. It was hard for me to excel in both worlds.

I wished I could embody my husband's confidence—so much like Forest's and Dad's. But I couldn't; I needed hard evidence. So I talked to others who made the commute. One didn't have children. Another lived closer to DC. The third had a husband who helped with child care. All agreed the job was demanding and erratic. I just couldn't envision it, so I withdrew my name from consideration. Joe said he understood, but I wondered if I had disappointed him.

A couple of months after turning down the promotion, we decided to have our second child, to give Brittany a sibling close in age, less than two years apart, just like Forest and Rachel.

Chapter 6

Miscarriage

My grief lies all within,
And these external manners of lament
Are merely shadows to the unseen grief
That swells with silence in the tortured soul.
—William Shakespeare

THE SPOTTING WAS light at first. I'd just had a sonogram the week before, so I knew the baby was fine. The heartbeat was strong, the fetus size appropriate, and the morning sickness was beginning to ease up a bit. I knew what to expect. I was almost at the twelve-week safe zone.

But when I arrived at work, the spotting increased. A strange cramping sensation rippled through my lower abdomen. I called Dr. B. He wanted to see me. Joe left work and met me there.

"Okay," Dr. B said with a quick smile, "let's see what's going on." I climbed onto the table, the crackling paper mimicking my every move. The cold gel shocked my tender belly, as we prepared for the sonogram's revealing look into my womb. The talking stopped. We strained to see the fluttering movement so wonderfully evident at last week's visit. Dr. B was quiet—too quiet—as I watched him study the screen.

"I'm sorry," he said simply. "There is no heartbeat."

"Are you sure? Can you look again?" I begged as I shut my eyes and tried to will that heartbeat back. "We just saw it last week. You said it was strong. You said everything was fine," I reminded the doctor with my eyes still pinched shut.

"I'm sorry." He moved the monitor, showing us the full screen. That marvelous sack so filled with life seven days ago was now empty, void of the new life we'd already begun to plan.

"What happened?" I whispered to Dr. B, afraid I'd cry if I looked at Joe.

And then he admitted the answer that all of his education and experience could not provide. "I don't know." He paused to look at the two of us. "I'll give you a minute." And he closed the door behind him.

The empty sack seemed to stare back at us. Our child was gone. Brittany's sibling was no longer there. I looked at Joe's soft brown eyes, my tears releasing. We hugged; his strong arms held me close. When the doctor returned, he explained the steps necessary to finish what nature had started. Three days later, the D&C was a crazed blur. I remember talking to the nurses and then counting until the twilight drug hit.

"How are you?" the nurse asked as I was coming out of the daze.

"Okay, I guess," I said, still trying to focus.

"My, you are a talker," another nurse remarked.

"Oh, no. What did I say?"

"No worries, hon," the nurse assured me with that word. This time I felt endeared. "Let's just say that you must really love your husband."

And I did. Joe worked too much and didn't help me as much as I would have liked, but I loved him. I was so very proud of him. I looked forward to our future together.

The drugs told no lies.

LIFE WAS DIFFERENT for me after my miscarriage. At the post-D&C visit to Dr. B's office, well-rounded bellies met me in the waiting room. Pregnant women were everywhere. Some were happy. Some were complaining. Some were alone. Some were with their spouse. Others bought their entire clan of kids along.

Their idle banter about their due dates, the nausea, the cravings, and what number pregnancy it was for them was like fingernails on a chalkboard, screeching in a vocabulary no longer mine. After my exam, I exited through the waiting area, this time making eye contact only with the receptionist and then gluing my eyes on my new navy pumps.

Alone in my car, I wept. As I drove home, a whole new respect for my mother washed over me. She'd listened to my play-by-play of the devastating sonogram and the D&C, but the reality of the loss hit me hard in that waiting room. I'd always known she'd miscarried. "Yes, I lost my first one, BB," she'd say with lowered eyes and a lingering sadness whenever I would ask about her pregnancy history. But we'd never really talked about it. I guess I never really listened or gave it much thought.

Until now. How brave she must have been to keep trying to get pregnant! I called her as soon as I got home. "How did you do it, Mom?" I asked. "How did you get through it?"

"Honey," she said, her voice soft but clear. "I had to tell myself that something must have been wrong for the baby not to grow. Give yourself and your body time to heal and try again."

But the march through grief was different this time. It was the first time I'd felt such deep sorrow since losing Forest. It had been eleven years since his death. Hundreds had wept with me after the loss of my brother; I, alone, knew this unborn child.

Grief is a strange companion, I'd learned. Even more private with this loss. Joe tried to empathize, but couldn't, not really. We both lost a dream, but my loss was physical. My body changed days after conception, my belly fluttering with life as I mentally measured each sign of growth progress, just like I had done with Brittany.

Yet, this time my body failed me. It was the first time it had refused to execute my plans. Doting on Brittany, then eighteen months, seemed to help. Instead of rushing her through our bedtime rituals to make our scheduled bedtime, I held her a little tighter, a little longer. I took extra time to marvel at her nonstop creative play. "What are you doing, honey?" I asked as she cradled an old cordless phone into her soft blonde hair, pushing the keys on the old IBM laptop I no longer used.

"I play, Mommy," she said as she blinked her daddy's curious brown eyes into the empty screen and mumbled excited gibberish into the phone.

Still, the sight of newborns seemed to torture me. When I looked at babies, I drank them in—the sound, the smell, and the imagined feeling of a brand-new life. To get through it, I created a game face with a plastic smile to protect me from the hurt and help me accept what I didn't understand.

⚬⚭⚬

IN DECEMBER 1988, only weeks after my miscarriage, Joe and I hosted our first holiday staff party in our new home. He had just been named Vice President of Black and Decker's Accessory Division at age thirty, the youngest vice president in the history of the company. I had already made my quota for the year, so we celebrated. We bought a white BMW with red leather interior for Joe and a Ford Taurus station wagon for me, Carolina blue.

We'd designed and built our new home with plenty of bedrooms for children and an easy-entertaining floor plan Mom called a circular flow, a feature she cherished in each of our family homes. As a minister's wife, she considered it part of her role to have a welcoming home for guests. And with Joe's rapid rise to the executive suite, we, too, wanted to entertain in our home.

But given the miscarriage, it was the last thing I wanted to do. Facing the people at work was hard enough. I knew I could do it, though, and should, for Joe and for my own sake of moving forward. I just had to "focus on the positives," as Dad always said, and of course "get my ducks in a row," like I knew my mama would.

"Hey Joe, take a look at this," I said, leading him to the foyer. "Do you like it?" I pointed to the small festive tree perched on the foyer table. "It's my 'Accessory' Christmas tree."

"Awesome!" he said, his brown eyes dancing. For a tool company, an accessory was a drill bit or saw blade. So, I'd taken dozens of gold-plated drill bits, tied gold-tinged red and green plaid bows on each, hooked them, and then hung them on a three-foot pine tree. "When did you have time for this project?"

"At night, when you were working late." I sighed, gently touching my belly. Then he put his hand over mine, its warmth comforting the emptiness. "Planning this party was actually a great distraction," I said, looking up at him. "Kept me busy and focused."

He gave me a quick hug, a potent squeeze that felt like a love and energy exchange in one short blast. I needed it. The plans were set, but I still felt uneasy. I was supposed to be wearing my new maternity dress, a purple satin with a large bow that draped under my should-have-been showing belly. Instead, I was in my figure-forgiving little black dress since I wasn't allowed to go back to the gym yet. At least I could have a glass of wine.

"House looks great, Beck! So do you," he said, releasing me then lifting his arms in the air as he turned and surveyed the rest of the entryway. "This will be fun. I think it will be good for you, right?"

"Yes, of course." I smiled back. "The peekaboo bar is ready, too."

His enthusiasm seemed to uplift mine a bit as I showed him one more unique creation. I'd asked the builder to gut a deep pantry closet and partially open one side that peeked through to the hall. A bartender could stand inside and mix drinks, serving them through the framed opening. "It's stocked and ready to go."

"Fabulous," he said, waving another hand.

When the caterer came, I relaxed a little more as I watched my kitchen transform into an upscale bistro with two chefs. Their full-service staff scampered up the steps with heavy coats and whisked away hostess gifts while passing hors d'oeuvres and tending bar. I'd never entertained that many, nor used a caterer, so I welcomed the help that promised to leave my kitchen cleaner than they found it. I also began to marvel at my mother's annual uncatered staff dinners hosted in their home. How did she do that? The circular flow worked well. Joe and I met guests at the front door and guided them left through the formal dining room or right through the living room and our office to circle around to my prized bar. Once there, a step-down family room offered comfy seating, overlooked by a two-story vaulted ceiling.

Most guests knew about our lost pregnancy. "Oh, you can try again," one mother of four gushed, discounting my loss as if it were an errant effort instead of an unborn child.

I nodded, returned her bubbly look with a noncommittal stare, and quickly changed the subject.

"Well, at least you have Brittany," another said, as if one child's presence could possibly replace another's—an impossibility I'd lived with for the last eleven years.

My daughter isn't a spare tire who could possibly replace my unborn baby, I wanted to fire back. I swallowed hard, stifling the words and focused on a swirly pattern in the hardwood floor. But the thoughts kept coming. *Just because you can't see it, doesn't mean it doesn't hurt!* I wanted to shout at her. *I'm entitled to grieve!* But instead I politely nodded, ground my teeth behind my plastic smile, and offered her an hors d'oeuvre.

Chapter 7

Undiagnosed Disease

> *Any human face is a claim on you. . . .*
> *But this is truest in the face of an infant.*
> —Marilynne Robinson, Gilead

ON FEBRUARY 28, 1990, I gave birth to Matthew Forest Galli. Five months after my miscarriage, we had conceived our son. I held close this beautiful, healthy boy who shared his middle name with my beloved brother, the uncle he would never meet.

He was such an easy baby. With his dark hair and deep-blue eyes, Matthew charmed us from the beginning, his dimples teasing us with every yawn and smile. He was a good sleeper who cooed far more than he cried.

So different from Brittany.

Sleep was a goblin for her, to be avoided at all costs. She was nine months old before she slept through the night. And even at the age of two and a half, she was often up at 4 A.M.—for the day. She fought sleep, never admitting to being sleepy or tired. "Not tired, Mommy!" she once announced in a restaurant, causing heads to turn and stare. And then she promptly fell asleep with two French fries in her mouth. I took a picture and showed her, since she tended to doubt my sleepy-time stories. I learned early on to seek out droning noises and rhythmic motions to calm her to sleep—a midnight car ride or lengthy backpack baby-carrier jaunt while vacuuming or push-mowing the lawn would often put her right out.

Waking up was equally abrupt. She would open her eyes as if a magician's snapped fingers had released her from a trance, jumping right back into conversation with whatever the last thing that was on her mind. She had extraordinary energy and a willful nature that kept me on high alert most of the time.

"That child has two speeds," my father said. "Overdrive and off."

And when she was up, she was on and searching for activity.

"Don't do it again, Brittany," I said during our Christmas visit to my parents' home. Joe had gone for a run, but Rachel had joined Mom, Dad, and me in the small den as we chatted before Brittany's bedtime. Rachel was lounging in an old upholstered rocker that had a quirk in its rocking mechanism. If you rocked too hard, you would fall over backward. It was a small rocker, low to the ground, so no one was ever hurt. Brittany thought it was hysterical and had fun discovering just the right push that would send Aunt Rachel tumbling backward out of the chair.

"That's enough," I said.

Brittany looked at me and smiled, pushing Rachel over again as Mom and Dad watched. I could see Dad's crooked smile out of the corner of my eye. Mom pinched her lips together to shut down her brewing laughter.

"Brittany, I said that's enough." I tried to mimic Mom's chocolate voice and Dad's steady stare. "You do it again and you'll have to go to bed. Immediately."

Brittany stopped, dropping her hands to the sides of her red silky nightgown with its matching lace-trimmed robe. She looked at her Nana, her Andad (the special nickname she'd given my father), and finally at me. Then she turned to Rachel and said evenly, "Night, night, Aunt Rachel," and pushed her over.

Although her eyes were a deep brown, their mischievous twinkle matched that of my green-eyed sister. "I've been through that set of genes once," Dad said, winking at Rachel, then watching his granddaughter head off to bed.

Once she'd given herself a haircut, snipping the cowlick in her bangs down to the root. "Brittany, you know better than that!" I scolded her.

"But Mommy," she shot back, "you're the one that left the scissors on the counter."

Unafraid of confrontation, she once sashayed into the kitchen, put her hand on her hip, and asked with a lisp, "Mommy, why do I have to *wisten* to you?" That one gave her Andad a sermon illustration, where he nicknamed his willful granddaughter "The Brittany."

Strangely, Brittany became the glue in our family, drawing us together as she played with our heartstrings. She craved attention and got it from all of us. I welcomed the support, advice, and insight from my parents as I began to experience some of those complex parenting feelings of an unconditional love versus the necessity for discipline.

After two years with a nanny, I had enrolled her in a nearby family day care so she could play regularly with other kids. She loved it, lamenting that Saturday was the only day without "school," given Sundays included Sunday school, where I was her teacher. But I also hired extra help at home, anticipating Joe's increase in travel and my return to work after Matthew's birth. Joe left for Europe only three days after Matthew was born. Thank goodness we'd planned for Mom to come stay with me for two weeks.

Bedtime was difficult enough without a new baby in the mix, so prior to Matthew's birth, I'd asked for my pediatrician's advice. "Structure Brittany's bedtime," he had advised. "Make it a simple routine and try to keep it consistent."

The routine worked most of the time. I agreed to stay in Brittany's room and sit in the pink rocker, the special rocker that Brittany had painted with her Andad. I could nurse Matthew while she was falling asleep—a twofer that somehow made me feel strangely productive. I just had to avoid the squeaky board in front of her door. If I stepped on it and she woke up, I'd have to start the whole process again.

⸙

"NITE, NITE, BRITTANY," I said to her as we began our litany. I'd been back at work for about a month. Matthew was three months old.

"Nit, nit, Mommy. Nit, nit, Bud-Bud," she said, wiggling down into the covers. We had brushed teeth, said prayers, and read *Goodnight Moon,* the customary three times. "Sit, Mommy, until I sleep," Brittany reminded me.

As I sat in the night-light-lit darkness waiting for sleep's rhythmic cadence to overcome my daughter, I rocked and nursed Matthew, her Bud-Bud. It only took twenty minutes that night. I avoided the squeaky board, walked down the hall to Matthew's room, and put my precious son, already sound asleep, into his crib.

Joe, home early—a rarity for him, was working in the office downstairs. "I'm going to stay up here, Joe," I whispered down from the upstairs overlook. He came out of the office and looked up at me.

"I'll be up soon," he whispered back and blew me a kiss.

A few hours later, I awakened to gasps and gurgles, and rolled over to see the baby monitor flashing in spasms. The sounds were odd and intense, unlike the sleepy whimpers that usually woke me for his 2 A.M. feedings. I looked at the clock. It was only midnight.

The lights and sounds continued as I slipped out of bed and

left Joe sleeping. I went into the nursery and flipped on the light, a soft glow from the sailboat-shaded lamp. When I looked into the crib, Matthew was face down, but had raised his head and stretched out his arms as if to reach for a toy. And he kept making that odd sound.

"Matthew?" I whispered, as I bent over to pick him up. "What's going on, little buddy?" I touched him to pat his back, and then realized he was stiff. I picked him up to cuddle, but he did not bend. He was rigid, frozen in a Superman posture—head erect and arms outstretched as if he were flying. I moved closer to the lamp to look at his face. His mouth was clenched, lips in a straight-lined grimace, seething bubbles of drool. His eyes were fixed in a wide-eyed stare that would not respond to my voice.

"Joe!" I said, rushing into our room and turning on the light. "Something's wrong with Matthew." We both looked at our son, still stiff, eyes wide and fixed.

"Is he breathing?"

"Yes, but barely," I said. "I think we should go to the emergency room."

Joe nodded, already out of the bed grabbing clothes.

I paused to think it through. "You'll have to wake Brittany. I'll call the doctor."

Our dazed family headed to the hospital. By the time we arrived, Matthew was in a deep sleep, limp and calm. The ER doctor was unsure what might have happened. He thought it may be a "night terror," an intense horrific sleep disruption that apparently some children experience. I'd never heard of it. He kept asking me to repeat what I saw, like I might change my story.

I returned to the lobby to Joe and Brittany sleeping. She was on his lap, nestled under her daddy's scratchy face, her favorite part of her *Pat the Bunny* book. I woke them with the good news. Perplexed but grateful for the benign diagnosis, we returned home and resumed our daily routines—Joe and I back to work, Brittany and Matthew to family day care.

Thirty days passed. Then Matthew had another episode. This time I videotaped it.

"He's having another night terror, Joe," I whispered. Even as I spoke these words, I questioned myself. "I'm heading to the ER. Brittany is sleeping. I'll call you when I know more."

With no time to transfer the video from the camera to tape, I packed up Matthew and drove to the hospital, my Taurus station wagon flashers announcing my caution and fear. Could it really be a night terror? I'd never heard of them nor knew anyone who had. But, I hadn't pursued it—and now regretted it. In those days, there was no Google to consult and I was still adjusting to life's new rhythm with two kids, a full-time job, and a globe-trotting husband. But, I'd let it slide—so unlike me— thinking it was a one-time thing. Maybe a video would help at some point. And maybe this time I'd get a different doc, one who might believe me.

But again, Matthew was asleep by the time we arrived. And again, they were unsure of what was wrong. Different doctors, same story. Probably another night terror. When I pressed one doctor, he suggested a specialist—a pediatric neurologist. I had to ask him twice and write it down. I'd never heard of such a specialty.

⋘⋙

TWO WEEKS LATER, I walked into a pediatric neurologist office with my son.

"May I help you?" the receptionist asked.

"Yes, I'm here for an appointment for my son, Matthew." I said, putting the car-seat carrier down next to her desk. "Do you mind watching him while I run to the car to get something to show the doctor?"

She agreed and I raced out and lugged back my "portable" twenty-five-pound television and video camera. "Thanks so much," I said, catching my breath. "I'd like to set this up in the examination room whenever the doctor is ready for us."

The woman looked up and over her glasses at me like I'd brought in a gorilla. We'd had the video camera for three years but I still didn't know how to get the dang recording off of the camera onto a tape. And even if I did, I couldn't be sure he would have a tape player. So, I just brought the TV and the camcorder. I knew how to connect those.

Surely this specialist would know what was happening to Matthew. But just in case, I had evidence. I'd about had it with "maybe" and "unsure" and "probably." I wanted to know what was wrong with my son.

Once in the exam room, I put the TV on the table, hooked up the video camera, and tested it while Matthew slept in his car seat. I sat on the edge of the cheap plastic chair watching Matthew's even breathing. So peaceful. After what seemed like an hour, the doctor shuffled in, slow as molasses. He barely looked at me or the TV on the table. He zeroed in on Matthew, examined him, and then began taking an excruciatingly detailed medical history.

"Okay, here it is," I interrupted him, his pace annoying me. "I taped it." And I stood up, pushed play on the video camera, and pointed to the screen. The television screen lit up with my son's night terror.

Only a few seconds into the recording, he said, "That's a seizure."

"What?" My arms dropped, dangling limp by my side. I sat down hard as I looked at his eyes, so certain. His words had an echo to them as I tried to make sense out of what he was saying. "A seizure?"

"Based on the video and your account of the earlier episodes, it appears as if Matthew has had two seizures. Because of the multiple occurrences, we now have a classification," he said, his tone flat and cadence even, as if he were giving a lecture—about someone else's child. "This is epilepsy," he said, retuning my shocked stare with disarming confidence. His gray unblinking eyes peered at me through thick wire-framed glasses. Everything about him was gray. His hair. His pants. His nonemotional tone. "I am certain. Epilepsy."

The word hung in the air.

But Matthew was a good baby. He smiled. He babbled. He goo-ed and giggled, just like Brittany. And he was such a good sleeper. These were just bad dreams. I struggled to sort it out.

"But, why? How?"

"We don't know," he began and then layered on all the "don't knows"—the cause, the cure, the prognosis.

But my mind was still stuck on the seizures. Yet, even in the shock, I noticed how *he* was certain, but *we* did not know, like he'd gained an army to shore up his ignorance. Ah, the royal *we* of the medical community. I'd heard it before with my miscarriage. I didn't like it then and I didn't like it now. I pressed my lips in a tight line and lifted one brow. "So how do *we* fix this?" I asked, annoyed but aware I needed this doctor's expertise to help me.

"There is a chance he could outgrow this before the age of two," he said, continuing the class lecture. "Meanwhile, we should manage it with medication."

⤳⅛↝

THE SPIRALING CYCLE of trial and error began. Our goal was to find the therapeutic level of medication that would stop the seizures. We would try one dose, do blood work to check for safe levels of the drug, and the wait to see if Matthew seized—or had signs of toxicity. We balanced controlling the seizures with a dosage that was safe.

Matthew and I were frequent visitors to the local diagnostic lab. We would arrive at 7 A.M. so I could still make it to work on time. At four months, his tiny veins were hard to find and soon became scarred with knots from multiple blood-work sticks. Each knot made the next blood draw more difficult, reducing the available area of the vein. Before each visit, I prayed for a gentle phlebotomist who was skillful with a butterfly needle and knew how to avoid the knots.

Matthew was quiet during these procedures. I cried more than he did.

At home, I learned how to give my precious baby phenobarbital, a bitter-tasting anticonvulsant, one of the oldest medications used to control seizures.

He hated it. So did I.

The early-morning routine exhausted me. "Here we go, Bud-Bud," I'd say, sitting cross-legged on my bathroom floor. I lined up the medicine, wipes, and syringes, and played a cassette tape of a lullaby to soothe both of us. After submerging a needle-less syringe into the liquid and drawing it up to the prescribed dosage amount, I'd cradle his sweet-smelling head in the nook of my arm to both support and restrain him. I'd squirt the medication a fraction of an ounce at the time into the side of his mouth, and then quickly offered him my breast to help wash it down. "Good job, Bud-Bud!" I'd whisper.

Most of the time he'd take it all down, but often the red sticky medicine would seep everywhere and I'd worry that he wasn't getting the right amount.

"How do other parents do it?" I once asked another neurologist, thinking she may have some special technique to get the baby to swallow the harsh medicine. I can still hear her no-nonsense response.

"In my experience," she stated, "success rests on the sheer will of the parent."

Like that helped. I wanted instruction and she gave me philosophy. The sheer will of the parent. I thought about it each morning when Matthew finished his feeding and then fell asleep.

I would kiss his forehead and hope my will was strong enough. Then I would get ready for work.

⤙⚭⤚

DAILY MY FACE was tear stained in those first six months of Matthew's life. My heart was torn by a relentless grief, an agony that cycled through my emotions every day. The anger, the crying, the resignation, the will to go on—and then, it would start all over again.

Little things would trigger my emotions. Brittany would ask to wear the same T-shirt as Matthew, to match the brother so unlike her. A healthy baby boy would hold his head erect in the grocery store. Matthew could not, even though he was six months old. I had to support the back of his head as if he were still a newborn. Someone would ask me if Matthew was crawling yet. "No," I would reply and change the subject. The truth was that he couldn't even roll over, much less sit up or crawl—but that was too painful to admit.

Once, I managed to prop-sit Matthew for a few seconds. I had dressed him in his Sunday best, a striped green-and-blue button-down with coordinating plaid clip-on bow tie. On the blanketed floor in my bedroom, I sat him down with his legs frogged in front of him. I tilted him forward, placing his arms to prop up his chest, tripod style.

I snapped a photo, just before his center of gravity shifted and he slipped sideways onto the blanket. The photo captured him sitting, just before the fall. My Matthew was sitting! I clung to it as proof of his progress. Still, he could never accomplish this feat on his own, no matter how many techniques I tried.

Joe and I grieved in silence with every missed developmental milestone as time continued to cruelly reveal our son's lack of progress. Beyond the seizures, something was terribly wrong.

No neck control. No rolling over. No sitting. No crawling.

The seizures continued. Phenobarbital did not work. We tried different medicines, Dilantin, Tegretol, Depakote, and continued with more testing, and investigated new doctors.

Matthew six months old

I PICKED UP the phone to dial Joe's office. "Joe, I figured it out," I said, bringing the medical report to the sunny window beside our desk. I'd come home early from work and had rifled through the mail looking for the letter. "The test results came in the mail this morning. Matthew's condition is listed as 'an undiagnosed disease of the central nervous system.' It's not Matthew," I rattled on, "it's the dimwitted doctor! If he can't diagnose him, we just have to find someone who will!"

Joe agreed, encouraging me. I hung up the phone, super-charged by my new focus to find a doctor smart enough to diagnose our son. Surely something treatable was causing the epilepsy and these developmental delays. After that, we saw specialists at Johns Hopkins and the University of Maryland, seeking that one expert neurologist who could accurately identify what was wrong.

But there was no magic underlying diagnosis. In fact, our son's prognosis seemed to change by the week. We might as well have used a crystal ball.

"Yes, he will be able to walk," the doctors told us in the early months. But after Matthew failed to progress physically, they explained that his condition was considered to be cerebral palsy, a disorder of body movement that affects muscle control, posture, and balance, and that he may never be able to walk.

"Yes, he may 'catch up,'" they told us about his verbal delays. But when the cooing did not evolve into the typical "da-da's" or "ma-ma's," they added "significant global developmental delay" to the list and told us he may never be able to speak.

Officially, our son had epilepsy, cerebral palsy, and was globally developmentally delayed—all broad categories of medical conditions with no true underlying diagnosis. We knew no cause. We knew no cure.

An undiagnosed disease of the central nervous system was devastatingly accurate.

Chapter 8

⌒⌒

Expect Obstacles

*Face your deficiencies and acknowledge them; but do not let
them master you. Let them teach you patience, sweetness, insight.*
—Helen Keller

MEANWHILE, JOE CONTINUED to excel at Black and
Decker as he prepared to launch a new product line, DeWalt
power tools. Our conversations at home became almost man-
ic-depressive. First, we would rev each other up as Joe animatedly
recalled each achievement at work.

"What do you think?" he said one evening late after work.
He fanned out Polaroid photos of different colored tools on the
kitchen table. He believed in revitalizing the trusted name,
DeWalt, with a new signature color: yellow.

"Love it! It's bold. Unique."

"Yes, but it's a hard sell inside. They say it's 'canary yellow' or
'banana,' or even 'lemon,'" he said, pulling the photo into the light.
"But I say it's hard-hat yellow. Perfect for the construction site."

"I agree. I'd go for it."

But when our conversations turned to Matthew, a soft sadness settled over both of us. My progress reports paled in com-

parison to Joe's sparkling strides at work. Even though I recalled in exact fashion all of my efforts to manage, control, and somehow press forward with Matthew's care, the weary truth was that there were always more questions than answers.

Oh, how I wished my focus could have yielded the same success as Joe's.

⤙⦇⦈⤚

THE GREEN LINES on the yellow paper began to blur. With Brittany and Matthew finally asleep, I curled up in bed with my favorite ink pen and a box of tissues and began to bare my soul to a tear-stained legal pad. Joe worked quietly downstairs in our office while my clashing thoughts erupted.

I was proud of him, I reminded myself. But I'd begun to resent his absence—and envy his freedom. How could he focus on work while our child was so seriously ill? Couldn't he see that I needed him? Oh how I longed for the escape that he had, into the rigors of a demanding job where problems were concrete and action plans worked! Why did he have that freedom and I did not?

Journaling helped, but that night, I needed my Dad.

"Why isn't Joe up here with me, Dad? Does he not care?" I said, pressing the phone tight into my ear.

"BB," he said softly. "I know you are hurting and you must feel very lonely. But, honey," he paused and I heard him swallow, "someone's got to drive."

My crying quieted as I tried to understand what my father was saying.

"Joe has been there with you through the crisis periods, right? He's supported you and helped you find the resources you needed, right? And although we don't know all the answers, it sounds like you have good plans in place to move forward, right?"

My jaw dropped to release the tight breath I'd been holding

as I tried to absorb his meaning. The words were true, but somehow not at all comforting.

"Yes, he's been there for me in those ways, Dad," I admitted. "No question about that."

"I know this must be so hard for you, honey," Dad continued. "But in a sense you are fortunate that Joe can drive and is doing a good job. If he could not, imagine the complexities that could result."

A heavy silence filled the long-distance line as my breathing steadied.

"Thank God he's driving, BB," Dad whispered.

"Oh, Dad," I whispered back. Leave it to my maddeningly insightful father to see all the angles, to know just the right way to look at a completely crazy, illogical, and ever devastatingly twisted situation and have it make sense! I tried to be grateful, but it was hard. It wasn't the answer I wanted to hear. I wanted a partner in my painful journey. Was that too much to ask?

Yet I couldn't find the words to ask for something I thought he should want to give.

So we pressed on through it silently, and I convinced myself we were stronger for it.

⚜

WHEN IBM OFFERED me an early-retirement incentive package after ten years of service, I decided to leave the company to be home full time with the kids. We could afford it and I was tired of the physical juggling and mental exhaustion of trying to be two places at one time.

Brittany had started preschool and we were engaged in intensive in-home therapy sessions for Matthew, who would soon be celebrating his first birthday. I thought we finally had the seizures under control, but then Matthew had a growth spurt and they came back.

"How many seizures has he had?" the pediatric neurologist asked. I described the intensity and duration of the major ones. "But, how many?" he repeated, his hand poised over the chart to write down a number.

"One, maybe two per day."

"And at night?"

I looked into his unblinking eyes, inquisitive but cold. Although we still slept with the baby monitor on, I was sure I missed some on the nights when I was exhausted. "I'm not sure," I said, my voice soft and cracking. I sighed and stared at the tweed carpet, jealous of its predictable pattern while its uniformity somehow comforted me. I was so tired. Joe's workdays often stretched to fifteen hours. Brittany was still up at 5 A.M., four hours before her preschool began. At least I no longer had my work schedule to juggle. "I'll count and call you."

That night I moved into the guest room and slept with Matthew tucked by my side so I could feel each seizure. Surely knowing exactly how many would be critical in our pursuit of an underlying diagnosis. I'd missed many, I discovered, and began to keep a log.

For weeks, I held my son each night, sacrificing my sleep for parental peace of mind.

Joe slept alone.

Ever silent, he never complained or questioned my actions. I thought he understood that my dedication to our child was an extension of our love. In fact, I thought he was silently proud of me for being such a good mother.

At the time, I thought that being a good mother was also being a good wife. Only later, I realized the hidden cost.

MY TRACKING HELPED, it seemed, and the doctor made adjustments to Matthew's medication. Once again the seizures were controlled and we were hopeful that Matthew's development could resume, too, despite the undiagnosed disease label. After multiple consults with doctors and geneticists, Joe and I decided to continue our pursuit of a large family. "Matthew's condition is unique and not genetically based," we had been assured by more than one specialist. I became pregnant again, but it ended in another miscarriage at eleven weeks. And the dark question kept haunting me—would we ever be able to have another healthy baby?

Soon I became pregnant for the fifth time. Because of my miscarriages and Matthew's condition, Joe and I sought genetic testing, chorionic villus sampling (CVS), used to detect chromosomal abnormalities at the eleventh week of pregnancy. The results came back negative for any known birth defects. We exhaled, looking forward to a healthy addition to our family.

As I approached my fourth month of pregnancy, Matthew's condition suddenly deteriorated. He was hospitalized for thirty-one days. Medications could not control his seizures, even in intensive care. He seized multiple times daily and soon lost his suck-swallow ability. Although he was closely monitored by specialists, he weighed only eighteen pounds at eighteen months of age. Based on our doctor's recommendation, we scheduled surgery for the insertion of a gastric button to assist in his tube feedings.

Gone were our hopes that he would "grow out of" the seizures and their devastating complications by age two. We found ourselves in deep waters of the unknown struggling to figure out the best thing to do for our son and our family.

"What would you do, Mom?" I asked one evening after dinner as we leaned against the deck rails overlooking our wooded backyard. She and Dad had flown in to help me during the extended hospitalization. Although I'd hired more sitter help with Joe's increased travel abroad, I longed for family support. I talked to Mom and Dad several times a week, and almost daily after

Matthew's birth, but had never found the right time to ask Mom what was on my heart. "What would you have done if Forest had lived, but been, well, not the Forest we knew—or like Matthew?"

"Honey," she said as she turned to me and took both of my hands in hers. "I'd find the best care I could for him."

"Really? You wouldn't care for him yourself? At home?"

"I would have tried to do what was best for Forest and the family," she said.

I was stunned, and then strangely relieved. I had resigned from IBM to try to provide the care that Matthew needed, but I'd made the sobering discovery that I didn't have the skills or the aptitude to do so. Brittany was an active four-year-old. I was pregnant with my third child. Joe was working hard to provide for us.

So Joe and I began to investigate alternative care. After considerable research, we found a hospital for chronically ill children who, like Matthew, were medically fragile and required round-the-clock specialized care. We were shocked to discover it was only a few miles away from the hospital where he was being treated.

"Expect obstacles," the neurologist had told me, the same neurologist who lectured me on "the will of the parent" technique for giving Matthew his medication.

"But this specialized pediatric hospital is only a couple of miles down the road from this hospital," I said. "We've been here practically all summer. Why did *no one* tell us about it and its services for children like Matthew?" I continued, meaning her, but generalizing to make it less pointed.

"Probably because you didn't ask," she said, not bothering to look up at me as she was reading through Matthew's chart, marking her place with a shiny red pencil.

"What?" I said, fighting my temper. "So they see us struggling here. Know my family situation," I gestured, pointing to my pregnant belly. "See me every single day with Matthew, crying, trying to figure out how to handle this complex and difficult situation. And no one tells me about this option? Not a word?"

"Well, Mrs. Galli," she said, glancing up from her paperwork, "Now you know. But I still say expect obstacles. They may not have a bed for him."

"Can't we check?"

"Yes, but there is an application process for that," she said as she got up to leave the room. "Let me know if you need any further assistance."

"Sure thing," I muttered to myself. As if this Queen of Negativity had ever been helpful before.

But she was right. The long, complicated process drained me in every possible way—mentally, emotionally, and physically. Joe was traveling, but was able to arrange for someone from his staff to help me. By that time, I was so confused and overwhelmed about what to do next that I welcomed any help.

From the very beginning of Matthew's seizures, I felt like I wasn't working hard enough to meet his needs. A testy exchange with the hospital social worker didn't help. At first I thought she was just being thorough, a necessary part of the process, as she probed the details about my care of Matthew. Then her questions sharpened, infused with a strange, almost accusatory tone. "So, you didn't do . . . you only did . . . and why didn't you think of . . . ?"

My fragile defense finally crumbled and I blurted out, "I'm doing the best I can! You make me feel like I'm a bad mother!"

Unfazed, the woman carefully placed her hands palms down in front of her, leaned toward me from her desk, and coolly replied, "*I* can't make *you* feel any particular way, Mrs. Galli." She paused and looked directly into my eyes. "*You* make yourself feel. Not *I*."

My hurt whitened to anger. This professional, who specialized in helping parents with critically and chronically ill children find resources, chose that moment to educate me on the source of my feelings instead of empathizing with me and trying to help. I was furious. She was supposed to give me guidance, not send me into a deeper tailspin. I stood up, left her and her heart of steel, and made it to the car before I broke down sobbing.

I called Dad as soon as I got home. He agreed with me that this woman was terribly insensitive and had "no business being in that profession," but then tried to help me see the truth of her words. "Others can give you information, BB," he said gently. "But how you feel about it and react to it is up to you."

"So it's okay for her to beat me up like that? I should just take it?" I shot back. "She's incompetent, Dad. An embarrassment to the profession. I think I should get her fired!"

"I hear you, BB, but you need to focus on *your* needs. Don't get sidetracked. If she can be helpful to you, great. If she can't, move on and find someone who can."

Although I understood this intellectually, I still could not entirely absorb it emotionally. I tried to stay true to the facts, to not let others' reactions create guilt. But it was hard, even after we moved Matthew to the new facility.

Joe and I truly felt Matthew was going to get better care outside our home; we made that decision together. However, doubts crept back for me. At some level, we were admitting a shortcoming, a defeat. We could not provide what we wanted for our child—a life at home with his family. Ambivalence refused to stop taunting me. Are we doing the right thing? Are there other alternatives? Is this a loving thing to do?

"When is Matthew coming home from the hospital?" a curious acquaintance asked one day.

My explanatory floodgate opened. I spilled out every detail of where he was and why he was not coming home as if presenting myself to a judge or jury to make my case. I relived the decision all over again, in front of a near stranger. When I finished, I was exhausted, tearful, and embarrassed that I had poured out far more than what the poor woman probably wanted to hear.

"I'm doing the best I can right now," I finally told her and kept telling myself.

But I'm not sure I believed it. How do we ever know for sure if we are doing our best?

Chapter 9

When Hope Hurts

To love at all is to be vulnerable.
—C. S. Lewis

"IT HURTS TO hope," I told Trish before I even sat down in her small corner office. I couldn't stop the tears. As the hospital's onsite psychologist, Trish's role was to support families dealing with chronically ill children. I met her the first day of Matthew's transfer, along with Matthew's impressive medical team. After a few weeks, I needed her help.

She shut the door and slipped around her desk to face me. She had long dark hair and light-blue eyes. She offered me a tissue urging me with a soft, "yes," to continue.

"I get so many mixed signals about Matthew's future. First, the seizures are nonstop and no one can make them go away and he is unresponsive to me. Then the seizures stop for no apparent reason and he starts to smile at me." I babbled on for another ten minutes. I could tell she was used to listening, her eyes inviting me to go on and share the pain, her hands laced and clasped in front of her as if she were praying.

Matthew's fluctuating progress had begun to overwhelm me, blurring my focus, the very thing I could count on to keep me stable and moving forward. We had made the decision, the good decision, the well-thought out decision, the best decision, we were certain, to admit Matthew to this specialized program. Yet his roller-coaster progress was tormenting me.

Was it the right decision? Am I being responsible? Or am I a coward? I couldn't see the future, or the path to it. There were just too many variables. I was drowning in uncertainty.

Trish listened to my account of each extreme and my attempts to address each, and took a few notes. When I took a breath she said simply, "It may help you to pursue parallel paths."

"What?" The odd words latched onto a different part of my mind. "Parallel paths?"

"Yes, think of the future with the possibility of two paths. One path preserves the hope that Matthew will outgrow these medical complexities; the other incorporates the reality that he may not."

The strange notion settled like a calming spa mist in the room. I dried my eyes and inhaled it. "Can I borrow a pen?"

She plucked one from the top of her desk and handed it to me.

"Pursue parallel paths," I repeated and scrawled in Matthew's notebook, a record of his doctors, nurses, medications, and logbook of seizures that I kept with me at all times.

"We may want one outcome, but we may get another," Trish explained. "Pursuing parallel paths prepares us for both."

Her advice helped to quiet the warring factions of hope versus acceptance in my singularly focused mind. My mission had been to "fix" the situation. Goal-oriented and results-driven, I didn't know how to do anything halfway, always tackling issues head on. Although my feet had never touched a wrestling mat, I was just as competitive as Joe. I wanted to win at most everything I set out to do.

But with no IBM quotas, sales contests, or awards to reflect my efforts, I threw myself into the details of Matthew's care with few, if any, measures in place to guide my quest for answers. Overachieving had always served me well in school and at work. Surely it would be an asset in handling my child's crisis. I wanted to win, to beat this thing. I knew if I put enough effort into it, I would prevail.

I had visited Matthew daily, checked his progress, and met with his medical team weekly. I called in after every blood draw to check his levels and questioned the doctor if I thought the dosage needed to be changed. I kept my logbook current and got to know the nurses by name for all three shifts. I was going to be the parent that cared the most and tried the hardest to understand as much as I could about my child's condition

But the terrible truth was that no one really understood it. And when "degenerative" was added to the diagnostic list, our goals for Matthew narrowed to just one—to stabilize his seizure-filled days, providing him with as much comfort as possible.

❧

OUR HOME LIFE was complex, but ran smoothly. I juggled the house and care for the kids and my pregnancy while Joe continued his extraordinary success at work. Brittany was happy with her jammed schedule of school and playdates. I regularly met with Trish during my visits with Matthew. Her "parallel paths" concept kept me stable.

Soon I would rely on her wisdom for my daughter, too.

"Let's play house," Brittany, then four, said to her friend. "But no boy babies," she instructed as they were creating their pretend families. "Boy babies have seizures."

I cringed when I heard her words, offered so matter-of-factly to her playmate. "That's 'magical thinking,'" Trish explained when I recounted the incident. "Brittany is looking for a way to explain why her brother has seizures and she does not. Creating the fact that boy babies have seizures helps her accept and understand her world."

The next week, Brittany began her own specialized play therapy sessions with Trish, who hoped to reframe Brittany's thinking about her brother.

When I told Joe about Brittany's new therapy, he listened, but then lowered his eyes and released a deep-weighted sigh. How well I knew it—the sigh of resignation. Yet we didn't share it. Instead, I felt him retreat, pulling away from me and the complexities of our family life as we both began to recognize the ripple effect of Matthew's fragile health.

That night, I journaled and cried for my daughter and her simple but profound way of dealing with the unknown. Magical thinking—I longed for it, too! Anything to help me make sense out of the senseless.

IT WAS WEDNESDAY...
...days after I mailed...

"A FLUKE" OR "bad luck" were words the doctors had used to describe Matthew's condition, and they kept playing in my mind as my pregnancy progressed. As the magnitude of my son's condition unfolded, I compared pregnancies to see if I could find any warning signs, despite the negative test results.

I had extreme morning sickness in the first three months with Matthew, and daylong nausea as well. This time my pregnancy seemed to be moving ahead just as Brittany's had, with little morning sickness, and none at all after the first trimester. I was certain this child would be fine.

After a full-term delivery with no complications, Madison Rae Galli was born on March 24, 1992. Her middle name was a playful tip of the hat to Rachel, my Sissy. A beautiful baby girl, with a wisp of dark hair and bright eyes, Madison captured our hearts instantly, but not without caution. Gone were my days of unbridled bliss around infants. I hawked every stage of her development; I knew all the tricks, the tests, and the vocabulary. We passed the critical three-month milestone with no seizures. I had learned that at that delicate age, the brain begins to develop in ways that can reveal abnormalities. Every night, I held my breath, fearful that the monitor would announce another foreign sound.

But it didn't, and we were grateful.

Physically, Madison was right on track. She smiled and enjoyed her Johnny Jump Up exerciser and music. She loved watching videos of Barney, the famous purple dinosaur, and would bounce and "sing" to his every tune. She laughed easily, amusing herself as she clutched to the side of her playpen, jumping to the beat of Barney's melodies. Her giggle was infectious.

Madison was not a good sleeper, but neither was Brittany, so I wasn't overly concerned. I wasn't sure I knew what normal was anymore, so I focused on more concrete indicators. She nailed the physical milestones so absent in Matthew's development—rolled over before three months of age, sat at five months, and was learning to crawl at six months. We were relieved.

Soon, Joe and I welcomed the news that we were pregnant once again. At thirty-four, we wanted to complete our family, keeping the kids close together in age. For the sixth time in five years, we were looking forward to another—our final—child.

Meanwhile, Madison, at eight months old, still hadn't babbled; she made noises, but not the "ma-ma" sounds of typically developing children of that age. She had an unusual cry, a nasal tone that was lower than a whine, but higher than a groan, almost sounding as if she were in pain. She slept very little, sometimes only a few hours each night.

"Beck, what's she doing?" Joe asked after we'd said grace and hand-squeezed during a rare family meal. I'd given the girls a snack to give him time to "run the steps," a version of his college workout he did weekly at a local hotel. I'd even allowed Brittany, then five, to "play Daddy" to keep her occupied. She loved doing "PREZenTAshuns," clicking and talking through the carousel of slides in our living room where Joe rehearsed.

"I'm not sure, Joe, but she loves straws. She's almost obsessed with them," I said as we both watched her ritual. She took the straw and stared into it as if she were x-raying it, holding it tightly in one hand and flicking it intensely with the other. She seemed to get lost in the quick flicking motion and groaned "EEEEeee" with delight.

"She likes watches, too, Daddy," Brittany chimed in, as she hopped down from her booster seat, her blonde pigtails flying, to get the plastic Barney watch for her sister. Madison took the watch by the strap and held it, and then flicked it hard and fast, holding it close to her face. Her wide-eyed stare was not unlike Matthew's eyes during a seizure. But she never seized. She locked her gaze into the blurred motion. She "EEEE-ed" again with delight.

"I have an appointment with Dr. Tellerman next week."

"Keep me posted," Joe replied, shooting Madison another quizzical look before stabbing the last broccoli floret and popping it into his mouth.

The following week, Dr. Tellerman, the developmental behavioral pediatrician I sought out when Matthew developed seizures, concurred with my concerns at her nine-month checkup. Further testing revealed that Madison was more than twenty-five percent language delayed, qualifying for services in a local Infants and Toddlers Program. At least I knew how to manage those services; they were the same ones that Matthew received. I began to replicate that process for my daughter.

Yet even with these interventions, Madison's speech did not progress. She continued to develop unusual mannerisms—spinning plastic bottles and lampshades, staring for long periods of time at the aquarium's water bubbles, flapping her hands, and repeating, "EEEE." All seemed to create a motion she could stare into, and get lost in, experiencing both exuberance and comfort in retreating into her world of flicking and spinning.

In April 1993, at thirteen months of age, Madison was diagnosed with pervasive developmental disorder—a generalized category of developmental delay that was later classified as autism.

I was seven months pregnant.

Joe and I had lost two children to miscarriage, and now, two of our three living children had special needs.

⚬᪥⚬

AS MY PREGNANCY with our last child progressed, the pace at home grew more chaotic. I struggled to manage it all, but kept moving forward. Joe traveled extensively as his role in the company expanded. I found excellent child care to help me and was fortunate to meet other parents whose journey with autism mirrored mine. We shared treatment ideas, therapists, and became sounding boards for new ideas and information.

I visited Matthew as often as I could with Brittany and Madison. Joe did not join us often, even when he was in town.

"Can we drop by and see Matthew?" I would ask him on our "date night" as we headed into Baltimore for dinner. I'd tried to steal that habit from Mom and Dad's routines, but it was difficult with Joe's travel.

Silence would fill the pause.

The answer was "no." I knew that. It had been "no" for quite a while, but somehow I couldn't accept it. Like in the early days of Matthew's seizures, I still wanted Joe with me in the painful journey. In fact, I wanted him to be like me, to feel like me, to think like me, to love like me. I tried to teach him by showing him my way and inviting him to join me.

"Somebody's got to drive," I reminded myself.

I still loved him, even though I did not understand him.

But slowly, an indignant self-pity slipped into my thinking. Why did I have to be the manager, the researcher, the decision maker, and the front line in our children's care? Joe was relentless in his pursuit of professional success. Why couldn't he apply those business skills to our home life? Why would he not engage in the way I wanted? His silence and detachment were maddening. I was hurt that he would not help me and angry that I was so alone. I wanted him to be the Joe I needed him to be.

Still, I could never find the words or the courage to ask for it. We soldiered on, once more, in silence.

TEN WEEKS AFTER Madison's initial diagnosis, Joseph Peter Galli arrived on July 6, 1993. His scheduled birth proved to be a unique and wondrous first for us. Joe and my mom joined me in the delivery room as an epidural let me feel more joy than pain this time around. It was an extraordinary experience—"holy ground," my mother called it.

Our newborn son was the smallest of my four children, but had the most hair and the longest fingers. His jet-black locks were over an inch long. While Joe and I celebrated the healthy birth, Dr. Tellerman examined our son and noticed some peculiar discolored blood vessels on his abdomen.

"I'd like to do some blood work," he said. "There's probably no cause for alarm, but these broken blood vessels, petechiae, should be checked."

We waited for the results, stunned at the possibility of another child with medical concerns. The petechiae were confirmed, a warning signal that our baby's platelet count was dangerously low. He was at risk for spontaneous bleeds anywhere in his system. And if one occurred in the brain or the spine, it could be permanently disabling.

Two nurses rushed our child to the neonatal intensive care unit (NICU), where the medical staff began to administer treatments to boost his platelet count. Because his veins were too small for the intravenous fluids, they shaved his beautiful dark locks and started the IV in his head.

The unusual blood disorder, alloimmune thrombocytopenia, was serious and could be life-threatening, we learned. Numb to this news while realizing the necessity of understanding it, we had no time for grief, only adrenaline-charged fear.

"What do you mean by spontaneous bleeds? Should I not touch him?" I asked.

I was assured it was safe and actually beneficial for me to hold him. Smocked in a blue gown, I held my breath to keep from trembling as the nurse put the small bundle in my arms, making sure the IV was unobstructed.

"You precious boy, you precious, precious boy," I cooed to him. "At least you had your picture made before your fancy haircut." I smiled at his soft eyes that seemed to be mesmerized by my face.

I must have asked the doctors, "Will he be okay?" but then, again, maybe I didn't. Who knew how much they didn't know this time. I trusted no one with my fragile hope.

Smocked but nowhere near ready to hold his son, Joe watched from a distance, his animated arms folded tight across his chest, eyes dark and remote. He paced, only a few steps— short and quick—refusing to sit, the gown's ties whipping behind him in his wake.

We were lost in a jungle of plastic where acrylic cradles housed fragile lives and IV bags hung like spaghetti from cold metal poles. The rhythmic humming of machines anchored the softness of the room, where whispers, almost reverent, floated over the babies who were hovering on the tender threshold of life.

We struggled with our son's name. It was hard to think in definitive terms with so much turmoil and unknown. Although we'd named him Joseph Peter Galli, we wondered what to call him—Joe, like his father and grandfather? Peter, like the brother Joe lost? Or Joseph Peter to avoid any decision—and dire associations—altogether?

We mostly called him Baby Galli.

After three days, I was discharged. I went home without my son. Joe left to go on a business trip.

⁓⚬⁓

I HEARD A tap on my bedroom door. I had just finished pumping for the second time that morning and had put a label on the breast-milk bottle, preparing it for the noon trip to the NICU.

"Yes?"

"You have flowers, Becky," a soft voice said. Pat, our newly hired nanny, had only been with us a few days, but I already loved this woman. Her melodic voice, just like her demeanor, was comforting yet focused, steadfastly helpful.

"Come in," I said, tucking the clunky breast pump machine and its suction cups in the corner of my sitting room. I sat down on the couch and placed a heating pad behind my neck.

"These just came," she said, and put the large bunch of yellow tulips and spider mums on the end table. She handed me the card.

"Wonder who sent these?" I mumbled. The house was still full of flowers from Baby Galli's birth five days earlier. Mom, Dad, and Rachel were here, helping me manage the postpartum chaos. Joe was still away on business. "Wishing you a speedy recovery. Thinking of you. Dr. Lamos," I read out loud. My hands dropped to my lap, my shoulders slumped down until a shot of pain tweaked my neck. I adjusted the heating pad again and looked up at Pat. "It's my doctor, Pat. My general practitioner. My doctor sent me flowers!"

He knew about Matthew. And Madison. And had followed

this pregnancy with Baby Galli, including the predelivery kidney stone saga. I'd gone to the emergency room with horrific back pain, thinking I was having "back labor." Nope. I had a kidney stone, of all things! After my OB suggested bed rest until my delivery date, I updated Dr. Lamos. "It's too risky to blast the stone or put a stent in to relieve the pain during this stage of pregnancy. To ease the pain, I'm on Demerol. It still hurts, Dr. Lamos, but I don't care!"

Dipped weekly at the OB office visit, my bloody pee, the evidence of the stuck stone and my pain, was the color of black-cherry Kool-Aid. My OB decided to induce labor one week before my due date. The plan was to put in an epidural, deliver the baby, and then have a urologist insert a stent with the epidural still in place. A twofer, just my style. But, apparently, I delivered the baby and the stone at the same time, a post-delivery test revealed, so a stent was unnecessary.

Three days after Baby Galli's birth, I developed an incessant neck pain so I booked an appointment with Dr. Lamos. "My son's in the NICU, I'm trying to pump so he can get breast milk, but my neck hurts so much I can't even sleep."

The towering man from the Midwest placed his warm hands on either side of my neck and pressed down evenly. "Drop your chin to your chest, Rebecca," he said, looking down through his bifocals.

"Ow, I can't." Pain ripped through my left shoulder up to the nape of my neck.

"I think you pulled a muscle during child birth, my dear. You need physical therapy at least three times a week."

"Great," I said, gingerly rolling my head from side to side. I looked up to smile at him. "At least my folks are in town and can cart me around. Per my OB instructions, I can't drive for two more weeks."

"Where's Joe?" he asked. He was our family practitioner so he knew us both well.

"Who knows, Dr. Lamos? Some business trip in Charlotte," I said, massaging my neck. "He's devastated. Can't believe we have more kid issues. Won't even hold the baby." I paused and looked at the caring man. "He's gone a lot, Dr. Lamos. A LOT. Spending more time down in North Carolina than he did when we lived there," I mumbled. "I'm just trying to get through each day. Mom, Dad, and Rachel are huge helps. And my new nanny, Pat."

Two days later, the yellow bunch of flowers arrived.

"What does it say when your doctor sends you flowers, Pat?" We both laughed, but I was grateful. Dr. Lamos had a rare perspective on my family, the medical complexities, and their influence on me—a true ally in my complicated life. "Tell Dad I'll be ready to leave in ten minutes for PT. We'll stop back here for lunch, pick up the breast milk, and then head to the hospital to see Baby Galli."

FOR SIXTEEN DAYS, the doctors worked to stabilize the platelet count. Baby Galli had one small bleed in his gastrointestinal tract, but thankfully, none appeared in permanently disabling areas such as the brain or spine.

Focusing on the details of his condition kept me going. I monitored every bit of information, listening closely to both what the doctors said and what they didn't say and reported it nightly to Joe, whether in town or out. I had to block out my other children's disabilities—for the moment—and cling to the thought that tragedy could not strike permanently for a third time.

Blood work became the barometer of our son's health—and our hope. When the results finally revealed a normal count, we took Joseph Peter Galli home. We decided to call him Peter, which means "rock." We believed our son's challenges were behind him.

After six years and six pregnancies, we finally had our four children, and our family was complete.

"Do you have children?" new acquaintances would ask Joe or me at the time.

"Yes, we have two girls and two boys, roughly two years apart—girl, boy, girl, boy," we would answer with our Teflon-coated game faces on.

"How perfect!" they would reply.

And our resigned and rehearsed plastic smiles would meet their bright gazes.

"Yes, just perfect."

Chapter 10

When Winners Fail

Don't cut what you can unravel.
—Dr. R. F. Smith Jr.

JOE WAS DIFFERENT after Peter's birth. His physical distance in the NICU lingered, then became something hard, finite—a retreat or was it resolve? His eyes were dark, Heathcliff dark, vacant yet troubled. It was as if something had broken inside, his heart light crushed by some mysterious alien.

I, too, had a broken heart. I, too, was a victim of these life-changing aliens who came into our life with no cause and stayed with no cure. But I couldn't retreat. How could he? We were so much alike. Winners. Fighters. Why weren't we on the same side anymore? I felt like I was on the mainland and he'd marooned himself on a nearby island. Even though he still called nightly, something was off. He was there—but he wasn't. I'm not sure if I gave him the space to grieve or he took it. I was so overwhelmed with the day-to-day logistics that I'm surprised I even noticed.

But I did. And I worried.

Half of all marriages end in divorce. But when special needs children are part of the family, that number can jump to 80 percent, I'd read. In the three years since that blaring baby monitor ripped through our lives, epilepsy, cerebral palsy, mental retardation, autism, and a life-threatening blood disorder pelted our marriage. Just when we thought we'd mastered one issue, another erupted. We were in trouble, I could sense it. But I didn't know what I could do about it.

⟿⟆⟆⟿

TWO WEEKS AFTER we brought Peter home, projectile vomiting reduced his body weight to near-birth levels. Dr. Tellerman sent me to a pediatric specialist who confirmed that Peter had pyloric stenosis, a thickening of the lower part of the stomach that prevents food from emptying out of it. Surgery enlarges the area and corrects the resulting vomiting.

Generally, we were told, this condition occurs with the firstborn male. Except in my family. Peter was the fourth born and second son.

Joe was traveling again so Mom came down to help me through Peter's surgery. It went well, and Pete, as we called him for short, finally had a healthy stretch.

But Joe wasn't there to witness it. By that time, I'd hired five sitters, including Pat, to help me with Brittany's camps, Madison's therapies, my doctor appointments, and visits to Matthew. Joe was rarely home, and when he was he was distracted—either working or working out. Thank goodness his salary kept pace with his travel and my child-care needs. I was grateful for that.

I continued to see Trish regarding Matthew, Madison, and now Peter after his precariously fragile start. Brittany's limit-testing had begun to escalate, an apparent response to all the special attention given to her siblings. She too began sessions with

Trish and we implemented weekly "Behavior Charts" to target six good behaviors, monitored daily with stickers and rewards.

"Okay, Britty, it's time for prayers," I said as I tucked her in bed one night.

"Aren't we doing happy-sad-mixed-up-mad first?"

"Oh yes, honey," I said. "I almost forgot." Trish had recommended that I spend extra time with Brittany at bedtime and to talk about a daily happy, sad, mixed-up, and mad feeling to encourage her to share her feelings. The hardest one was always the mixed-up one.

"So what was your mixed-up experience today, Britty?"

"I don't know, Mom. What's yours?"

"Well, let's see. I'm happy that it rained today because we needed it. But sad because it caused your soccer game to be canceled."

Although our family functioned—problem-solved, analyzed, gathered resources, and just kept going—slogging through each crisis *du jour*, after a while, an emotional fog settled in. I was worn out and lonely, but had trouble telling Joe I needed him without somehow provoking a fight, most often a standoff of silence. He breezed in and out with barely a kiss or time for an update. I told Trish about Joe's upsetting behaviors and she suggested couples counseling with her mentor, and now colleague, Dr. A. A. Lucco.

"Sure, Beck," Joe said when I'd asked him to go. "Whatever you want." Then he left for the gym.

⚶

I POPPED INTO Dr. Lucco's office, unannounced, nabbing him between his sessions after I'd finished mine with Trish. "Dr. Lucco, I'm Becky Galli. I know I'm being terribly rude but I wanted to introduce myself and my crazy situation," I flashed a smile and kept talking. "My husband, Joe, and I will see you next week for a two-hour session, but I wanted to give you a heads up. We have four children, ages six and under, two with special needs. My youngest is two months and has just recovered from a rare blood disorder, sixteen days in the NICU," I rattled on without taking a breath. "Anyway, I don't know what's wrong with Joe. I have all these kids and need his help but he's rarely here and when he is he isn't and I gave up a ten-year career with IBM to be home with the kids and now I feel like I'm not even married," I blurted out, finally taking a quick breath. "It's not fair and I'm going nuts and it's like he's in this huge daze and doesn't even know it and needs to snap out of it and, well, well . . . you need to fix him!"

I paused to take another breath, surprised at my desperation. The kind man looked at me, his bushy gray eyebrows up and brown eyes alert; but the rest of his face was unreadable.

He said nothing.

"I'm so sorry," I said, taking a step back from my invasion, hoping some of the words would retreat with me. "I do that, babble on, that is." I shook my head to clear my thoughts and swallowed hard. "Look, I'm grateful that you're willing to see us, Dr. Lucco. Really. We love each other, we do. We've just had so much," I whispered, my voice cracking. "I hope you can help us. I'm sorry if I've made you late for your next appointment."

"I'll see you next week, Mrs. Galli," he said evenly, his tone warm but professional. I offered my hand and he shook it, firm, still holding my gaze with those alert eyes that seemed to record every bit of what I'd said and somehow more.

I exited without a sound, looking down at my moving feet, my long unkempt bangs shading my eyes as I passed waiting clients. The carpeted floor guided me out of the office into the building's lobby where it changed to a dark-gray marble. My heels clicked with each long stride. I stared at my shoes, last season's boots, cute but dated and in need of a shine as they led me to my car. I plopped in the "mom-mobile," my trusty Taurus station wagon where the smell of my Starbucks welcomed me. I shut the door and cried.

Had I lied? Did I still love Joe? Did he still love me? His business trips were longer. He spent more time working out, even started peck-dancing in the mirror like the wrestlers did in college while a new hand-gripper routine bulged his already Popeye-sized forearms. And he kept sunning himself on the deck, something he'd never done before. More than once, I noticed he was talking on the phone in his car, idling in the driveway. Business calls, he said.

Mixed-up feelings were rampant in our household. Brittany wasn't alone.

⚘

"OKAY, DR. LUCCO," I said in our first counseling session. "We need to come out of here with either an amazing marriage or an amazing divorce," I said, raising both hands in the air to indicate the extremes. "Let's go."

There, I'd said it. The D-word. Maybe that would shock Joe out of his daze. No one in either of our families had ever divorced. It was not our way. We were strong. We did not give up. His parents had survived the loss of a child. So had mine. Surely we could weather these issues with our children, too.

The weekly sessions helped at first. "Come from the hurt, not the anger, in your exchanges," Dr. Lucco told me with Joe listening. "Don't forget to put out your price tags," he said. "When something is important, be clear about its worth to you."

And I tried. But I felt like I was whining. Did I really have to tell Joe I was hurt when he was late for dinner and didn't call? That I'd busted my butt to get the kids ready, the table set, the candles lit, and a hot dinner prepared for our family? Did I need to tell him that I needed him to care about us and not just about work and working out? That he needed to show up at home as consistently as he did there? That family time was important to me? Didn't he know that? Couldn't he see that? He was a smart man. He certainly had no problem seeing issues at work. All he needed to do was apply some of his business acumen at home. Didn't he love me enough to understand what mattered to me?

Despite the counseling, I felt Joe pulling away even more. Slowly my anger at his distance turned to a fear of his leaving me. Lucco must have sensed it.

"Becky, what are you afraid of?"

I'd been quiet in that session, my crossed arms holding me tight. But with this question, my arms flung open to my lap, my mouth, agape. "No disrespect, Dr. Lucco, but ARE YOU KIDDING ME? If Joe left me, I would be an *unemployed, single, mother of four*," I said emphasizing each word. "*Two* with special needs. How could I *possibly* support them?"

Joe tried to assure me that would never happen. But Lucco could see I was still upset.

"I've seen a separation agreement work well in this situation," Lucco said. "Even if it's never used—you never separate—it can be helpful to clarify the financial arrangements."

"Can we do that, Joe? Please?"

"Ah, we don't need that, Beck. Really, I don't think it's necessary."

But when my tears welled, he relented. "Ok, sure, if that's what you want."

Lucco had described Joe as "loyal," but not committed, whatever that meant. It felt good to be gaining some commitment at least in one area of our marriage. I jumped into the process. I may have been hurt, angry, and silent, but I wasn't stupid, much less a victim. Our kids' future depended on me. So I analyzed our household expenses, did five-year spreadsheets, read William Ury's *Getting Past No*, and listened to his book on tape, *Getting to Yes*, before I even sat down with Joe to review the agreement. Surprisingly, with very little discussion, he signed it. Relieved of the financial uncertainty, I plugged back in to our Lucco sessions. Joe and I were still hard-charging firstborns, but so different from one another now. My calendar was filled with the kids and doctors and sitters while his had dinner meetings, board retreats, and first-class tickets to Lake Cuomo and regular trips to Europe, often on the Concorde. Although still living under the same roof, we began to pull away from each other even more as I began to feel resentful of the weight of our family issues.

I talked to my parents nonstop. Dad's counseling background was helpful, but he would always steer me back to Lucco for professional advice. He subscribed to his doctor friends' philosophy that "you can't do surgery on your own kids."

"Trust the process," Dad kept telling me.

"But I think I'm going crazy, Dad. Joe's buffed body shows up, but his mind is elsewhere. Travels so much. Vacant eyes, empty promises," I rattled on.

Dad listened and then said simply, "Don't cut what you can unravel, BB."

Again, I tried. But the more I tried to unravel the situation and understand my husband, the more mystery I found. Despite the counseling, life at home became increasingly volatile. Joe's erratic absences and behaviors sent me spinning into a hyper-vigilant state of investigation. I caught myself routinely riffling through his wallet, his briefcase, even the bottom of a messy overfilled garbage can, to piece together evidence of my suspicions. A seething anger began to take root as I began mentally to underline all of the injustices of the situation.

Forget telling him I was hurt and needy, I reasoned. We were *married*. These were *our* kids. I was his *wife*. Couldn't he just *man up* and be responsible? *Engage*, for crying out loud. Engage in the life we have. It's not the life we wanted, dang it, but it's the life we have!

But the more demanding I became, the more he disappeared. Where was he? Who was with him? Why was he not here, where he needed to be? A slow rage began to consume me.

After one particular frenzied but fruitless search, I caught a glimpse of myself in the mirror. Who was that crazed woman, so misguided in her relentless pursuit of what—the truth? The truth was I was a mess with him. This had to stop. I could not stand one more uncontrollable thing in my life.

"I CAN'T DO it anymore." I'd called Mom and Dad, asking them both to get on the line. The kids were asleep. I had cried. Journaled for over an hour. Even attempted prayer. Joe was gone again. I wasn't even sure when he'd be back or when I would hear from him. "I feel stuck, trapped. I have to do something. I don't like who I am becoming." I paused, gathering myself. "We've both signed the separation agreement. I've found a furnished apartment for Joe not too far away. And now," I took a deep breath and said in a steady voice that even surprised me, "I need space to clear my head and think. I'm not ready to divorce Joe, but I can't live with him in this house anymore."

They both understood.

Lucco guided us on how to tell the children. Brittany, then six, helped her dad move out. Matthew, still cared for in the pediatric hospital, had just turned four. Madison was two. Peter was nine months old. Joe was compliant, willing to do whatever Lucco suggested. He moved through each transitional scene as if he weren't in it. Aloof. Stoic. Dumbfoundingly trusting.

I still managed all the money. Paid the bills and gave him cash when he asked. I would arrange child care for his weekends and then promptly leave to visit friends and family to avoid being alone in what used to be our home.

As we began our new every-other-weekend routine, the great irony hit me. I had fought hard to get away from the loneliness in our marriage. I had accomplished that, but now I was even more alone. The resentment of being alone led to being alone with resentment.

What had I done to my family?

Chapter 11

The Closure Party

*There is a time for departure, even when
there's no certain place to go.*
—Tennessee Williams

THE SILENCE OF loss filled my house on "his" weekends. Empty echoes reminded me that I still had those overwhelming family responsibilities. And now I had no partner, not even a silent one, by my side for support.

However, I reminded myself that I'd had enough unmanageable things in my life. Let someone else deal with the crazy calendar, unpredictable schedule, and vacant stares.

And they did. Women waltzed into Joe's life like heat-seeking missiles, targeting a successful executive who no longer wore a wedding band.

I bought a new car, a mink coat, and gym membership. I lived on Starbucks cappuccinos and fruit-on-the bottom yogurts. I shed my post-maternity wardrobe and found a personal shopper at Nordstrom's to help me shop for my pre-pregnancy size-six figure. I was down to my fighting weight and ready for a new life—either way.

Now that we were legally separated, I dipped my toe back into the dating world. I remember my first time out to a bar with a girlfriend. After a fifteen-year absence, I felt like I had an "I'm a mother of four" neon sign blinking on my forehead. I met a few men, but could find nothing to talk about besides my family—like that was an uplifting topic. I kept hearing Dad's words about the importance of "appropriate self-disclosure" in building relationships and realized how little of me there was beyond my children. So, with good child care and supports in place, I went back to work to help ease my troubled mind.

As an outplacement job developer, I counseled clients who had just lost their jobs about the next steps in their lives. The words I spoke to them, applied to me, too:

- Assess your strengths and move toward them.
- Become a free agent, knowledgeable of what you have to offer beyond the confines of your job (marriage).
- Recognize the different facets of your life that may have been dormant in your last work experience (marriage) and include those in your plans.
- Reflect and create your "what happened" story and practice it. The more comfortable you are with your explanation, the more at ease others will be.
- Stay away from anger-tinged comments about your former employer (spouse).
- Bitterness can color your qualifications (and is unattractive!).

Despite all my efforts to adjust to the idea of the single life, I could not ignore one core thought, the one underneath all the changes and plans and positive thinking: *I did not want to be divorced.*

Joe and I had deep roots. We had been through so much. For so long. Surely we could work through this together.

⁓⧸⧸⁓

FOR THREE YEARS, we tried. Our sessions with Lucco continued weekly, sometimes more. But living apart gave us space to explore the single life. His world seemed to get simpler while mine got more complex as the single-parenting realities began to kick in. Although neither one of us wanted to end our marriage, we never could fully reconcile, either.

We talked through our respective issues of what we wanted and needed, but nothing seemed to stick. The more I gave, the less I got or at least that's what it felt like. And he'd developed this uncanny ability to twist things around and always make it my issue. Never his. My demands justified his disappearances. It was maddening.

"I want to be in the room with someone who wants to be in the room with me," I admitted during one of our sessions.

Lucco was silent, but looked to Joe to respond.

"I'm here, Beck," he said. And I caught a small sparkle from his still mysterious eyes.

"But I'd make dinners for you and you'd run the steps instead, and I'd tell you about doctor appointments and you'd say you're too busy. I'd ask you to help and you'd forget. . . ."

And his beautiful eyes went empty. It was like punching a cloud.

The next day, I wrote a letter to myself, part of my scrapbook of notes from our Lucco sessions that included copies of the cards and letters I sent Joe, and the pro and con lists I made for staying married or getting divorced.

AUGUST 26, 1996

Three years ago today we started working on our crumbling marriage. It's time to stop rereading your history, Becky. Make your plans and stick to them. December 31, 1996, is your target date. Your freedom date. Your life-changing date—a commitment to yourself. How energizing! Shoot for it! Know these three years of notes are the truth and can be used to support a renewal or a divorce. You're coming down the home stretch. You can do it, B. I know you can. He's not who you thought he was, but you've known that for quite a while now. You know you can live with him or without him. Do it, B. Do it with STYLE. Teach your children how to handle adversity. Show them your commitment to family, your faith, your belief in yourself and the ability to make things better.

That was what my brain was telling me to do. And by my deadline, my heart caught up.

⚭

"HE DIDN'T WANT to sign the final papers," I said to Dr. Lucco six months later in January 1997. "Joe asked me if I was sure, if maybe we should give it some more time."

"Of course he did, Becky. What else did you expect?"

I winced at his comment, on target as usual. Ever loyal, Joe never ever said he wanted to divorce me, yet he didn't seem to want to be married to me either, at least not in the way I thought about marriage. In my mind, we weren't a couple; we'd become two individuals sharing a mutual life. I wanted more than that. I grew up with more than that, and I couldn't settle for less. Not anymore. It was too painful to feel disconnected from the one who was supposed to be with me and face our life together "until death do us part." I knew Joe still cared for me, but I had to decide if I wanted that life.

Maybe he needed more from me, too. The kids took so much of my time, of me. Maybe he needed more of me than I had to give.

"I've tried everything," I told Mom and Dad. "Both my parallel paths are blazing with pain. It hurts to hope. It hurts to give up. But I am dying inside. I can unravel no further, Dad," I swallowed hard. "When the kids are older, I can honestly tell them I did everything I could to try to save our marriage. But I can't do it. I just can't." They understood.

The more I tolerated, the less of me there was, it seemed. I had to hold fast to what was left of me and try to rebuild a life without Joe, the one I wanted. Yet, when I brought the final divorce papers to Joe's office, he kept asking me if I was sure.

"Yes," I said firmly, but still wondered if I were lying. After another lengthy discussion, he signed them.

⊷⧓⊷

THE NEXT DAY, I brought the document to my attorney's office for the official filing. "You need to sign here," she prompted, pointing to the yellow sticky arrows.

I hesitated, shuffling the papers and my feet, and then glanced at my friend, Barbara, who'd come to support me.

"Take your time," the legal counsel advised. "I'll give you a few minutes." And she closed the door as she left. The room was quiet, shadowed by partially drawn shades, a massive mahogany conference table its anchor. I sat down, placing the pages in front of me. A single black pen rested nearby. The words blurred. My hands started to shake. More shuffling, this time in my mind. I am getting divorced. I will be on my own. I have four children.

What am I doing? Why couldn't I make it work? What didn't I try? I have failed.

The debate began, one last time. But then that other voice, the strong one, came back: But you cannot be you, being married to him. I took a deep breath.

"Are you okay?" asked Barbara, my friend I'd known since grade school. She stood beside me, letting the space and stillness do its work. As she waited for my response, she moved to sit down across the table from me. Another dozen could have joined her and still not made a dent in the emptiness.

"I'm fine. Really," I said, exhaling a bit. "Still battling the demons, but I'm ready." I looked up at my friend and found comfort in those compassionate eyes, the same eyes that could look left and go right on the basketball courts in our youth or roll with wide-eyed indignation at poor judgment or an off-color joke. She was a refined woman of the South, a Wellesley grad who was as comfortable throwing an elbow on that basketball court as she was throwing an Emily Post–perfect luncheon for eight.

I picked up the pen and in one smooth motion pushed down hard, but evenly, signing my name. "Done," I whispered, brushing back my hair as I sat up a little straighter.

Barbara pressed her lips together, lowering her eyes as if bidding farewell to a departed soul. We paused, absorbing the moment, and then stood up and walked from the darkened room to the reception area's awkward brightness. I put the documents on my attorney's desk near a fresh bunch of daisies—strange for that time of year.

A yellow-sweatered assistant wished us well. "The official decree will be mailed in a few weeks," she said as if it were a piece of art or honored degree, suitable for framing. "Good luck, Becky."

I smiled at her cheeriness, ready to leave that world of black and white that so crisply reduced my past and defined my future with a single dotted line. The January afternoon clouds allowed a few shreds of light to greet us as we bundled up with our hats and gloves, heading to the car. Barbara had insisted on coming with me a little harder than I had insisted that she didn't need to. As usual, her radar was accurate.

"We just weren't good for each other anymore, right?" And then we had the same discussion we'd had for over three years. I'd gone through the I-can't-believe-all-this-crap-that's-happened-to-me phase, faced it, and put on my big-girl panties and was ready to move on. She listened, as she always did, for the twenty-minute ride home, then helped me refocus.

"Oh, I loved your invitation, Becky. You know I'll be there. A *Closure* Party. What a great idea!" We pulled into the driveway and headed up the steps to the back door.

"Yep, well, we celebrate the firsts, so we might as well celebrate the lasts. The plans are 'coming along,' as Mom would say." We plopped down at the kitchen table. I grabbed my Franklin Planner from my briefcase and flipped past the work and children tabs, to the new section, Friends. "I have lists."

"Of course you do!"

"Pizza, booze, music from my '70s stash, X-rated movies, oh, and some cigars!"

Barbara's eyebrows shot up and then we both laughed as we remembered the last time we had tried cigars. I'd had a little bit too much to drink at our club's last Mardi Gras event and had given her date, a friend of mine too, a big smooch.

"So sorry about that," I said, reliving the embarrassment of the moment. "It was that snake-skinned sequin dress. Just made me feel a bit too wild, I guess."

"It was fine, no harm done," she said and we laughed again. "It was actually good to see you having such a good time."

"We had a blast, didn't we?" I leaned forward on the table and looked into the eyes of my dear friend. "I do hope I can find someone who wants to share my crazy life with me," I said, the tears welling up.

"You will, Becky, you will," Barbara said. "Your heart is so large. You deserve so much."

Barbara was more than my childhood friend; she was practically family. She was Rachel's age and her friend first, and part of that tightly knit high school group that included Forest. She loved Dad's jokes, Mom's Southern grace, and grieved with us through the loss of Forest. Then after college, in the strangest of coincidences, she was hired by the IBM Baltimore office and was assigned as a trainee to me. For the last thirteen years, she'd worked with me at IBM, watched me battle through six pregnancies, and witnessed firsthand the demise of my marriage.

"Thank you for being here for me," I smiled hard, a determined grimace, and then hugged my steadfast friend. "And now," I said as I popped up and pointed to the hallway, dabbing my sleeve to my eyes, "let's figure out how to use my peekaboo bar again."

⚬ৡৡ৽

SEVEN OF MY dearest friends came in for the festive party and sleepover. Five of them I had known for over twenty years. Four of them were in my wedding. All of them knew Mom, Dad, and Rachel, and knew about Forest. They knew the premium I placed on family and had supported me as I struggled with the decision to break mine apart. Yet we had never been together in my home in Baltimore, nor ever had the occasion to gather for this purpose. I had invited my friends to a "Closure Party" to mark the end of my fifteen-year marriage.

OCCASION: MY CLOSURE PARTY
DATE: SATURDAY, JANUARY 11TH TIME: 6 P.M.
COCKTAILS, DINNER, GAMES
PLACE: MY HOME
GIVEN BY: TO BECKY FROM BECKY WITH LOVE!
BRING YOUR FAVORITE CLOSURE SONG,
YOUR DANCING SHOES, YOUR IMAGINATION
AND YOUR INNER CHILD!! LET'S PARTY!

Barbara arrived early, helping me set up while I welcomed my guests. "Hey, Joy!' I hugged my potluck roommate as she entered the kitchen door.

"You look great, B," she said after I finally released her from the hug.

"Thanks! The gym is paying off." We could wear the same clothes and in fact did in college. One Halloween we passed for twins with our long-legged builds, blue eyes, and matching Farrah Fawcett hairstyles. She'd let me borrow her black dress for Forest's funeral.

"Bing!" I squealed as the lanky brown-eyed blonde scooted around Joy to give me a hug. "So great to see you, roomie!"

"And come on in, Cynthawea!" I teased my funny friend, the fashionista of the bunch that my daughter had renamed in her snaggletooth stage of speech. "You look great!" A striking brunette with Elizabeth Taylor brows, Cynthia's dark eyes sparkled with her signature playful thinking. You never knew exactly what was coming out of her mouth other than it would be unscreened—whether hilarious or deep. Although always fashion-forward, Cynthia sported the same hairstyle—cropped short to stifle unruly curls—since the day I met her our freshman year in college.

"I'm here, too," piped my "big sister" Robin. Although a year older, she was a good six inches shorter and delighted in telling everyone I was her "little" sorority sister. We Mutt-and-Jeffed-it through many a mixer. A petite green-eyed blonde, she had once modeled in her teens and still carried herself, all five foot two of her, with a notably erect posture, a tribute to the classical ballet training of her youth.

"Everyone, this is Kim, the Dukie," I said, teasing UNC's archrival. "But you guys will love her anyway. Kim, a Mensa-brilliant Duke grad and IBM colleague, had cranked out babies with the same rhythm I had. Then we both went through three-year separations. As did Bing.

They both reconciled. Kim had a baby. Bing had twins. I had a closure party.

"And this is Skipper, Barbara's friend and now mine."

"Hey, ya'll. So nice to meet you," my newest friend greeted and hugged everyone with her New Orleans charm.

"I smell pizza," Bing said. So funny because she was string-bean thin with the appetite of a nit.

"Wait, I need a tour," Robin chimed in. "Got to see the redecorating I've heard so much about." The Martha-Stewart wannabe had spoken. So they all gathered around me for the tour.

As I looked at my friends, I realized why I needed the party. Although my father disliked the word, closure, even lectured on its overuse and misleading message, it seem more than appropriate for me now. Closure might not be the magic word that helps one get over life's tragedies as he suggested in his columns and lectures. But for me, now, I needed some mark of finality, some way to close out what could never be again. And what better way to do that than with friends who knew me when.

"So how are the kids?" Bing asked when we passed some photos in the hall.

"Well, let's see," I paused to condense my thoughts. "Brittany's great, nine years old now, and in fourth grade. Headstrong as ever. Madison's four and doing well in her new autism outreach program. The bus comes to the end of our driveway to pick her up—so helpful. Pete's three and just had tubes put in his ears before Christmas, so he's finally talking—yeah! He's still not potty-trained—but that's not unusual for a boy, right? And little Matthew," I caught my breath, "he's seven now, believe it or not. He is stable and very well cared for. He still functions at about a three-month-old level and is tube fed. I visit with the kids when I can." I pressed my lips together and gave them a quick smile. "All under control—at the moment."

I smiled again at my friends, so relieved these gals knew better than to push for more. No questions. Just seven sets of caring eyes, compassionate eyes. They'd seen me live through the losses—most even knew Forest—and all knew the private way I moved through the pain.

"That's great, B," Bing said.

My kids are fine, I kept telling myself. I can do this divorce thing. I can make my family what I want it to be.

"Joe has them this weekend." I continued as we circled through the living room, office, and back to the hall. "They are 'visiting his parents' in Pittsburgh," I said, using my fingers for quotes. And I tied a bow on that conversation.

⚬⚬

"ANYONE READY FOR margaritas?" I fired up the blender inside my prized peekaboo bar.

"To good friends and the best that is yet to be," I toasted. And we drank. And talked. And drank some more.

Then the dancing began.

"A little blast from the past, ladies. From our DJ neighbors, seventeen years ago!" And I punched the cassette tape to play.

Do a little dance, make a little love . . . get down tonight! Boomed KC and the Sunshine Band. Then Michael Jackson. Then Madonna. Then Marvin Gaye. One funky baseline blended seamlessly into the next.

And we started dancing, on my coffee table. And in the bar. And from the upstairs overlook. Barbara grabbed her camera. "Smile, ladies!"

Then Gloria Gaynor's words stopped us all.

"It's your song, B!" Cynthia shrieked.

At first I was afraid, I was petrified. Kept thinking I could never live without you by my side. But then I spent so many nights thinking how you did me wrong. I grew strong. . . .

Every girl knew every word. Every note. And we belted it out, confident of the diva's message.

I've got all my life to live. I've got all my love to give. And I'll survive. I will survive!

And I knew I would. But not alone. I also knew that I'd put the best spin possible on the situation. I could only bear to tell them so much.

I didn't tell my girlfriends that my life felt like a simmering pot of kid issues, even though I was determined to manage it. That I was still worried about Pete's development. That despite twelve months of speech therapy, he still had an open-mouth posture with excessive drool—a possible sign of further developmental delays.

I didn't tell them that Madison was still nonverbal. That she was not responding well to her new therapies at school. That she was still only sleeping a few hours each night.

Or that Matthew was in his second specialized foster care home for medically fragile children. That even though we'd found good care for him after his hospital placement was discontinued, each move tore me apart.

Or that Brittany, although excellent in the classroom, was still a handful at home, a "masterful limit-tester," Trish had acknowledged, despite their counseling sessions. That to appease my willful daughter and her nonstop questions about the ever-changing future, I'd promised her this was going to be the "best year ever," a thought I kept telling myself as well.

I did, however, tell them that Joe's time "visiting the parents" seemed to be code for his place to take the kids where he could leave them and get on with whatever social life he had going, which was apparently robust and time-consuming given the tales the kids came back with.

But I also didn't share what was really on my heart. That I knew I shouldn't care about Joe's personal life—I did divorce him. But despite my best thinking and planning and bright-side attitude, the reset button that I kept trying to hit could not clear out our history. That I still cared for Joe and missed the man I married. That whoever or whatever had invaded our marriage and taken what I thought was mine forever had left my heart battered and scarred with anger, betrayal, and abandonment. That in my soul I secretly wondered: Was it me? Had I had become unlovable?

I didn't tell my dearest girlfriends that I was having a hard time letting go. That I was scared of this single life. That I didn't know if I could do it.

⚮

A FEW DAYS after the Closure Party, I decided to create a special gift for all who attended. The party did more than just celebrate an ending and a new beginning for me. It brought together my friends in a way that I wanted to sustain for the sure-to-be rocky adventure ahead. So I designed a hot-pink nightshirt, one we could wear and remember our bond.

On the front it read: LEARNING TO LOVE THE JOURNEY. And on the back: WHEN WAS THE LAST TIME YOU DID SOMETHING FOR THE FIRST TIME?

I mailed them Monday morning, February 10, 1997, just in time to arrive for Valentine's Day. That afternoon, I went to see Dr. Lamos for a lingering flu bug that would not leave me alone.

Chapter 12

One in a Million

Life is either a daring adventure or it is nothing.
—Helen Keller

IT WAS WEDNESDAY. Ash Wednesday, to be exact.

Two days after I mailed the pink nightshirts.

Nine days after my divorce was final.

I awakened around 2 A.M. with a dull gnawing ache in my lower back. Strange shooting sensations rifled down my legs, firing like electrical surges. I got out of bed and shook each leg, but the flickering pains continued.

I headed downstairs, thinking exercise might help. A runner's stretch on the bottom step quieted my legs, but the dull ache in my back deepened as if someone was grinding brass knuckles into my spine. Gingerly, I walked into my office and eased myself behind the desk and into a chair. The pressing fist relaxed a bit.

I fumbled through some bills, and decided to pay the mortgage. I stuck the check in the envelope, licked the stamp, and sighed as I pounded it with my fist, *bam, bam, bam*—three staccato blasts—just like Joe used to do. Saturday was bill-paying day when we were married. Joe sat on one side of the oversized desk; I was on the other. We searched for a desk big enough for both of us and found one, discounted at a local office warehouse. I'd open and sort the bills. Then Joe would write the checks and stuff, seal, and stamp—*bam, bam, bam*—stacking them for me to take to the mailbox. Who knew that pounding sound would be one I missed, one of those married sounds that settle in the background and gently remind you that you are not alone?

I studied the stamp. Would I always be the one to pound it in place? Then another outage shot down my legs, like someone hit my funny bone with a razor blade, an erratic cocktail of numbness, tingling, and blistering pain.

I called Dr. Lamos. The answering service promised a swift reply as I let both pain and fear show in my voice. "Don't wait to get this sick to see me, Rebecca," he'd lectured me at my appointment the previous Monday. "We'll do blood work to confirm, but I think this is pneumonia. I'm prescribing an antibiotic."

I stared at the phone. I felt guilty, but I hadn't been irresponsible. We'd talked the week before my appointment and agreed my symptoms sounded like the flu. I slowed down at work, like I promised, and was much better, well enough to go to the Mardi Gras event on Saturday night. I wanted to keep that commitment; it was the third one I'd chaired.

I went solo, but met Barbara and her boyfriend, Mark, there. I felt fine when I arrived, but after pumping juices with two virgin sea breezes and a screwdriver, I started to feel worse. Even the perfect dress, a sequined collage of purple, green, and gold, and matching sequin shoes couldn't boost my energy.

I danced through the first set and tried to keep pace in The Isley Brothers' classic, "Shout," and its mesmerizing effect on the dance floor as it wooed each dancer's unison response to its lyrics. With raised hands, we obeyed the prompts, "Shout!" I made the rhythmic squat all the way to the floor with "a little bit softer now," when suddenly I felt a weird prickling sensation shoot up my spine, like I'd pulled a muscle—except more electrical, like a spark. It vanished as soon as I stood up but then I grew tired. So tired that I made my apologies, said good night to Barbara and Mark, and was home by 11 P.M., rare for the one who was usually the last one off the dance floor and ushered lingering guests out.

The phone rang and Dr. Lamos's calm voice snapped me back. I described each symptom. "Sounds like a potassium deficiency," he said. "Drink a glass of orange juice, Rebecca. Continue to take the antibiotic and call back if you don't improve."

I drank the juice, went back upstairs, and crawled into bed. The cubed clock beside my bed glared 5:34 A.M., its red numbers the lone fixture in the dark. As I lay in the stillness, the knotted fist pressed harder into my back. I curled up my knees to my chest to try to release it but that set off more outages down my legs. Then an icy numbness set in. Was it another kidney stone? I knew that skewering pain well, but never lost sensation. I waited an hour, knowing Dad— a kidney-stone veteran—would be up by then and called him.

"Sorry for the early call, Dad, but I think I'm having another kidney stone," I said with a fake breezy tone. "Did you ever have numbness?"

"Numbness? No, never numbness, BB," he said. "Better call the doctor on that, honey."

I didn't tell him I already had. I hung up the phone.

⚬⚭⚬

"HI MOM," BRITTANY said, peeking into the room through the partially opened door. "Are you better?" Although nine years old, she was still the earliest riser of the bunch—Peter and Madison were still sleeping. Pat, on site by 7 A.M., joined her at my door. Knowing I'd not been well the past few days, they had slipped up to my room to check on me.

"Hey, Britty," I said, motioning them both to my bedside. "Mommy's not feeling that great today." I smiled hard, teeth clenched to cover the pain. "Oh my!" I said, interrupting myself. "I've got to go to the bathroom." I swung my legs to the side of the bed and placed each foot on the floor, easing upwards to stand.

I reached the bathroom, only steps away from my bed. Brittany followed me in. I lowered myself slowly to the toilet seat. I tried to urinate. "I need to go—but can't," I said more to myself than to my daughter. "I'll try later." And I stood, or tried to. My legs buckled, and I landed back down on the toilet. Flustered, I adjusted my feet to get a better stance. "Britty, can you help me to the bed?" And I pushed up from the seat, hanging on to the door frame, with my daughter leaning into me to support the other side. We made three, maybe four steps back to my bed.

"Thanks, sweetie," I said, as I dragged each leg into bed. Pat helped me tuck the covers around them. "Britty, can you please get me a glass of orange juice?"

When she left the room, I told Pat I'd called Lamos. "I'll call him again, but we're going to have to call 911, Pat. Something's terribly wrong." I exhaled slowly and looked at the clock, then back at Pat. "Madison's bus will be here at 7:45. Let's get her on the bus and then run Brittany up to school early. See if you can switch the playdate with Pete and have him go to Jack's house today, then call for the ambulance." I bit my lip to stop its quiver. My eyes filled. "Thank you, Pat. I really don't want the kids to see it take me."

"Of course," she said in her gentle caring way, her eyes never wavering off mine. "I will make sure of it. Just rest, Becky." She left the room, quietly closing the door. Her soft voice comforted me in that moment. Who knew what was ahead, but at least we had a plan for now. I knew I could count on her.

A few minutes later, Brittany brought in the orange juice and I explained the new plans. For once, she didn't question me. Not a peep.

"I'll be fine, Britty. Give Mommy a kiss." I smiled hard again, and hoped I wasn't lying. "I love you, Britty."

Pat brought Madison up and then Pete. I kissed each good-bye. After they left, I made one more call.

"Joe," I began in the most even-toned voice I could muster, "I don't want you to worry, but something is happening to me." I took a deep breath. "I can't move my legs."

The pause lingered, its silence stripping away the clutter that had smothered our relationship in the last few years. We'd known each other for over twenty years. He was my friend long before he was my husband.

"Stay calm, Beck," he said, his own even tone matching mine. "Get to the hospital. I'll be there as soon as I can."

The ambulance's arrival interrupted our conversation. Two paramedics ran up the steps, lifted me out of bed onto a folding stretcher, and carried me back down. Once we left the neighborhood, the lights and sirens started. But I focused only on my big toe. My left big toe, freshly manicured with a sparkly snowflake. The only part of my lower body that I could still move. "That's good, right?" I said to the paramedics, as they watched me wiggle the glittery toe.

"Very good," they said.

Then I could no longer move it.

And the excruciating pain began.

❧

DR. LAMOS MET me in the emergency room. I could not feel or move my legs. The knotted fist was now a spiked skewer, twisting and grinding deeper and deeper into my lower back. The ripping pain came in waves, taking my speech from me at each crest.

Lamos said we should call my parents and my sister.

"But Mom and Dad are in West Virginia, eight hours away. And Rachel is in North Carolina," I answered between waves.

"I know," is all he said. And he stood there, close, right beside me. The big, brilliant lumbering man looked through his square-framed glasses into my eyes. He didn't move.

I swallowed hard. "Am I going to die?"

His gaze was unwavering, just like his presence. "It's not likely, Rebecca," he said. "We are not sure what this is," he continued in his steady Midwestern voice, "but it is serious. A Hopkins specialist is coming in. Your family should be here with you." He patted my hand and left to huddle with other white coats.

Warm blankets covered me as I stared into the bright lights of the ER's dingy, speckled ceiling. Hushed conversations floated by as the rhythmic beeps of machines broke the monotony.

Was I going to die? Was this it? Was it my time?

Then Forest's last written words came to me.

I would change nothing.

A kaleidoscope of colored memories began turning, churning through the pain. Was that true for me? The kids were in good hands. Pat was wonderful. Joe would provide. My family would be there for them. My friends, too.

I would change nothing.

Did I have regrets? Yes, I hadn't wanted to end it with Joe—I did love him, but I couldn't live that life. I tried my best; I was sure of that. And yes, I wanted to be married, but it couldn't be to him. Despite our shared history, I was right in what I'd told Barbara. I couldn't be me being married to him. It was time to let that go.

I would change nothing.

The colors began to fade and blur. More waves. I *was* ready if it were my time. Not that I wanted to give up or give in, but I was at peace with my life, no huge regrets. No desperation.

I would change nothing.

And I understood them, my brother's words. His contentment. All good, but oh the pain it caused in the life I'd had without him! Suddenly, I wanted more. I had no regrets, but I wanted to live. To fill my heart again with love. I was ready to fight for that.

And the colors went dark. The waves won; I could surf them no longer.

I slept.

⁓ᛥ⟶

WITHIN THE HOUR, Barbara arrived in the emergency room and did not leave my side. She kept my family members updated via phone as they cleared their schedules, packed, and headed to Baltimore. Mom and Dad traveled eight hours from West Virginia while Rachel drove six hours from her home in North Carolina. Joe raced to the hospital from his workplace in nearby Towson and immediately began talking with the medical team.

After hours in the ER, they finally moved me to the intensive care unit where a bloody spinal tap result brought two young doctors in to assess me while nurses started IV antibiotics, painkillers, and massive doses of steroids. Joe and Barbara hovered in the waiting area.

"Can you wiggle your toes?" one doc asked.

"No," I said. "But I've been trying ever since I got out of the danged ambulance. Don't you love the snowflake?" I tried to joke as the drugs began to mask the pain and the steroids artificially lifted my mood.

He smiled back, but quickly resumed the tests. "Can you move your legs at all?"

"Let's see." I exhaled, willing my knees to come up to my chest, my best Pilates move. I'd worked so hard to get my belly flat after Peter's birth; Pilates was my secret weapon. "I can't," I said. "Really, I am trying, but I can't."

"It's okay, Ms. Galli. Let's see if you can feel this." He

unfolded a paperclip, pressed the pointed end into my shin, and looked up at me.

"No."

"This?" And he poked my thigh.

"No."

"Let's check your abdomen," he said as he placed the sheet back over my legs.

I lifted up my hospital gown to reveal my belly, my taut belly that cranked out five sets of crunches every morning on the fuzzy pink bath mat in the middle of my bathroom floor. He took a black Sharpie pen from his shirt pocket and uncapped it.

"What's that for?"

"We need to mark your level of sensation. Can you feel this?"

"Yes!" I practically screamed as he gently touched the area just above the elastic of my Victoria Secret high-cut briefs. "That's good, right?"

"Oh yes, Mrs. Galli. Very good." And he marked it.

And then another wave of pain blew through the meds and skewered my back, drilling down deeper and deeper. And words and tests weren't important any more.

❧

THIRTY-THREE SMALL bones house the spinal cord. Starting at the bottom of the spinal column, the paralysis moved from the sacral to the lumbar to the thoracic section.

"We may have to put a tube down your throat to help you breathe," the doctor explained as he marked another level of sensation loss. Soon three inches of tracks marked my belly as the paralysis advanced.

As I flowed back and forth between managed and unmanaged pain, I could overhear the speculation about my diagnosis. At first, they thought it was ALS (amyotrophic lateral sclerosis), or "Lou Gehrig's disease," the devastating motor neuron disease from which there is no recovery. Then they thought I had Guillain-Barre syndrome, a disorder in which the body's immune system attacks its own nerves but usually reverses itself. The conversations waxed in and out, depending on my pain—and the drugs.

Finally at 5 P.M., the expert arrived.

"I'm Dr. Moses," I heard a soft but clear voice say after one bout of short but deep sleep. "From Hopkins." Balding with small rimless glasses, the aging gentleman shuffled around to the side of my bed clutching my file in one hand and his well-worn but classic black medical bag in the other. He asked questions and gave me the same exam as the other young docs. Then he asked to look at my belly. He ignored the black lines and gently touched my tummy with his fourth finger, slowly moving it from the top of my underwear upwards. Then he stopped. "Your sensation level stops here, correct?"

"Yes, how'd ya know?" I mumbled, trying to clear the drug fog to focus on the man's words.

He explained the difference in the way the skin feels—where there is no sensation, the level of moisture changes. It slows the skimming finger.

"So what's wrong with me?" I asked, not really caring as long as he could make the ridiculous pain go away and fix it.

"I've reviewed your tests. It appears you have transverse myelitis, or TM. An inflammation of the myelin sheath across the spinal cord."

"Oh, okay." That's all I could absorb. Another blast of painkillers kicked in and a dull fog suffocated the pain as well as my thinking. I could hear Joe in the background peppering the man with questions as they headed out to the waiting area.

I finally slept.

"HEY THERE, BB," a deep, soft voice said. A large, warm hand covered mine as the monitor's steady beep became clearer. A hint of Old Spice helped me open my eyes.

"Dad?" I could see him, but not clearly.

"Yes, BB. It's Dad. Mom's here, too." His voice trailed on like he was slurring his words.

"Slow down, Dad. I can't understand you." His next words were slower, but still smeared.

"We got here as fast as we could. Rachel's here. Joe and Barbara updated us. They are doing everything they can. We love you, honey. . . ."

"But, Dad, I can't see you, Dad," I interrupted him. "Not with this eye." His deeply etched face was there, right beside me, but parts of it were missing, gray.

"Okay, honey. We'll let the doctors know," he said in that soothing tone of his. "How is the pain?"

"Awful, but I have this button." I smiled, then winced, pushing the morphine twice.

"You rest now, pumpkin." His massive hands squeezed mine and he turned to leave. I could hear him sigh and see the shadow of his shoulders round a bit more as he moved slowly to the door.

"Dad," I called out to him. "It's going to be okay." He looked so worried. So tired. "I just know it's going to be okay. I've been in the wilderness before, you know. I've been here so many times that I have paths down here," I managed to smile as the drugs lifted a haze of hope above grim reality.

He turned and smiled at me, coming back to my bedside. "Yes, you do, BB. Yes, you do." He gave me a quick kiss on the forehead before he left, his step a little quicker.

I grabbed the morphine button and rolled it in my hand. The wilderness. Far too much time there—losing Forest, two miscarriages, Matthew's seizures, Madison's autism, Peter's fragile first weeks of life, and a divorce that nearly drained my will to live. Joe, oh, Joe! What a tortured path that was! And I pressed my thumb down on the morphine button once more.

Then the young docs came back to mark my belly and began testing my left eye.

AT 9 PM, the paralysis stopped. The Sharpie notation read, T8, or thoracic 8, just short of the next and final grouping of the spinal column, the cervical section, that would have necessitated the "tube down your throat," or ventilator, to breathe. I could still breathe on my own and use my upper body. But my legs were lifeless, bowel and bladder control lost.

"My stomach is so flabby," I said to one of the young docs as he checked my belly's railroad track. "When I recover, will it be LIFO or FIFO?"

"Excuse me?"

"You know, last in first out or first in first out?" I tried to joke, remembering my old accounting class that I promptly dropped after the first test. "Will I get back the last thing lost or the first thing lost?"

"First thing lost," he said.

"Nuts," I exhaled and rolled my eyes. "I guess I'll have to wait even longer for my flat belly to return. Took me six years to get it back. I suppose a few more months won't matter."

Months. How stupid I was. How naive. How blissfully ignorant.

Although the paralysis stopped on the first day, the raging pain intensified. Forget a skewer, I felt like I had a razor-tipped jackhammer chiseling through my back. This attack on my spine and my eye had to "run its course," I overheard the doctors say. I hated those words. Why couldn't they make it stop?

But the assault and its cause refused to be managed. Life in intensive care became a merry-go-round of chaos. Day and night had no distinction for me. Pain shattered through any semblance of order, warping time.

Mom, Dad, Rachel, Barbara, and Joe tried to comfort me, but I could barely focus on what they were saying. Their words continued to slur, running together as if in slow motion with an echo. They became students of my disease, absorbing every detail, learning far more than they wanted to about this vicious virus. Ever present, Joe was attentive to each detail of my symptoms, progress, and prognosis. He became the "TM expert," constantly cross-examining doctors on the range of outcomes and best resources for my care.

Finally, three days after I'd arrived at the hospital, the pain subsided.

"What is this transverse myelitis anyway," I asked Joe once I could think a little more clearly.

"It's rare, Beck. Happens one-in-1.34 million."

"I'm one in a million?"

"Yes, you are," he said, a small twinkle lit up his dark, tired eyes.

"So I can beat this?"

"Oh sure. Two-thirds of people recover. You will, too." I'd later learn that he'd fudged the truth a bit. In truth, only one-third of TM patients recover fully. Another third recover partially. And that last third have no recovery at all.

"And this blindness?"

"They think it's Devic's syndrome, an inflammation of the optic nerve. It's even rarer than TM, Beck. But, that, too, has good odds for recovery."

"Great!"

"Yes, Moses says that both illnesses were probably kicked off by your body's response to that flu bug you had. Turns out it was pneumonia. Good thing Lamos got the blood work done when you went in to see him. Apparently, as your body was fighting this pneumonia, a *mycoplasma* pneumonia," he said, emphasizing the word to show his newfound expertise, "it began to attack itself, the good cells both in your spine (TM) and in your eyes (Devic's)."

"Oh wonderful. My body was attacking itself?"

"Yes, some call it autoimmune. I'm still trying to understand that more."

"Oh good, you do that. I've got to take a nap."

"Sure, Beck." And he squeezed my hand and kissed me on my cheek.

GRADUALLY THE BLUR of life in intensive care assumed a rhythm with nursing shifts, doctors' rounds, and medication schedules. Simple hospital routines set my expectations for the day while family and close friends coached me as I began to re-engage with the life I left at home.

Seven A.M. wake-up calls from my hospital bed to my children connected me to their world since they weren't allowed to visit me yet. Mom read cards and letters to me from the morning and afternoon mail deliveries. Meals bookmarked the sections of the day into "after breakfast" and "before dinner" periods. Physical and occupational therapies began. Goals were set, and structure returned to quiet the chaos.

Joe visited daily, often staying hours.

"So do you think I can still beat it?" I'd asked him again one morning. My vision was getting better, but I still could not wiggle my left toe, my daily test for recovery. It was an odd sensation, trying to mentally will a body part to work. I would think the thought—*move, toe, move*—and shut my eyes hard and imagine my toe going up and down, curled under as if to pick up a stone, or a sock like I used to do with Brittany's laundry. Sometimes my upper abs would flinch, and I thought I felt an impulse going down through my thigh, my knee, my shin into my foot, and out through my toe, and I'd be sure I'd done it, moved my toe! But I'd open my eyes and I'd be wrong. Again. Everything below my belly button just lay there, stupid and disobedient. "My big toe is still not minding me yet."

"Oh, it will. You will beat it, Beck."

"I want a big party when I do. I want to dance all night."

"Absolutely," he said, spreading his hands wide and starting to pace. "We'll do it in New York. Rent out Studio 54. Invite anyone you want." He swatted the air with each phrase.

"I just need to get to that top third and recover fully."

"You will, Beck." He came close to my bed and put his hands on mine. I smiled. Just when I'd made my peace letting him go, the man I'd fallen in love with steps up to the challenge. Now he peppers the docs with questions, engages the situation, and is willing to learn. I knew he had it in him. I'd forgotten what it was like to have Joe fully there for me—both comforting and comfortable. Part of me felt restored.

Days later, I fully recovered my vision loss. One lone neuro-ophthalmologist said that because of the course of the Devic's in my eyes, I should have recovery in my spine as well.

Not everyone was as optimistic, I later learned. Dr. Lamos and Dr. Moses prepared my family for the worst. And even with Joe's persistence, he could find no one who'd ever even had TM, much less recovered from it. So despite his never-ending positive outlook with me, Joe had a very different conversation with my family.

"Dr. Smith," he told my father, "I want you to know that whatever happens, I will take care of Becky. You don't have to worry about her."

Dad swallowed hard. Mom teared up, Rachel told me years later. They listened to Joe, sizing up every word the young man said. Mom and Dad had witnessed Joe refuse to engage in a struggling marriage for three years. "We believed him, Becky," Rachel told me. "Although we didn't know exactly what he meant, we knew he was sincere. He was showing us, daily, that he would be there for you. He was so concerned for you in a way we'd never seen."

"That must have been so strange to hear after the hell we'd been though, wasn't it?" I'd asked.

"We were in shock, raw with disbelief in what had happened to you. But his words put a floor underneath us. We were grateful. None of us wanted to think that you would never walk again, but we knew it could happen. Dad thanked him as did Mom. I think we all cried. I know we hugged and then said nothing for quite a while."

I never knew they talked about me like that. Never knew their struggle, their hurt, or the loss they'd suffered because of mine.

I do know that if positive energy and love could have healed me, I'd have walked out of that hospital seconds after my family arrived.

Chapter 13

A Useless Master's Degree

When we long for life without difficulties,
remind us that oaks grow strong in contrary winds
and diamonds are made under pressure.
—Peter Marshall

MY MONTHLONG STAY in physical rehabilitation, or rehab, was a different world from my ten days in the intensive care unit.

"Is she a quad?" one attendant asked another when transferring me from the hospital's ambulance to the rehab center's stretcher.

"Am I a what?" I interrupted their too-loud private exchange.

Unfazed, the girl blurted out, "You know, quadriplegic."

I must have looked dumbfounded even after she clarified her question because she cracked her gum a few more times, sighed with impatience, and raised her voice as if I couldn't hear. "Can you move your arms, hon?" she asked, that Baltimore twang annoying me again.

I obediently raised both hands to show her as another attendant pushed me down the hall. I couldn't believe she spoke about me in such banal terms. No, I wasn't a "quad." But I quickly learned I was a "para," or paraplegic. Those labels foreshadowed the tone of the weeks ahead in rehab, or more accurately "boot camp," where schedules and orders ruled. I learned to check any expectations of sympathy at the door, because these folks were no-nonsense, mission-driven drill sergeants. They pushed every limit I had. Get up. Get out. Move. Practice. Practice. Practice.

I learned to "transfer," rehab-speak for moving my body from one surface to another, sometimes with the use of a board to bridge the gap. They taught me how to transfer out of the bed and into the wheelchair. Out of the wheelchair and onto a work-out table, then into a car, and into another chair, and onto a sofa, and even onto the floor. I learned how to open doors while in the wheelchair, to pop wheelies to get over obstacles such as sticks, hoses, or ropes, and how to back into an elevator so I could still reach the buttons.

I learned all about the foreign term, "bed mobility," or how to be mobile in the bed using my upper body to move my lower body. Without sensation or the ability to move my legs, I could lie for hours in the same position which over time would lead to "skin breakdown," a disastrous and even deadly condition those with limited mobility and sensation fight daily since we can't move our paralyzed parts as others do.

Our skin, the largest organ we have, needs good circulation and relief from continued pressure to remain healthy, I learned. If a sock is too tight, for example, it may leave a red crease on the ankle. Normally, we would feel the pain from it, adjust the sock, and the red mark would eventually disappear. With paralysis, however, we can't feel the pain of the creased skin, so it can go unnoticed. If left too long, that continued pressure will "break down" the skin, even cause it to open. If left untreated, the healing process can stall and the opened skin can become a wound. We were taught how to do "skin checks" daily and were given a specialized mirror to help see the skin areas we could no longer feel.

I worked out hard with free weights, pulleys, and a rickshaw rehab machine to strengthen my upper body while stretching my lower body to prevent stiffness and spasms. Spasms mystified me. For no apparent reason, my knees would spring up to my chest, or my foot would jerk forward, falling off the wheelchair's footplate. It reminded me of the reflex test, when the doctor makes your foot kick by whacking your knee with a rubber hammer. These spasms felt like I had invisible rubber hammers randomly assaulting my paralyzed parts, provoking uncontrolled responses. Meanwhile, I had to learn how to bathe, toilet, and give myself shots to prevent clotting in my legs.

It was exhausting.

Even the simplest routines changed. One morning I attempted to put on mascara. But when I raised the wand to my eye, I toppled backward into the bed. I laughed, but then the tears welled up.

"Let me help you, BB," my father offered. He pulled me back up, putting his hand on my back to steady my trunk, something my abdominals could no longer do. He'd come for a rare morning visit. He and Mom continued to tag-team their visits as they had done in the hospital.

Mom, ever the early riser, usually came in for my 7 A.M. breakfasts and calls home to the kids before Pat took them to school. Pat, now the anchor caregiver, worked her shift and, along with Joe, Mom, and Dad, scheduled the other caregivers to assure full coverage for the kids. Joe popped in daily both at the house and at rehab. He was most encouraging at the rehab gym during my physical therapy sessions, marveling at my upper-body strength. I was in great shape; that was true.

But I was frustrated with my abdominals.

"It feels like you are sitting in a bowl of jelly, doesn't it?" a veteran physical therapist asked me once when I'd struggled to describe the lack of control. I had owned my abs, practically named each one in my quest to get back in shape. I had won that battle as my Nordstrom personal shopper could attest. Now, though, my body was not responsive.

Frustrated, I refused to fully engage in the rehab program, feeling like it was a waste of time. Why should I bother to learn all this if I planned to fully recover? I was going to beat this thing, why clutter up my mind with things I would never use?

"Think of your rehab stay as a master's degree," one doctor suggested. You may never use it, but it can't hurt to have the education." A master's in rehab that I would never use—I loved that idea. But my mindset was clear: this was all an academic exercise.

"HOW ARE YOU today?" the hospital chaplain asked during one visit. My father joined him at my bedside as we chatted. I'd had a good day and was feeling particularly optimistic.

"Great! Getting ready to go home soon. Getting ready to get my legs back, Chaplain. Easter's coming," I said, slapping my legs frogged in front of me under the covers of my bed. "You know, I gave them up for Lent."

The chaplain's mouth hung open for a second as he looked at my father, relieved at his deep smile.

I flashed a quick grin at him and winked at my Dad. "I know, I'm a character. But hey, a little optimism never hurt anyone, right?"

"Oh BB," Dad said as he stroked my hair. "Yes, you are quite a character."

Still, staying upbeat was a fight. When the rehab staff flooded me with spinal-cord injury information—hotlines, support groups, magazines, and resource lists—I deemed it useless in my mind. I wanted to throw it all in the trash. But when Joe brought in some file folders from work, I took one and labeled it "Plan B." I shoved the papers in, stuffed the folder under my "going home" pile, and vowed never to use them.

Going home terrified me. Surely I will be walking by then, I kept telling myself. It was a sensitive nerve for me, one young occupational therapist found out.

"Don't you want to get back to your home?" she said when she was trying to teach me how to get dressed in bed. "To take care of your kids?"

I sat straight up in the bed, propped myself with both hands behind me so I wouldn't fall backward, and looked hard at her, straight in the eyes. "Are you kidding me? Take care of my kids? I can't even take care of myself!" I fired back. "I can't stand. I can't walk. I can't even pull my underwear up by myself! That's what you're supposed to be teaching me to do!" I then lifted my arm to shake my fist at the young woman and her stupid comment.

Or that's what I meant to do.

Instead, the minute I lifted my arm to shake it at her, I lost my balance and plunged backward into the pillows. I gasped, and then burst into tears. "Just leave me alone. Go. I don't want you in here. You aren't helping me. I want another OT, one that will help me get better, not make me feel guilty. Don't come back!" I shrieked at her and then turned into my pillows to muffle my crying.

How could I possible take care of my kids? What kind of mom could I be from a wheelchair? I didn't even want to think about it.

I released the pillows and looked back at where she once stood, letting out a long sigh. I'd let her get to me. She'd hit that nerve, the one where I let others' inane comments affect me. I overreacted. What was she, all of twenty-two? What could she possibly know about being paralyzed? About being a paralyzed single mother? I'm sure I scared her to death. I scared *me* to death! It was the first time I'd ever put words to those fears.

But on the other hand, she wasn't being sensitive and I didn't need any more obstacles in my healing plan. So I spoke to her supervisor. The young woman then apologized to me.

"I know you were trying to help me," I said. "And I'm sorry I raised my voice at you. But I'm fragile right now. Most of us are who are in here. We can't quite imagine our future," I paused. "It's frightening. Overwhelming."

The kids only visited me once in rehab, on my birthday, my thirty-ninth birthday, February 26—fourteen days after my paralysis. It was the first time they'd seen me in the wheelchair. Pete was fascinated by my light-up wheels. Madison loved riding in my lap. Brittany made a special banner for my room.

Then Joe gave me the most surprising gift—a sapphire and diamond necklace, heart shaped. It was beautiful.

Barbara baked my favorite, the Waldorf Astoria red velvet cake with a special cooked icing, so hard to make but uniquely delicious. We lit the candles, and they sang "Happy Birthday." There was no doubt what my birthday wish was for.

The visit was short, but it wore me out more than any rehab routine. I loved them, and missed them, but had no idea how I was going to manage it all if I had to stay in this wheelchair. It's early, I reminded myself. You have at least three more weeks before you will be going home.

I vowed to work harder.

⚭

"DO YOU NEED help, ma'am?" The hospital security guard offered his assistance as he watched Rachel struggle with the transfer board she was trying to position between my wheelchair and the car.

"We're fine," she replied to him quickly, then turned to me. "I promise I won't drop you, Sissy." It was just the two of us siblings now, such a small number compared to three, it seemed.

"But, what about your back?"

"I'm fine," she said again, her eyes bold, confidence brimming.

"I will not drop you and if I do I will pick you up. Promise," she said, planting herself between the wheelchair and the opened car door. "You can do this." She double-checked the wheel's brakes and pushed down hard on the armrests to make sure the wheelchair wouldn't move.

"Okay, here I go." I pushed up from the wheelchair onto the board and then slid over into the passenger seat, sinking down hard with a muffled thud.

"Yeah, Sissy! I stuck my landing!" I said, raising my hands like an Olympic gymnast. We both busted out a laugh as we pulled my cumbersome legs onto the floorboard. "Maybe you can help get the wheelchair in the car," I called out to the kind guard, who continued to hover.

And he did, assisting Rachel in taking out the cushion, removing the footplates, armrests, and pulling up the seat of the wheelchair to collapse its frame.

"Fits perfectly, Sissy!" she hollered to me from behind the trunk.

Great, I breathed to myself. At least one thing went as planned.

"Have a good evening," the guard said as he shut my door.

"Thanks so much," my sissy and I said in unison. After six weeks, I was coming home. I'd mastered the rehab goals, but fallen short of mine.

"You are going to walk again, Sissy," Rachel said. "I know it."

"What did you do, Sissy? Pray for signs again?"

She smiled that confident smile of hers. "Maybe."

In the third year of my separation, I'd told Rachel how hard it was for me to make the decision to divorce. "What are you afraid of?" she'd asked me, so shrinklike from the master of mischief. I was impressed.

"Well, beyond the single life in general, I do worry about the money," I'd said. "Even though we have a separation agreement, I'm not sure I can handle the kids and our future financially." Joe's career had taken off. I remembered the poignant evidence, the business card collection his father posted in his small scrap-yard office. Joe had been promoted twenty times in nineteen years. He was well compensated and had always been generous with any family needs.

Rachel had suggested we pray for "signs." I'd never done that before. I'd always thought that practice was a little "out there," far from my traditional prayer life, one I'd gradually resumed after Forest's death. But Rachel, still a little bit of a wild child, didn't mind experimenting, and we'd talked it through with Dad. So we prayed.

Two days later, I went to an ATM to withdraw some cash. When I got back in the car I looked at my remaining balance. It was supposed to be about $700. Instead it read, $47,751.46. It was a bank error, corrected within twenty-four hours, but the timing was remarkable.

I still have the receipt. I kept it in my wallet for years. I didn't know what signs Rachel was praying for this time, but I hoped they would be as clear as that one.

⊸⧏⧐⊶

THE RAMP TO the back door wasn't finished, so Rachel efficiently bumped me up the three steps at my front door just like we practiced in rehab. After one small wheelie over the threshold, I landed in the foyer of my two-story colonial home. Barbara, Joe, an aide, and the kids met us.

"Welcome home, Mom!" the kids exclaimed.

Brittany led the group with her take-charge voice. Pete, only three, joined in faintly since he was already midair en route to my lap to give me his famous neck-crushing hug. And then there was Madison. Four and still nonverbal, she added to the commotion with her hand-flapping and "EEEEeee" sound, both unvarnished indicators of her rare, but intent, engagement.

"Thanks, guys!" I managed to reply.

"Here's your room, Mom." Pete hopped down to open the new door to my former formal living room. I wheeled in. It seemed my upstairs and downstairs had awkwardly collided.

Still elegant with the white marble fireplace and intricately carved mantel, the room now housed my master bedroom's mahogany armoire and a small chest of drawers that was once Peter's changing table. The Queen Anne side tables remained along with the welcoming pineapple fabric of my wingback chair, my navy brocade couch and its sofa table now hosting matching vases of fresh flowers. One thoughtful soul had brought down my favorite bedside lamp, a fringe-trimmed lace-shaded beauty, whose glow mellowed the room's most striking addition: the totally unchic hospital bed.

I stared at the bed, then looked down quickly to the beautiful powder-blue oriental carpet, letting its soft pastel design settle my mind and stifle the tears.

"Do you like it, Mom?" Brittany asked.

"Oh, sure, sweetie. It's great!" I lied.

⚭

I HAD RETURNED to a world that was not my own. Although Joe and I discussed every step of the remodeling, the ongoing transformation still shocked me.

My home's artful flow was now dammed up with doors—double doors separated my room from the foyer and the office to give me privacy. A foyer door had been installed to separate the front of the house from the family room area as I had to wheel to the other side of the house to use the bathroom. Construction workers continued to be onsite daily as they gutted and enlarged a laundry-room half bath for an accessible shower, sink, and toilet. To avoid an unsightly ramp at my front door, a zigzag ramp at the back door was underway, soon to be camouflaged with landscaping.

I didn't have a family. I had a friggin' organization.

Adjustments permeated every part of my ridiculous new life. Family, friends, and neighbors brought meals, took me to doctors' appointments, and carpooled my kids. Aides helped me with personal care while in-home therapists and nurses helped me adjust to managing my changed body and its demanding schedule. I learned to self-catheterize, emptying my bladder every four hours, and mastered the unpleasant but necessary daily bowel program.

Meanwhile, my children adjusted to their reconfigured mom. Even though they recognized I was different, they still expected me to be there for them. Those demanding darlings didn't let me wander too far into the past or gaze too far ahead to the future. The here and now was their unyielding reference point.

Brittany needed help with her homework. Madison was just learning to talk, benefitting from a new specialized therapy. And Pete wanted playtime with his mom, as well as playdates with his friends. One of my goals was to be dressed and ready for the day by breakfast so I could sit with my kids before they headed off to school. In rehab, they told us twenty-five percent of our time would be spent managing our bodies and the adjustments to paralysis. I determined to finish the majority of those routine nuisances by the breakfast hour.

I began to keep a journal in an oversized calendar book, recording all the "firsts" after paralysis: lunch guests, a dinner out, going to church, baking a cake. Each was a major milestone as I struggled to put back in my life those things that mattered most. Each piece had to be reconfigured for my new circumstance.

I bought different-colored pens to match my mood, taking more time with my annotations when a reflective muse struck me. I then began to use the journal as a depository for worrisome questions. I would flip ahead in the calendar and write down my current concern—a doctor's appointment, a child issue, or a caregiver situation. Somehow whatever the issue was quelled a bit once I wrote it down and put it on a calendar.

Then I started using the calendar to make predictions, a gentle kind of goal setting that let me look ahead and envision possibilities. I hoped I could go out to dinner with a friend. I hoped I could attend one of Brittany's softball games.

I still hoped it was possible to wiggle my left big toe.

⚜

IN LATE MAY, three months after my paralysis, I opened a note from my friend, Julie, a power broker of a woman who had befriended me after my separation and encouraged me to join the Center Club, the site of the Mardi Gras events she'd asked me to chair. She'd even set me up on a few dates with some high-powered executives as I began to find my footing as a single woman.

I opened the letter, her fine-grained personal stationery paper clipped on top of a newspaper article.

"You trendsetter you!" she wrote.

I took the paperclip off and unfolded the clipping. "Barbie's newest girlfriend is wheelchair-bound Becky," the headline read.

My hands released the folded paper, dropping it on my desk as if it were contaminated by a lethal ink. My jaw dropped as I squinted at the photo of the dark-haired, light-eyed woman and read its caption: *Share a Smile Becky: Mattel and Toys"R"Us believe the doll will help improve attitudes about people with disabilities.*

At least her wheelchair was pink; mine was red.

I glared at the article. How in the world could it be? What a horrible coincidence. Couldn't they have named her something else? Anything but Becky. Wheelchair-bound Becky. I hated even seeing those words in print, much less knowing my name and this disabled doll would be linked forever in toy stores.

Although I realized Julie was trying to be lighthearted, I didn't know what to do with the article. Keep it? Trash it? Did I want my kids to see it? Was it anger, or fear—or just plain horror at the timing of it all? What did it mean? Why now?

Dr. Moses said most patients with TM get full return of function in the first three months after paralysis. I was paralyzed February 12; Share a Smile Becky debuted three months *and ten days later*, May 22, 1997. Was this a sign? If it was, I decided to ignore it. It was still early, very early, in the healing process, I told myself. After all, Moses said, "most," not all.

So I dug out my Plan B folder from the back of my deepest filing cabinet, jammed the clipping in it, and told myself it meant nothing. It was not an omen. I was going to beat this thing. Joe had said it. I believed it. After all, I got my vision back. That was the sign I was going to cling to. Besides, I had no room in my life for that kind of negative thought. My kids needed me. And that took all the positive energy I could muster.

ASSOCIATED PRESS

"Share a Smile Becky": Mattel and Toys R Us believe the doll will help improve attitudes about people with disabilities.

Barbie's newest girlfriend is wheelchair-bound Becky

ASSOCIATED PRESS

WASHINGTON — A new member of the Barbie doll family was introduced yesterday to the public — one that uses a wheelchair and is intended to change attitudes about people with disabilities.

"Share a Smile Becky" is the new 11½-inch friend of Barbie who comes in a bright hot-pink wheelchair. The strawberry blond doll wears a turquoise outfit with a white shirt underneath decorated with a flower.

The doll, made by Mattel Inc. and sold at Toys R Us stores, will help dispel uneasiness some people have around those with disabilities, the companies said.

The bendable joints are an exclusive feature of Becky.

James Brady, the former press secretary to Ronald Reagan who was paralyzed in a 1981 assassination attempt, said he planned to use the doll as a "teaching guide."

"Barbie is still the same Barbie. She's still cool," Brady said.

The doll is being sold exclusively in Toys R Us stores nationwide and hit the shelves without an announcement almost two weeks ago at an estimated retail price of $19.99.

Between 4,500 and 6,000 dolls have been sold nationwide, Mattel officials said.

"Barbie's world reflects the real world. Barbie has African-Ameri-

Chapter 14

Finding My Words

*Your life is like a mosaic, a puzzle. You have to figure out
where the pieces go and put them together for yourself.*
—Maria Shriver

THE KIDS WERE asleep. Pat had said good night, leaving me
with a steaming mug of tea at my office desk and my treat for the
evening, a raspberry Nutri-Grain bar. It was the end of August,
four months post-paralysis. I pushed up the sleeves and snuggled
into the softness of my favorite fleece sweatshirt, the one my kids
gave me that said, "Give me chocolate and no one gets hurt." I lit
the vanilla-bean candle in the shadow of my computer monitor.

It was my habit to open the mail in the late evening, after
the kids had gone to bed. In the quiet glow of it all, I would open
my cards and letters, saving my bills for daylight. I welcomed the
soft tunes of Mozart, a nice change of pace from the earlier jam
session with the kids. They loved the CD I'd chosen. After Joe
moved out, I joined several CD-by-mail clubs, jumpstarting my
mission to reinvent myself beyond the mother-of-four label I felt
I had plastered on my forehead. I stocked up on current artists as

well as oldies and classics. Then I bought a six-CD station boom box for the kitchen dining area and a small one for my bathroom, remembering how Mom and Dad seemed to always have music on—and how it never failed to brighten the mood.

Our family loved music. In the furniture pocket of North Carolina, one church member offered to build a custom cabinet Dad had designed for his prized stereo collection. The unique three-compartment French provincial piece was large enough to house Dad's turntable, receiver, amplifier, tuner, woofer, sub-woofer, and tweeter, along with special storage sections for his albums. He wanted music to fill the house and took great pride in running stereo wire and speakers throughout each home—three levels in most cases. In one of the larger parsonages, we had a designated "music room" for Mom's piano, Forest's drums, and Dad's revered stereo cabinet.

"Let's turn on some pretty music," Mom often said during dinner or on lazy Saturday mornings. "Pretty music" was usually Perry Como or Andy Williams, but often Boots Randolph and Simon and Garfunkel were in the mix as well. Later on, James Taylor, and even Forest's favorite, The Doobie Brothers were featured.

Dinnertime became an even more important family ritual for me after Joe left. Each night, I would put in a CD, light two tapered table candles (changed for each season's decor as Mom used to do), and then have the kids make our family circle as we held hands to say grace. I rotated the music, from jazz to pop to the classics, often finishing up with family funk time in the step-down family room where we danced before my paralysis struck.

I'd tried to teach Brittany and Peter how to shag to my native Carolina "beach music," but they enjoyed my disco and pop tunes more. Brittany caught on easily to the Electric Slide and Macarena while Madison mostly jumped up and down non-stop—always on the beat. When Pete wasn't shaking his boo-tie (diaper, at first) to KC and the Sunshine Band, we played "airplane." Lying down on the floor, my knees to my chest, I grabbed his hands while he leaned his tummy into my bare feet. I sometimes wiggled my toes to tickle him. Then I would push my legs up, lifting him high in the air to "fly him," pumping him up and down to the music. It was a great leg workout and tired him out as well.

I put down my cup of tea and tried to lift my knees as I remembered the pumping motion, thinking hard with all my might, "Knees up! Knees up!" I commanded my body, but to no avail. Then I closed my eyes and tried to wiggle my toes, scrunching them in and out inside my shoes, once again imagining picking up Brittany's lacy socks. Was it working? Was I doing it? It felt like it. Surely I was moving my toes. But I opened my eyes and my feet were still, exactly as they had been. They wouldn't mind me either, at least not yet.

I picked up the mug again for another sip and let Mozart's "Serenade in G, Andante" calm the angst. I was tired and I ached. A five-inch-wide band of pain below my level of sensation pressed around my waist like a giant rubber band two sizes too small. "Dang nerve pain," I whispered to myself. They never did explain that term very well other than apparently I can hurt where I have no feeling. Mixed-up nerve endings, I guess. I put the tea down and unbuckled my seat belt, placing both hands on my armrests. I pushed up, raising myself from my seat and then tucked my chin to my chest, trying to stretch out my spine to reduce the pain, while the lift gave pressure relief. I could still hear the rehab PT barking at us about "wheelchair push-ups" and "pressure relief."

"Every fifteen minutes you need to relieve the pressure on your bottom to prevent skin breakdown," she lectured daily. "Your bottom is the most at-risk part of your body with paralysis. And, watch for friction, too. In fact, let's remember that this board," she held up the three-foot-long wooden board used to bridge one surface to another, "is not a *sliding* board." "Don't even use that word. It's a *transfer* board. We lift up and over, people, never *sliding* across," she said, using her hands to mimic the arched movement. "Sliding is the quickest way to acquire skin breakdown." I remembered one rehab group session where they showed us a slideshow of horrible pictures of wounds that had started out as skin breakdown. I vowed then never to let that happen to me. "I'm too active—and too careful," I muttered to myself as I lowered myself back down into my wheelchair's seat.

I reached in my desk drawer for two Advil to ease the band of pain. I took another sip, then a big gulp of tea to wash down the pills. I was staring at one last envelope of the mail pile when the e-mail chime sounded.

Barbara and her boyfriend, Mark, had just helped me upgrade my computer and connections for the latest craze: e-mail. "Is that you?" flashed in my inbox. I clicked it open.

Becky? It's Gibson.
I got your e-mail address from your dad's column in the Hickory paper. I've kept track of you through the Hickory rumor mill over the years and so I knew you had been hit with that strange infection. I know you will recover.
 It's OK not to respond. I know you are busy. I wish we had not lost contact, but I do not forget you. Maybe the telepathy still works and we just don't know it. Take care.
Your (aging) friend,
Scott

It was Gibson. My long lost friend, Scott Gibson.

Gibson and I became friends in our church youth group in our early teens. Dad was his pastor for six years so he knew my family, including Forest. Gibson, a redheaded tall and lanky fellow, was known for his quick wit, dry humor, and animated theatrics at the golf course over missed shots during our games. He, too, went to UNC. During my freshman year, I joined him on his biweekly trips back home to Hickory. The two-a-half-hour drive cemented a tight friendship. We dished professors, our latest romances, our dreams, and our thoughts about life in general. We lost touch after college.

Seventeen years later, he popped up with a question I'd been wondering about every single day for the last six months: *"Is that you?"*

Although I had recovered reflexes in both legs and some slight voluntary movement of my knees, I was still paralyzed. I smiled at my friend's note, excited to reconnect with him, but it was getting late. The Advil had kicked in to ease my band of pain and I needed to sleep. But first, I wheeled across the house to my bathroom, flipped on the light, and shut the door to catheterize. The massive wall-long mirror greeted me. I looked up and into it, hearing Scott's question, "Is that you?"

My renovated bathroom was huge, large enough for all three kids plus me to fit in and perfect for working out, wheelchair dancing, and general horsing around. They had joined me earlier that day when I was doing my arm exercise routine. Peter had attached a green Dyna-Band to my wheelchair and pretended it was a guitar as we boogied to Michael Jackson's "Working Day and Night." Brittany had used my hairbrush as her microphone to sing while Madison jumped up and down, hand-flapping at her reflection. It wasn't the family-room funk night of six months ago—certainly no leg-pumping airplane leg rides. But it was fun and we were happy. That part of who I am was still intact.

I finished my bodily chore and wheeled back across the house back through the office to my bedroom. I looked forward to writing Scott the next morning.

SCOTT. OH, MY gosh! I can't believe it's you, my
buddy Gibson!! How wonderful to hear from you. I do
think of you, too, and am sorry we lost contact. How
did that happen? It shouldn't have. Thanks for the note.
I would love to catch up with you. My life is a bit like
a soap opera—if I were to write an autobiography I
know they would put it in the fiction section!

   Thanks for the positive thoughts about recovery.
I am determined to walk again. It is NO fun being in
this wheelchair. Thank goodness for wonderful friends
and family and two superb nannies! It makes this
journey so much more bearable. The good news is it has
provided a wonderful opportunity to reconnect with
folks from the past—like you!

   I'll catch you up on my life a chapter at a time.
All in one sitting would be too overwhelming. Hang on!

⁓⁂⁓

LATER THAT NIGHT, I wrote my first story to Scott, beginning with "the strange infection," as he called it. By the time I
finished, it was almost 2 A.M. After I clicked "send," I returned to
my homepage to a shocking headline. Princess Diana had been
killed in a car crash.

   I was stunned.

   She was more than Princess Di to me; she was my inspiration, a strong woman who had survived so much. She'd been
married four months before me and divorced six months before
me. I watched her wedding on TV and saw her survive a far-too-
public divorce. I always had a hopeful, watchful eye on Di—just
knowing she could rise above it all.

   Her life story resonated with me—her quest to start over, to
discover a life beyond the fairy-tale she thought she was living. But

she had been stopped in her pursuit. Tragically stopped. I cried that night for her, for her family, and for the future taken from her that she never had the chance to have. Life can be so terribly fragile.

❦

"YOU WILL NEVER be alone," Joe told me when I first came home from the hospital. "Don't worry, Beck, I'll take care of it."

And he did. He made sure the COBRA insurance covered the personal aides I needed and even had his secretary help manage their schedule. He and Pat hired an additional full-time nanny, Krista, to ensure twenty-four-hour coverage for the kids. With two in diapers, Madison's speech delay and her unique needs, and an inaccessible upstairs and basement, I could never be left alone with the children.

I struggled to figure out a way to parent from the wheelchair while defining my evolving role with caregivers. I was on-site and in charge, but often I needed help, too.

Krista, a former teacher, was bright, articulate, and great with kids of all abilities. A curly-haired blonde with playful eyes and smile that both calmed and invited mischief, she managed all my kids well, but adored Madison. She took extra time styling Madison's hair and matching every piece of her teal, pink, and yellow Gymboree clothing from her hair ribbon down to her socks.

It took a few weeks, but Madison finally adjusted to my homecoming and all the changes. She was puzzled by the aides at first, but then memorized their schedules and would often hand them their keys five minutes before the end of their shift. She would still climb up into my lap for a ride. Other times she would push me where she wanted to go to avoid using words. "Use your words," I trained every caregiver to prompt Madison when she acted like she wanted something. Autism scrambled her ability to communicate, so it was far easier to show us what she wanted rather than struggle to speak.

But she understood far more than her words revealed.

One morning Madison saw me wheel into the laundry-room bathroom to brush my teeth. She looked me in the eyes, giggled, and then quietly shut the door. Inside the bathroom, I could hear her turn the deadbolt to the laundry-room door that led outside. There was a pause and then I heard her heavy footsteps quickened, muted by her loud, "EEEEeee!" as she ran outside.

"Krista!" I hollered. "Madison's escaped!"

"Where are you?" she called back from the family room.

"She shut me in the bathroom!"

Krista bolted out the back door and found our Madison racing up the street to the neighborhood school playground. The next day I had a keyed deadbolt installed on the back door and put the key in a nearby cabinet far above her head—and mine, I realized. So I had another key made and kept that one in my wallet.

Another evening, I tried to help Madison with a Barney tape, a routine task I often did before paralysis. She loved her Barney videos, engaging with that purple dinosaur far more than any human. She memorized each characters' words, songs, and dance steps. Although her fine motor skills were not on track, she was an expert on pressing rewind and play buttons. She would sit in front of the family-room TV for hours and hit rewind, then play; rewind, then play—if we let her.

That night, the tape was stuck and Madison was getting frustrated. Krista was upstairs putting away laundry and the other kids were with Joe. Madison came into the kitchen and started pushing my chair toward the sunken family room to help her. "Wait, Madison," I said, locking my brakes and taking her hands off my push handles. "Mommy will help you. One minute please." That's the last thing I needed—to be pushed over that one step down into the family room! So I took her hand and guided her in front of me and onto the step. "Madison, stop. Stay there." I said. Short phrases worked best with Madison. Kids with autism need extra processing time, I'd learned. Too many words at once are confusing, like an overlapping echo.

I wheeled down the ramp to meet her. I had added ramps to the outside of the house as well as from the laundry room to the driveway and from the kitchen to the deck. I scaled these ramps daily, unassisted.

"Here I come, Madison. Stay there," I reminded her.

She watched me back down the ramp, just as they taught us in rehab. Then I spun around to meet her. I was unable to fix the tape so I called for Krista to help. She was putting a new tape in for Madison when I decided to go back up the ramp. I got halfway up when I lost my grip, fumbled with the wheels, and slowly began backing down the ramp. No big deal. I knew that if I were to tilt backward, my anti-tipper wheels were in place to prevent a fall; I'd added them on to my wheelchair for that very reason. Attached to the back of my wheelchair, these small wheels reside behind the large wheels and touch the ground in the event the wheelchair tips backward. They exist to prevent tipping backward, hence their name.

But this time my anti-tippers caught between the hard surface of the ramp and the carpet on the family-room floor. With the momentum of coming back down the ramp and the tippers being stuck, I pole-vaulted backward over my tippers and landed on my back with a gentle thud.

I could see it coming. All I could say was, "Oh, noooo!" When I opened my eyes, I turned my head to the right and saw one knee and to the left I saw the other knee. I felt like a gymnast or diver stuck in the pike position—except upside down and with bad form. My seat belt kept my hips tied into the wheelchair, preventing a backwards flip out. When I looked up at Krista, her eyes wide and mouth startled open, I began to laugh. For some strange reason, all I could think of was the crash position instructions that flight attendants give, "Put your head between your legs," I added, "to kiss your sweet rear end good-bye!"

Surprisingly, even Madison noticed, stepping away from the VCR to hand-flap and "EEEEeee" at my spinning wheels. Krista helped me adjust my legs and we managed to right the wheelchair.

"Thank you so much, Krista! I do believe they need to rename those anti-tippers," I said. I smiled, but my mind was still absorbing the scary reality of it all.

Never alone, Joe had said. And I was grateful.

~§§~

ALTHOUGH I WENT back to work for a few weeks after the paralysis, I decided to stay home full time after more health issues cropped up. I developed carpal tunnel in both wrists from the repetitive wheelchair pushing and had another bout with a kidney stone. Deciding to allow plenty of time for healing and "listen to my body" was a choice I could make. Thankfully, we had good insurance, had invested well, and Joe continued to be generous financially.

The e-mails I sent to Scott about my daily life and adjustments helped focus my mind. His responses were almost immediate, often two to three times a day. He could type faster than I could think. And when Barbara's boyfriend, Mark, showed me how to scan in photos, I started including photos of my life—before and after paralysis.

Subject: Your Surprise Date
Date: Thu, 04 Sep 1997 12:24:31-0700

Hey Gibson!
Thanks for the newsy note and the thoughts about my recovery. I, too, know healing is coming. I just wish I could move my toe. Do you know what joy that would bring? I really want to move my toe.

Here's your surprise. I've been working hard on it. Hope you like it. It's part of a series. My pre-morbid functioning state! Like that techie term? It was used in a questionnaire during my admittance to the rehab hospital. It describes one's "capabilities prior to the injury or illness" So, I guess that makes the hospital a morgue. And me— dead? Lovely message. Life after paralysis is death?

Here comes the tough part—yes the picture is of me in the stander. I'm not as fat as this looks. The idea here is to see me as I am and envision better days by looking at the past. I am creating a collage of photos that show me standing. One set of photos is grouped strategically. The first photo shows me in a wheelchair. In the second, I am standing in the stander. And the third shows me in my black evening gown months prior to the paralysis. I study these, daily. Mental imagery is so important to me now. I am purposeful in what I place in my mind. I only want positive images stored.

In my huge bathroom, where I spend so much of my time, I had three shelves built to display the photos. The massive collage hangs under a small window on a wall between the toilet and the roll-in shower designed for wheelchair access.

To the extreme, I have become selective in my exposure to potentially negative situations. For example, it is difficult for me to watch another person in a wheelchair. At some level, I am afraid I will envision myself as doing what they are doing. And if I can envision it, then, maybe it will happen! Is that weird or what? Magical thinking? Maybe. But for now, I've decided to indulge myself. It is a workable outlook for the moment.

My feelings are quite defined on this image-management mentality. I don't want to talk to other

*paraplegics. I don't want to learn to drive. I don't want
to put in a lift or elevator that would allow me to get
to the second floor of my home. I don't want to send
my body any messages that I am accepting my situation
or to imply it is OK not to get better. I am setting the
expectation for healing. Total healing. I am thinking
it, feeling it, and living it in a way that indicates my
expectation of recovery. Permanent paralysis is not an
option. I must reinforce that to my body in every way.
That's where my head is at the moment.
Take care. —B*

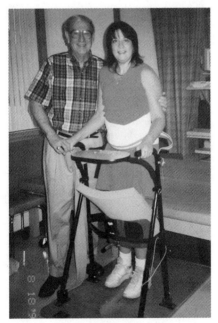

In the stander

Last time I danced at Mardi Gras

Black Evening Gown Attire, December 1996

Scott asked about my family and he updated me on his. He was married and had a son.

Here's a picture of me with all four kids. It's a rare one since we see Matthew so infrequently. This was taken a year ago. And an impish moment with Brittany and Peter. Note the construction material in the background—my house is morphing by the minute!

Scott continued to ask about the details of my physical therapy sessions and my escapades from the wheelchair. As I updated him, I decided to forward my stories to family and friends, who then forwarded them along to their family and friends. Soon I had an e-mail audience following my progress and e-mailing back with encouragement.

"Becky," wrote Barbara, "do you realize you have *readers?*" I hadn't thought about that. Although I was busy with the kids' schedules, physical therapy, acupuncture, cranial sacral therapy, massage, and even swim therapies, I made time to share my stories. The wheelchair was shutting down so many parts of my life. I'd finally found one it couldn't touch.

Subject: An Update with a Smile
Date: Mon, 22 Sep 1997 20:26:18-0700

Hey Gibson!
I had another great therapy session tonight. I stood in the stander four, yes count them, 1, 2, 3, 4 times! It was unbelievable. Three weeks ago it took two men, one holding me up from the front and one pushing me up from behind (thank goodness they were cute) to support me, as well as three sets of straps buckled around me and the stander to lean on.

Tonight, I only needed the assistance from one therapist and he only used one hand on my hip to keep me from falling backwards! Don't misunderstand, I clung onto the stander for dear life, but I could balance myself fairly well. I even shifted my hips back and forth and my shoulders from front to back—kind of walking style. Yes!

Did I tell you the deal between Dave, my PT, and me? He asked me one time what my goals were for the upcoming therapy sessions. I told him my goal was to kick him in the shins! He said if and when I kick

him, we'd all go to Chili's and drink margaritas until
he couldn't walk! Tonight, he said he was really looking
forward to those margaritas. I think I have convinced
him. He was a tough customer, too. Just hope I can
deliver—the sooner the better!

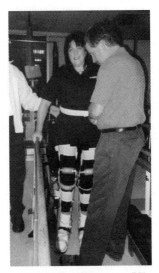

"Walking" with Dave, my PT

The therapy sessions were a three-hour ordeal that ran right through my dinner hours. My ride would come at 5 P.M. and I'd be home by 8:00 P.M. depending on traffic and Dave's agenda.

Peter, then four, would often tag along with me when Brittany and Madison had after-school activities. He'd cheer when I would stand and then hop back in my lap for a ride when I'd returned to my wheelchair. Dave included him in the workouts when he could, allowing Pete to throw a large therapy ball to me to strengthen my abs.

Pete loved counting my dips. Dave would park my wheelchair between the parallel bars, strap my feet together with a band, and lift and hold them up to the bar height. With my hands on the bars, I lifted up and lowered down. And up. And down, raising and lowering my entire body weight with my arms. We started out with one set of ten dips. My record was 150.

"Keep going, Mom! You can do it," my son coached me. He sounded like his father, so positive and encouraging. But there was tenderness about Pete, a caring warmth and sensitivity far beyond his age that reminded me of Forest.

But there were days I couldn't do it.

Therapy was difficult tonight, Gibson. Dave made me work on stuff I hate—learning how to get down on the floor and to get back up again. I see no value for that if I walk again. And, it's hard. From the floor, I have to put my arms back behind me on the upper surface and lift my body. Heave ho, buddy. I couldn't do it. I hate that. We tried alternative ways. I turned around to face the upper surface and tried to lift my lower body and push up and quickly pull up the rest of my weight. Better, with assistance, I did it. Finally, I suggested the ol' army crawl to pull myself up. Much better. But very strenuous.

Then we worked on the barrel. I pulled myself up from all fours to just my knees with my arms on top of a foam barrel. I tried to straighten my hips, which has been difficult for me. My hips tend to get stuck in the flexed position from sitting so much. I need to be able to extend them to stand up straight. I did OK on that. I was getting tired.

He then checked the movement in my legs side to side. Lots of thinking and trying so hard to move my legs. Just a trace of movement, Dave says.

Then he stretched my hip flexors. Lots of pressure pain in my hips and thighs. All in all, he pretty much

beat up on me tonight. I will sleep well. He must have
felt guilty because he called me at home twice to make
sure that I was all right.

Dave wasn't the only observant one.

"Are you okay, Mom?" Pete asked when I got home. He'd
jumped up in my lap and I guess I'd winced a bit.

"Sure, buddy. I just had a tough workout," I said, letting
him crush my neck with that hug of his.

"That means you'll get stronger, Mom." He released my
neck as those eyes of his father's beamed love at me.

"Yes, buddy. I am getting stronger."

"Is that you?" Scott had asked me.

Yes. I suppose, underneath the layers of the years, I was still
in there somewhere.

But where was that life I wanted, the one I'd planned?

Six months post-paralysis

Chapter 15

Pain Is Inevitable

Any idiot can face a crisis; it's day-to-day living that wears you out.
—Clifford Odets

IT WAS A year of many firsts. Every outing was an unpredictable adventure, despite the best of preparations. Logistics were a constant issue as loved ones and caretakers tried to transport me safely from one location to another.

The first time Mom and Dad came to visit after my month-long stay in rehab, we decided to go out for dinner. By then I was experienced in car transfers. They taught us in rehab to take control of the situation, to let others know what you were doing and what you expected of them. For me this was a good but not necessarily new way of behaving in the world.

We proceeded to the car. I rolled up to the passenger side, opened the door, and locked my brakes. Dad positioned himself to my left, ready to "help." Mom was to his left, ready to empathize and encourage, two of her stellar strengths.

The brakes were locked. I took the left footplate off. I

handed it to Dad. He handed it to Mom. Mom put it in the trunk of my station wagon.

I wheeled up even closer to the door and again locked my brakes. I took my right footplate off. I handed it to Dad. He handed it to Mom. Mom put it in the trunk of my station wagon.

Then I steadied my feet on the ground, placed my hands on my armrests, and did a wheelchair push-up, pressing down on the armrests to lift my body up and forward to the front of the chair cushion. Dad moved closer to help. Mom groaned sympathetically—the only sound to break the silence. I landed safely on the edge of the seat.

Then I removed my left armrest and I handed it to Dad. He handed it to Mom. Mom put it in the trunk of my station wagon.

Still, none of us uttered a word. I looked at my parents and started to snicker.

"What is it, Becky?" Dad asked.

"You'll never believe what this reminds me of."

"What?" they both asked in unison.

"Communion," I whispered. "Holy Communion." And we all busted out with laughter. I'm not sure why the image just popped into my head. But there was something about the routine of taking apart my wheelchair and passing it along in silence that reminded me of Dad and his precision-tuned ritual of Communion, one he controlled with pursed lips and head nods. Paralysis hadn't been able to rob me of my humor. At least not that day.

Although they were ever present in my life in so many ways, Mom and Dad could not visit often given Dad's church commitments. Before the divorce, Joe and I usually visited them. We drove with the kids to Huntington for Christmas, then to New Kensington for New Year's, and had at least one family summer vacation together with Mom, Dad, and Rachel. Mom was the master scheduler, who kept us together with her calendar, Hampton Inn directory, and predictable newsy notes. Weekly she would take time while under the hair dryer at the "beauty parlor" to write a letter, often including stamps or a stick of gum, just like she'd done in my college days. Now, after the paralysis, her notes were even more frequent; Dad preferred e-mail. But together they phoned me at least once day.

"You're doing mighty well," Mom would always say.

"You're a winner, BB," Dad would add.

They also regularly called Joe and Pat directly to ask their opinions on my progress, physically and emotionally. And when they were able to visit me, they met my doctors, therapists, and aides, and remembered to ask about them by name on our calls.

⚬⚭⚬

MEANWHILE, I TRIED to make room in my family life for my danged wheelchair. At my first teacher conference at Peter's preschool, there was no parking available in the narrow carpool drop-off zone. Two cars (with no handicapped tags) had taken both spots in front and in back of the only curb cutout leaving no room for us to park near the cutout. Pat and I decided to park between them so I could get out of the car and roll up the cutout to the sidewalk. Traffic could be blocked, but my transfer out of the car was down to a ninety-second routine. And since school was closed for conferences, we didn't anticipate any traffic issues.

All was going as planned: flashers on, handicap placard hung from the mirror. Pat unloaded the wheelchair from the trunk and wheeled it around to my opened door. With my feet planted on the ground, I locked the wheelchair brakes and put the transfer board under my thighs. My next move was to push my body up, over, and land into the wheelchair seat. I would then put my footplates on, unlock my brakes, and go.

But not this time.

As I was about to push up and over, someone blew their horn at us—a good solid two-toot blast. Startled, I rose up, but didn't launch myself far enough over. I caught myself between the car and the wheelchair. I was wedged precariously; if the chair had moved at all, I would have tumbled to the ground. I hung suspended, shaking. One arm was on the car's seat. One arm was on the wheelchair's seat.

Peter was in the back of the car, strapped in his car seat. "Mom, what happened?" he said, straining to see. Out of the corner of my eye, I could see his mop of dark brown hair bouncing back and forth as he tried to get a better look.

"I'm okay, buddy," I said giving him a quick half smile while staring at my wedged legs. I had never missed a transfer. Pat, who had seen me transfer dozens of times, looked at me bewildered. "What do you want me to do?"

"Just hold the wheelchair steady," I said evenly. "I've got this, Pete. No worries," I said a little louder. "I can do this," I whispered to myself.

I prayed my arms had the firepower. I didn't need to do 150 dips. Just one. A big one. I knew if I could not lift my body, I would be on the ground. Once on the ground, I could not remedy this situation by myself.

On my mental count of three, I went up. Way up. Airborne, and then way over. I landed back in the center of the seat in the car, not on the edge where I started out. I was grateful, but it didn't last. I was still blocking traffic. The horn-blower was still lurking. I had to make another attempt to get in the wheelchair. I breathed in deeply and commanded my body parts that still listened to me to perform. Transfer board placed. Up. Over. A perfect landing.

"Nice job, Mom!" Pete cheered. "You nailed it!"

I smiled back at him, but the horn-blower's presence still had me on guard. My hands trembled as I reached for the footplates. Then I caught myself. I quieted myself. This is not your problem. This is the horn-blower's problem. Relax. Take your time. You will hurt yourself if you try to run on someone else's schedule. Someone else's misguided reaction will only affect you IF you let it. Don't let it.

About that time, another parent who'd witnessed the whole scene came up to me, glared at the horn-blower, and offered to assist me with my footplates before helping me get into the school. We scooted out of the way to the comfort and quiet of the hornless halls of academia.

At last I felt safe.

Safety was a priority for me. I thought about it all the time. As a single mom, I had no strong-armed man who could rush in to scoop me off the floor. My missed landings would result in a 911 call. I lived carefully, fully aware how my mistakes would impact my family.

I didn't want to create any more havoc; they'd had enough.

Peter, age three, with Becky

AT BRITTANY'S NEW school, I had been invited to a Salad Supper and program for the mothers of incoming students. I had called ahead to ask about wheelchair access for the building and was told there was one small step. "No worries," a cheerful voice assured me. "We have a small portable ramp we will put in place for you. And someone will be on the lookout for you."

A new sitter, Chrissy, drove me to the event along with Brittany and Peter. When we arrived, there was no ramp. Chrissy finally found someone who could help.

"Oh, I didn't know you would need a ramp," the woman told us, peering through my car door window at my kids.

"Yes," I said, "I called and spoke with someone about my situation in a wheelchair. She assured me there would be a ramp available."

"Oh really. Whom did you speak with?" she asked. I knew she was going to ask that. I just knew it. I came very close to asking the woman on the phone what her role in the organization was but then I'd thought better of it.

"I really don't remember," I replied, frustrated but keeping my cool as I could feel Brittany and Pete watching me. I am teaching them, I kept telling myself. Take the high road. So I faked a smile and asked if perhaps she knew someone who could help her find the ramp. Although she couldn't find the ramp, she located another woman who was familiar with wheelchairs. She bumped me up and over the step as Chrissy and the kids followed me in. I kissed the kids good-bye and told Chrissy to come back by nine o'clock.

As I wheeled inside, I saw no one I knew. The room was crowded with moms of all shapes and sizes: petite blondes buzzing around in their sneakers and tennis skirts; tall long-legged brunettes with sixties colored shifts and matching flats; portly middle-aged moms with gold charm bracelets and sweeping skirts and pumps. All were chit-chatting so warmly. The room had a hum of a relaxed contentment.

I rolled into the crowded main room. Everyone seemed to know everyone else. I finally saw one familiar face. She offered to get a soda for me and introduced me to her friends. I learned that this was a dinner to honor the new mothers given by the other mothers in the Mother's Club. Over 130 people were in attendance, far bigger than the intimate gathering I'd envisioned.

Suddenly, I became acutely aware of my disability. I never realized how much we rely on our mobility to socialize. A slight turn of the shoulders and hips can include or exclude someone in a conversation. Just shifting your weight from one foot to another to come closer to someone can change the level of intimacy. Returning an empty glass or throwing away your napkin gives a break to the dialog—or you can always excuse yourself to go the ladies' room.

None of those techniques for socializing work from the wheelchair. You can't shift easily. Yes, you can pivot, but you better make sure no one is behind you or you'll run over a toe! And, you can't move closer to the speaker—you have to allow room for your lap that protrudes out farther than any pregnancy. Sometimes if you look like you are straining to hear, folks will squat down next to you to ease the awkward distance. But that's generally only when they know you well.

There were no squatters that night.

Accepting a drink makes you even less mobile. You can't wheel with both hands if you're holding a drink, and you certainly can't risk putting it on your unstable lap where those invisible hammers could strike and set off a spasm.

So, I sat and drank my Sprite. In the same spot. For forty-five minutes.

At last, dinner was announced and we moved in mass to another room. A buffet—of course. My least favorite way to dine. I couldn't reach the food and I had to be careful not to run over the tablecloth as I moved along in the line. I'd caught my wheels once before at a buffet and had almost taken down the entire buffet line.

There must have been at least seventy-eight different salads. On a thirteen-foot table draped with an oversized tablecloth.

On an oriental rug. A thick oriental rug. I cringed when I saw how plush the pile was. I'd just had all the padding removed from my carpets at home. The thicker the carpet, the harder it is to push the wheels as they sink down into the soft pile like a bike tire in mud.

I knew there was no way I could roll on that carpet using one hand while the other steadied my plate as I tried to steer clear from the tablecloth. I could see a disaster brewing. I wheeled over to a far corner.

I'm not sure which thought made the tears come to my eyes. Was it the energy of these beautiful mothers and the graceful way they moved among themselves? Was it the content of their chatter about their daughters' latest softball game or field trip— parts of Brittany's life I could not share with her because of the wheelchair? Or was it just those gorgeous clothes, those skinny size-six clothes in styles I used to wear.

I touched my permanently relaxed abs, my stubborn bloated belly that refused to shrink, and sighed. My hands started to shake. I could hear my heartbeat in my ears. I used to be like these women and now I was not, separated from them by useless legs and a cumbersome wheelchair. Maybe I should wheel into the next room, I thought. Maybe there was a large coat closet where I could wait until the whole thing was over. My sitter would be coming soon. No one would miss me.

The heartbeat thudded louder, drowning out everything. I felt so alone. And the word I hate and try so hard not to use kept flashing in my mind: *UNFAIR. UNFAIR. UNFAIR.*

I started to push down hard on my wheels to make my escape when I felt a touch on my shoulder from behind. I turned and found a smiling woman, who offered her hand, introduced herself, and then began asking me about Brittany. She soon told me about her daughter, who was a year older. Although my eyes were full, looking up prevented the tears from spilling. I knew that if I had looked down, they would have gushed.

So I kept talking and looking up. My new friend offered to prepare a plate for me. Grateful for the sturdy oversized plate, I placed it in my lap and wheeled slowly onto the hardwood floor into the dining area. I found a table and moved a chair so I could park mine in its place. I wheeled in but was stopped short.

I didn't fit.

I lifted up the tablecloth and found the culprit—the table's three-inch apron, hidden from view. My knees had banged into it. I backed out, replaced the chair, and started poking and peeking under each table's cloth until I found one with no apron. I scooted in, put my plate on the table, and exhaled.

Once parked, I tried to forget about my legs and focus on Brittany. I learned about the drama club, the chorus, the summer reading program, carpools, homework expectations, orientation dates, the "big sister" program, and the schedule for the upcoming year. I wrote down the name and number of a current sixth grader who had many of the same interests as Brittany. One mom confided how much more difficult it was to keep connected with her daughter once she transitioned into middle school. So I studied the twenty volunteer opportunities even harder, looking for a role that could accommodate my wheelchair.

I would find a way. I was not going to lose out on this part of my daughter's life.

⚭

THE HOLIDAYS WERE going to be tough. I knew that. It would be my first—and I hoped only—Christmas in the wheelchair. But I had to deal with the changes, no matter what the future.

I remembered the feelings of the first Christmas after Forest's death. Although the details were a vacant blur, I remembered well the pain, the emptiness, and the wish for the day to be over and done with. Not unlike this Christmas.

By the time I got through Christmas Eve and Christmas Day, I felt fragile, on the verge of losing it. Last year at this time I had made the decision to finalize the divorce, to get on with my life. I'd even promised Brittany that it'd be the *best year ever.* Oh my, how I'd failed her. I had to stop the thoughts, to catch them, plant them on paper, and try to disarm them.

Dear Gibson,

It's Thursday, December 25th at 10:43 P.M. Pete and Brittany are asleep together in Brittany's bed tonight. Last night it was Pete's bed, a first for them both. What better time to try out sharing a bed than Christmas Eve! They were so cute. Brought back memories of the Christmas Eves when Rachel, Forest, and I crammed into one bed.

Joe came over about 1:30 on Christmas Eve. He was very helpful. Played with the kids outside. Wrapped some presents. Reorganized the dining room to accommodate the unwrapping rituals. Then Pete, Brittany, and I were off to church. The service was a children's cantata. The living nativity scene was preceded with caroling and dramatic readings. Brittany's choir sang three times. Pete sat on my lap and was in awe. We lit candles at the end, singing "Silent Night" (my personal favorite) and "Joy to the World." I just love seeing the church begin to glow when we pass the light from one to another. That makes Christmas for me. The sharing of light.

Joe watched Madison during the service and then came to pick us up. I actually cooked Christmas Eve dinner. I decided to try an old favorite of Joe's, roasted pork loin with potatoes and carrots. The kids helped me prepare it. Joe had to help me get it in and out of the oven. It was wonderful. So strange to all be sitting

*around the table, candles lit, holding hands, saying
grace. I wonder if we could have made it. . . .*

*We got the kids down for bed and then played
Santa Claus. Joe chewed several bites off of the celery
and carrots that were left for the reindeer. And we
both nibbled at the huge S- and C-shaped cookies
that Brittany and Pete had designed. M&M cookies,
of course, with red and green M&M's. Stockings were
stuffed. A bottle of Cabernet was shared. Then we
had a brief reflection on the year and then a frank
discussion about the future.*

*Joe still thinks I will walk again. He hasn't seen
my legs in a while. They look fairly toned and much
more muscular than "legs would look after ten months
of not being used," so he hypothesized. He was amazed
at the spasms. I can tickle my upper thigh and get my
foot to flex and knee to bend almost up to my chest.
The moves are powerful and very consistent. Still can't
feel a damn thing.*

*Joe thinks that I would not continue to get small
increments of return if recovery wasn't on its way.
He read so much about my illness during the acute
phase. He feels very confident that a lengthy recovery
is reasonable. He discounts Dr. Moses's suggestion at
my last visit that most recoveries are within six months
of onset. I should have never asked that question. It
haunts me daily now that I'm ten months post onset.*

*But, I can't seem to surprise Joe with any of the
comparisons I make with others who have recovered
more rapidly. He says my body is giving me signs it is
still fighting. And my positive attitude and focus will
enable healing to occur.*

*He's big on attitude. I think that is why he was so
extraordinarily helpful. He even cleaned out the garage*

and the gutters today. He never did that when we were married. Ran the dishwasher. Put the dishes away. Washed the pots and pans. He even changed Madison's diaper! (Yes, at five, she's still in diapers.) Mr. Helpful. He actually seemed to enjoy it. And it did lift my spirits, too, to see him so engaged.

Joe gave me a Canon Sure Shot 35mm camera, knowing how much I enjoyed scanning my pictures in and sharing them with my e-mail buddies. Pete played with the Playmobile all day. Didn't even mention the Jurassic Park campsite that I couldn't find. Brittany loved her American Girl doll and clothes. And the animated Barney was a hit with Madison.

Joe took off about 5 P.M. "for the weekend." Said he thought he'd be back on Sunday, but he doesn't like to commit much. I try to be grateful for when he is here. He plans to take Pete and Brittany to Pittsburgh on Monday for the New Year. We'll see. His plans change quickly, it seems.

And now, Gibson, I'm in my danger zone. Transitions kill me sometimes. My mind wanders back to other days, mistakes, opportunities lost, hard choices, and the game of "what if." I have found if I focus, I can get through these times. I have to keep structured, busy, talking or writing to make sure this analytical, creative, ever-optimistic mind of mine stays on task and doesn't wander down that pity path OR that anger path.

So thanks, Gibson, again, for being there for me. It's 11:37 and time to go to bed. I made it, dear Gibson. I made it through Christmas.

᠁

WRITING TO GIBSON kept me focused. I continued to share my wheelchair escapades with friends and family, who continued to pass them along to others. E-mail addresses were precious to me; I cherished each one. In that pre–social media era, sending out an e-mail to my "list" was a laborious task, where I copied and pasted my story into an e-mail for each individual, adding a personal note.

I didn't mind, though, since it kept me connected in a world in which I felt so distanced from others. Most folks wrote me back, either encouraging me or reflecting on how the story helped them. To my surprise, a few suggested I write a book to share my journey. I was both shocked and flattered to learn how my writing seemed to touch people, even those I'd never met. I started researching that prospect as my e-mail list grew to over one hundred.

However, never was the disconnect between my reality and my hopes more apparent than at the dreaded one-year marker. I'd survived the three-month Becky Barbie omen. And I'd made it through Christmas with Joe's encouragement, despite Moses's six-month rule. But twelve months was a marker I could not ignore. Grateful for my ever-growing e-mail audience, who was so generous and caring in their replies, I wrote to them. My subject line was "Swinging Through."

> *Hi Folks,*
> *I knew it was coming, the anniversary, that is.*
> *Reflections abounded. Time just hung that day,*
> *remembering the details. The calls to my parents, my*
> *sister, Joe, and my kids. The endless tests, multitude*
> *of doctors, and unknown specialists in the intensive*
> *care unit. And the eternal question, will I walk*
> *again? I thought I would be at a different place in*
> *this journey on my anniversary date—one more*
> *vertical, to say the least.*

But, on February 12, 1998, Becky Galli was not vertical.

So I "made contact" with that date. I looked it squarely in the eye. I was angry and sad and enraged and devastated all over again. I let myself get in touch with all the feelings that I'd learned to so effectively sort and manage and put in benign little buckets that somehow eased the pain.

But when memories flooded, all those buckets of feelings spilled and ran into one another. And they began to combine and blend, creating a mass of emotion that can take on a life of its own. Dad calls these swirling together of emotions little "Pity Pools." Pity Pools can be a very effective way of dealing with lots of volatile emotions, he told me. You can vent and cry and holler and just sit there and feel sorry for yourself if you want to! It's OK. You allow yourself the luxury of wallowing in your own self-pity. You are entitled. Go ahead, experience your pain.

But don't stay down there too long because you can drown, I've learned. At some point, it is time to move from "pity to power," as Dad says. I just love that! From pity to power. Can't you just feel the change in perspective? The sense of the tide turning? The shift in momentum? That wonderful sense of control that begins when you realize you DO have a choice about something—your attitude! No one can take that away from you. Life in all its unfairness can never take your attitude. That alone is yours to keep and change. No one does that for you. That is power.

But how do we move from pity to power? For me, the imagery of "swinging through" helps me focus. Swinging through is the advice the baseball coach or golf pro gives you when you are working to improve

*your swing. "Make contact, and then swing through,"
they drill. The power of the follow-through is critical
for a healthy, solid swing. You meet the ball, and then
power it through, increasing its speed and energy with
the strength of your follow-through.*

*I have swung through February 12th. I powered
up with attitude and worked through all the emotional
charges that day set off. I made contact with February
12th. I sat in that pity pool and wallowed in it an hour
or two. Then I slowly began to feel the need to move
from pity to power. I needed to put that anniversary
date behind me, to move through it on the way to a
larger target.*

*As Dad says, "Don't judge a performance in the
middle of the act."*

*So stay tuned, folks. I am proud I have powered
up and swung through this most difficult anniversary
date. I do hope the second act is about to begin. I have
so many more roles I want to play.*

*Keep the faith, the prayers, and the e-mails
coming.*

⤸§§⤳

DESPITE JOE'S ENCOURAGEMENT, I became increasingly aware of the lack of progress in my recovery. In the next few months, I began to seriously consider how I could manage my life as a paraplegic.

The parallel-paths concept that Trish had drilled into my thinking came to the rescue again as I pursued two outcomes at once. On the fearful path of no recovery at all—my current reality—I took driving lessons, learned how to swim, and joined two advisory boards for the disabled. And on the hopeful path of full recovery, I bought a power stander machine to help lift me to practice standing, a workout table so I could continue the exercises I'd learned in rehab to avoid further muscle atrophy, and started dietary supplements to address bone-loss issues that could complicate any future hope for walking. I also heavily researched nerve regeneration progress and subscribed to Internet lists to keep current on all spinal cord–recovery research.

As I became more engaged in the present, the process of acceptance brought with it its own pain. Letting go of dreams was loss, just as real as the loss of the use of my legs. I found a new motto: "Pain is inevitable; suffering is optional." It became my mission not to suffer. I found that parallel paths kept suffering in check. Pursuing two paths required a vigilance that left little time for suffering.

I wanted to walk again; meanwhile, life was still moving forward. Time did not wait with me for my hopes to become realities.

⁓⚮⁓

IT SOUNDED RATHER simple. Pick Becky up and take her where she needed to go. People had been doing this for me for almost fifteen months. But this trip was a little different. And this trip was a little special. This trip was eight hours away from Baltimore, for three overnights. Barbara and Mark were getting married on May 9, 1998. And, I was in the wedding.

It'd been 545 days since I'd slept in a bed other than at my home or the hospital, but I was ready. My friend, Beth, would drive me. A church buddy who lived nearby, Beth had plugged into my life in a steadfast way after the paralysis. For the last year, she'd taken me to physical therapy weekly, as well as other jaunts to the acupuncturist, doctors, and my shrink. The mother of four, she would be away from her kids on Mother's Day. But, in her undaunted, gracious way, she offered to drive me back to my high-school hometown, Hickory, and she meant it.

I started packing and thinking. I hadn't been to Hickory in years. After Forest's death and Mom and Dad's move to West Virginia, I had no need to visit. At least the wedding was in a different church than the one where we had Forest's funeral.

The reception would be held at the country club we'd belonged to when I was in my teens. As a minister's family, we were offered a complimentary membership. Forest, Rachel, and I used to make a day of it, hanging out at the pool and eating an early dinner. Forest loved their steak fries; all three of us were fans of their famous cheeseburgers. I wondered how much it had changed in the last twenty years. Had Forest really been dead for twenty years?

Traveling with paralysis was a new experience for me. I felt like I was packing for a newborn with all the paraphernalia I needed. We needed to allow room for both the wheelchair and luggage. Everything fit, but snuggly, and that was before I realized I would need to take my potty chair. When I mentioned the addition of the potty chair to Beth, she didn't skip a beat. "Sure, we can handle that," she joked. "We'll just put it on top of the car." Unflappable, that woman was. Just unflappable. Of course it fit inside, but we had fun with the mental image of it strapped to the roof.

So we were off at 9 A.M. We had great plans of listening to books on tape, flipping through magazines and catalogs. But I do believe we yakked the whole eight hours. We made it to the hotel room and settled in for the night. Rachel met us there and was in an adjoining room next to mine. Beth was down the hall.

The next day was filled with events. The bridesmaids' luncheon, the rehearsal, and rehearsal dinner were on the agenda. But first, I had to get ready. Time to shower.

The bathroom layout was functional; Barbara's pictures were accurate. However, the shower bench was narrow. We decided to have both Rachel and Beth help me with that tricky transfer from the wheelchair to the shower bench. Beth and I had reviewed all the elements of transferring with Dave, my PT, before we left. With a belt around my waist, Rachel was positioned in front of me and Beth was in the shower to my side. I transferred from the wheelchair to the bench, no problem. The shower bench was a little rickety, so I basically held onto the grab bars while the two girls washed my hair and rinsed me off. I made sure Beth was in charge of rinsing with that adjustable showerhead. Visions of childhood garden hose attacks from Rachel kept popping into my head.

With the shower complete, I had to get back into the wheelchair. Again, Rachel was in front. Beth was in the shower to my side as I sat on the shower bench. The distance back to the wheelchair was a healthy three-inch height difference. I was slippery, but, I psyched myself up.

On the count of three, I was supposed to lift up and move over. Rachel would hold the wheelchair in place and Beth would help me lift. However, when I lifted up, I did not lift myself high enough and I didn't make it onto the seat. Beth caught me on my way down and lifted my rear end up with the belt and then over onto the seat. In the meantime, my "over" motion knocked the wheelchair sideways, pushing Rachel up against the door and down to the floor. Beth was standing, I was sitting, and Rachel was sprawled on the floor. It wasn't pretty, but I did stick my landing.

Once we all realized we were safe, we could not stop laughing. I can still see Rachel on the floor yelling, "Sissy, are you all right?" And, "Beth, you sure are strong!"

There I was, naked as a jaybird, with these two nutty women, totally at their mercy. Where had my modesty gone? I smiled, shaking my head at the scene replaying in my mind as they helped me wheel out of the bathroom. We made an executive decision to bypass the full shower on the next day. Beth was quite firm about that.

The rest of the trip's mechanics and logistics went beautifully until we got to the reception, more specifically, the dance floor. I wheeled into the gorgeous room with Rachel and Beth flanking me. I had recognized nothing about the club or its layout when we first arrived. The only thing that had looked familiar was the swimming pool. Rachel and I spotted it at the same time and then looked at each other, our eyes softening. The last time we were together here, Forest was with us. We didn't have to say what was in our hearts.

Mark was the one that got things rocking. The booze was flowing and we were all "relaxing" a bit, ready for the dance floor to start moving. He had arranged for the band to accompany him on his rendition of "My Girl" as his groomsmen came up on stage with him. Microphone in hand, Mark belted out all the words to that Motown tune to his beaming bride.

Not to be outdone, the band's lead singer told Barbara he had a song she needed to sing to Mark. He motioned for all of the bridesmaids to come up on stage—four steep steps. I watched the girls climb up each step, but I knew I wasn't about to allow anyone to bump me up that many steps, especially since everyone was becoming so "relaxed." I guess the bandleader felt sorry for me since he handed me a microphone as well as Barbara.

Our song was Aretha Franklin's "R-E-S-P-E-C-T." We jammed! It was great! I guess I started bopping around in my chair. I looked back to the girls and they were into it, too! Everyone clapped. The band dude told me I looked like I was enjoying this and asked if I had any requests?

The next thing I knew, we were all singing, Wild Cherry's, "Play That Funky Music." And, I danced. In my chair. With my sister. To the same song I danced with my brother twenty years ago.

My body may be paralyzed, but my soul was a movin' on.

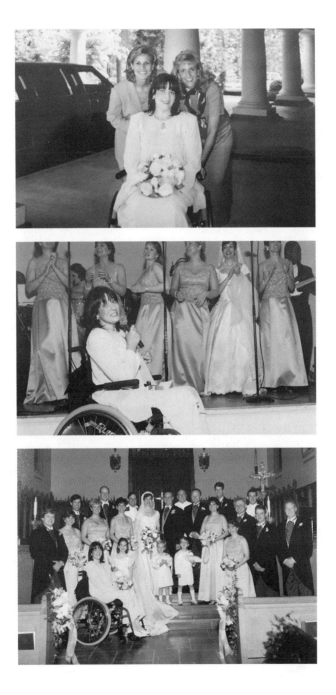

Chapter 16

The "C" Word

"Nevertheless" has a strange and amazing power—
the power of determination; the power of resolution; the power
of getting on with life, despite the circumstance.
—Dr. R. F. Smith Jr.

THE PHONE'S SHRILL ring woke me from an early-afternoon nap. It was June 1998, four months after my paralysis anniversary date. I had just turned forty. Both of my parents were on the line. They asked if it was a good time to talk.

"BB," my father began, "We've just come from the doctor. I'd had some tests done and the results are back." The tone of his voice, although even, alarmed me. It was the same tone he'd used so many years ago when he called about Forest's accident. I sat straight up in bed, fully awake, and braced myself for his next words. "They found a tumor on my kidney," he said.

My heart began to pound. This wasn't happening. Please, please don't let the next words be ones I don't want to hear. I held my breath.

"It's malignant, BB," he said simply. "I have cancer."

I could not breathe. I absolutely could not breathe. My weakened body was so stunned, it forgot how. Tears welled, but I could not speak. I finally gasped for air. "No!" I whispered through the sobs. "No!" I said again and again.

I looked up on my fireplace mantel at a picture of my beloved brother. Another photo showed my precious Matthew. Madison would soon be home from her specialized school. And my lifeless legs lay on my bed before me. My sadness rapidly turned to rage. "Damn!" I said to my parents. "Just damn it all!" I seethed. "Can't they pick on another family for a change?"

I don't remember what my parents said, if they said anything. But I do know it was all I could do to hold back the other four-letter words I was so ready to unleash. We were raised to be polite, to choose our words carefully, respectfully. So I choked down more forbidden words, like a good PK, so I could take in what my dad had to say.

The tumor was about the size of an apple. They thought they had found it in time. There would be surgery. There would be chemotherapy. There would be a six-week recovery period. The prognosis, although uncertain, was "good." We talked and talked until there wasn't anything else to say. No words could make things better. When I hung up the phone, the sobs began in earnest.

How much more could our family take?

What a ridiculous question. I had asked it many times before. I should know the answer by now. "Uncle already!" I hissed in the solitude of my makeshift sleeping quarters, its cheap bed and odd dressers creating a paltry substitute for my gorgeous master bedroom upstairs. My venom thickened. "Can't you hear me screaming?" I ranted to the hodgepodge Spartan room. "I said, 'Uncle'!" I collapsed back onto my pillow, tucking my heavy legs beside me. I cried until I could cry no more, until the calm of spent emotions could rescue me.

Then I got up, shoved my body into that contraption of a wheelchair, and powered my way to the keyboard where I pounded out my heart to Gibson and my e-mail friends:

Hi Folks!
Yep, it's me again. Time to write. Time to vent. I did something today I have never done before. I swore in front of my parents.

Hypernephroma, adenocarcinoma, Grawitz's tumor, clear cell tumor, renal cell carcinoma . . . what an education I have had this evening surfing the net and learning about the latest unwelcome, unwanted, unchosen path that my family will be taking. My mom and dad called today telling me that they have found a tumor the size of an apple on Dad's kidney. It is malignant.

"Damn," I said to them. "Just damn it all!"
In the weeks and months that followed my paralysis, I read many inspirational books and books on healing. It's an odd zone you slip into when you are trying to find the formula for the will to live. You look for meaning in everything you do, everyone you meet, everything that happens to you. You seek the highest level of interpretation, looking for the greater goods, the loftiest ideals. The details become minutiae that have no merit alone, but together form a pattern that you stretch and pull and twist into some shape of reality that finally makes sense if you stare at it long enough. That thought haunts you, the one that everyone so solemnly confides in you as you face your latest challenge, "Everything happens for a reason."

"Everything happens for a reason." Ugh! I've often thought I would create a book of myths and this one would be the first one I attack. The second

*would be, "God doesn't give you more than you can
handle." I've heard them all, dozens of times in dozens
of circumstances from Forest's death, to Matthew's
seizures, to Madison's autism, to my divorce, to my
paralysis. "There is a reason for these tragedies," the
theory cries, "and God is behind it!"*

*Great. Just great. With this theory I envision
God as a card dealer, taking stock of all the players,
assessing their "tragedy threshold." He has so many
tragedy cards he is forced to deal. And he must give
them out to those who can best handle them! How can
this be a loving God?*

*"How Mean Is Your God?" was the title of a
sermon Dad preached years ago. I've never forgotten
it. It always puts into perspective who God is and what
God represents. God is Love. How could he willfully
deal untimely deaths and unknown diseases, accidents
and heartbreaks to his children? I love what Dad has
written in his book, Sit Down, God . . . I'm Angry. He
talks of looking for God not at the point of cause but
at the point of cure. Not to blame God, but to lean on
God to get through the healing process.*

*He created a world where man has free will, the
power to choose. He created nature with all of its laws
and limits. He created a world where there would be
great joy and laughter and sorrow and pain. Bad things
happen to good people. That's the way it is. We do not
have all the answers.*

*Dad says we have to learn to live life with the
questions.*

*Yes, learning to live life with the questions—
again, a much-too-familiar pattern for me and my
family. How we would all love to be rookies in this
game of adversity. But we are not. We are veterans,*

seasoned. And in truth, we don't cry "uncle." We don't
give up. It is not our way. It is not our style. We are
survivors. And, unfortunately, we are damn good at it.
Please keep us in your thoughts and prayers.

~§§~

LATE THAT NIGHT, I wheeled back into my office where I
parked in front of my keyboard with my trusty mug of tea and lit
my writing candle, lavender. The heat of anger had burned itself
out, yet the cold reality remained: my father had cancer.

I sipped the tea and closed my eyes, trying to envision the
future. Was he going to survive? How long did he have? What
kind of life was ahead for him? And for the rest of us? The questions began and ended with no answers, a frustrating loop of
rhetorical pain.

Then Dad's wise words broke through the mess. "Find a
peg in your mind, BB, and put that concern on it," he often suggested. "You can't solve it today, and I can tell it's bothering you.
So hang it on a peg."

So I did. I put my burdensome questions "on a peg," not
to be forgotten, but to be managed. I smiled at my father's sage
advice and the comfort it brought me. Then an e-mail chime
sounded. I opened my eyes to an e-mail from my father. I clicked
it open.

The day before he learned of his diagnosis, he had con-
ducted the funeral of a young woman, Terri, who had succumbed
to breast cancer, He wrote to me about his remarks.

Dearest BB:

So sorry I had to give you the news this afternoon.
We've always been open and honest about what's going
on in our family, so this time was no different.
 I read the following at Terri's funeral yesterday.
Someone had given her a little stuffed lamb named
Faith that had this attached:
  Cancer Is So Limited:
     It cannot cripple love
        It cannot shatter hope
           It cannot corrode faith
              It cannot destroy peace
                 It cannot kill friendship

  It cannot suppress memories
     It cannot silence courage
        It cannot invade the soul
           It cannot steal eternal life
              It cannot conquer the spirit

 Even as I read this yesterday, BB, I had a strange
feeling it would become a very special message to me.
For some months, I have had this strange feeling that
I had cancer. As I did various things, e.g., roofing the
house here and in Lenoir, changing banks, getting "my
house in order," I sensed something was afoot. Now I
know what it is. But I am so glad that the future looks
brighter than it could have been given other factors.
I do feel this is but a detour on my journey, and I am
even now asking, "What will I learn from this?"
 We will make it. We are survivors.
 I love you.
DAD

I winced at his words that stared back at my weary eyes. I remembered his signature challenge, the one he used in each church service: "No experience is ever wasted unless you let it be." Each time he used that phrase, he would set the stage for learning while sending the message that we must take responsibility to learn from what we experience.

As he had just done, once again.

❧

AFTER FOREST'S DEATH, I watched my father struggle to learn how to accept the good in life while living in the shadow of the best that could no longer be. In his typical pulpit sound-bite style, he had boiled down his philosophy to one simple word, "Nevertheless." "Nevertheless," he would explain, "implies that given a certain situation, I will behave contrary to its implications. I may not like my circumstances; *nevertheless,* I will find the good in them.

As I thought more about the next steps for my father, I realized I needed the power of that one-word philosophy. Frustrated that my paralysis and ongoing medical issues prevented me making the eight-hour trip to West Virginia to be with my family, I wondered, what could I do? Yes, I was devastated, angry, and sad about Dad's news, but *nevertheless,* what could I do? There must be something I could do!

As I thought about the needs of my parents and my limited ability to physically help them, I realized the answer lay just beneath my fingers. I could "tell the story." By soliciting e-mail addresses from friends and family and updating them on Dad's progress I could help Mom and Rachel by fielding the inquiries and at the same time capture every response for Dad to read later as he was able.

The next day, I told Mom and Rachel I would be the official e-mail press agent for the family. E-mail addresses poured in from friends, family, church members, and the community.

⚬⚬⚬

DAD'S PROCEDURE LASTED almost three hours. The doctors removed a mass about the size of a football, much larger than expected, along with my father's right kidney. The official diagnosis: renal adenocarcinoma, stage II, no evidence of invasion of capsule, pelvis, or vessels; no evidence of lymph node metastases. According to the experts, this was the "best diagnosis possible" for renal adenocarcinoma, as the tumor appeared to be contained and not in the renal vein.

The recovery was lengthy, as expected, and frustrating for Dad. He missed his energy and was impatient for its return. After he stabilized at home, he and Mom left West Virginia to complete his recovery in Lenoir, North Carolina, at the "Ophelia-Forest," my father's childhood home, named after his parents. Dad's father, a lumberman, had built the home, and upon his death, it became the perfect nostalgic retreat for my parents. Dad had preached his first sermon in the church next door. And a half mile down the road, its cemetery was filled with Smith relatives, including his parents and Forest.

During his four-week recovery there, we talked daily. He always gave me something to think about.

It was 9:15 one Saturday night. I knew if I wanted to talk to Mom and Dad I would need to make my call right then, or I would not make their bedtime curfew. Mom answered on the first ring and Dad joined in the conversation. He said he had an "okay" day. In Dad-speak, that means not-so-hot. Mom translated his hesitancy and acknowledged he'd had quite a bit of pain and discomfort. His sleep patterns continued to be irregular. "But, it's nothing to be worried about," she assured me. "He's progressing, it's just a slow pace for him."

They asked about my dinner party that was in progress. I had gathered some friends together for a cookout, many of whom Mom and Dad knew from earlier visits to Baltimore.

"How's Beth? And Barbara and Mark? Is Mark grilling?" they asked. "Tell them all we said hello." They loved to plug into my world. "And how's your ice cream?" Dad inquired. During their last visit, I had purchased an ice-cream maker and we had made some delicious ice cream together—strawberry, Mom's favorite.

"Well," I began, "I don't know what I've done wrong, but it has been churning for three and a half hours and it is still soup!"

Without skipping a beat, he said, "You can always serve milkshakes."

I just had to laugh and shake my head. Milkshakes, indeed. He didn't ask if I had used enough ice. He didn't ask if I had changed the recipe. He didn't ask if I used the right rock salt. He just made a helpful suggestion of how to use what I had to its best advantage.

That was his gift, to see the possibilities. To assess right then and there the issue, the person, and the situation, and to suggest how to use what is available to its best advantage.

Even though a critique may be in order, moving forward with a positive approach was always his lead. It was almost an automatic response with him. If you watched him carefully, you could almost see the sifting and sorting going on underneath that steady gaze, allowing only the most positive of possibilities float to the top of his mind.

Using what you have to the best advantage. I liked that thought. I may not have liked where I was, stuck in this dang wheelchair, but there were ways I could still use what I had.

❧

ON SEPTEMBER 13, 1998, almost nine weeks after his surgery, Dad returned to the Huntington pulpit and a new silent battle with the calendar began as we were told to "bide our time" in the five-year critical period of waiting before claiming total victory.

But "bide" he did not! Dad expanded his newspaper column, "Looking Homeward," from North Carolina to Huntington's *Herald-Dispatch*, sharing the lessons he'd learned in his personal valleys with new readers. As a family, we lived fully, gathering family together as often as possible for holidays, vacations, reunions, and even a special Caribbean cruise.

Between scans, imaging, and blood tests, we did a good job of holding the unforgotten threat of returning cancer at bay. Second and third opinions kept us grounded, though. We knew we could be traveling through borrowed time.

Chapter 17

Rejected Again and Now Replaced

*I was trying to reimagine my life. You have to be willing to let go of
the life you planned in order to make the life you're meant to live.*
—Maria Shriver

AFTER EIGHTEEN MONTHS of dealing with my paralysis,
my kids decided it was time for me to get back into their world of
sports. Peter, now five, had started T-ball games in the spring. I
learned I could pitch to him if I angled my wheelchair slightly to
the left and leaned way over to the right, steadying my body with
my left hand on my right armrest as I threw.

Brittany, now a five-foot-three eleven-year-old energetic
blonde, excelled in softball as a pitcher and had made the All-
Stars. I learned I could still swing a mean bat as long as my brakes
were solidly locked and my arm rests were swung around to the
back of the chair. I could give her a good target as a catcher, as well.

But Pete wanted me to play soccer.

I could still spiral a football and dribble a basketball. It
wasn't pretty, but I could do it.

But soccer?

My sensation level had not changed. I could still only feel about an inch above my navel, still T8. Although some tone had returned, my hips and legs remained immobile and numb, void of any voluntary movement. So my thoughts of soccer were as a spectator. However, Peter had other ideas.

"Mom, I have a soccer game on Saturday. I need to be the best. I need to practice," he told me, his deep-brown eyes intense and determined.

"Well, sure, Pete. Let's go!" I spoke before I thought. About halfway down my three-level zigzag ramp that led outside, I began to wonder how I could possibly play with him. I could only use my arms and hands, the very things that are illegal to use in soccer.

Pete had suited up for the occasion. His team was the "black" team. Black T-shirts. Black shorts. Black socks and black shoes.

"Pete, you forgot your shin guards," I told him. Right, like I was going to kick him in the shins! I laughed out loud at the thought, but Pete nevertheless obediently put them on. They were huge, covering not only his shins, but also a good part of his ankles and knees. It was hysterical, but I solemnly praised his attire. "Now you are ready, bud. Let's go."

As I rolled into the driveway, it hit me. "Pete, I'm the goalie." We had two single garage doors beside each other. "You try to kick the ball past me into this garage door," I directed. "And the other garage door will be my goal," I added as a passing thought. I knew I'd never score, but the idea sounded good. We had to be fair about this.

So we played. He'd kick and I'd roll. He'd shoot and I'd block. He'd shoot and he'd score. He'd shoot and I'd block—and it would ricochet into my goal! He'd shoot and he'd miss and he'd score in my goal! That was the best, his unintended score. I'd do my Elvis Presley imitation of, "Thank you very much!" and Pete would erupt into waves of laughter, each round starting a little higher pitched than the last. His whole body quaked, Nana-style, as he lost his neck in the rhythmic shake of his shoulders. I'd have to remind him, "Breathe, Pete!" And he'd suck in a quick breath and start again. Twice he ran to the bathroom to relieve himself. There seemed to be a direct connection between the giggle muscles and bladder control.

Pete sharpened his shooting skills and I got the best workout I'd had in a long time. My trunk was sore and my thumbs had tread marks on them, but the fun was worth it. Plus, Pete scored twice.

❧

THE NEXT MONTH, I ventured out to a seminar designed for and by spinal cord–injured patients as part of an outreach program. The topics were selected from a recent survey that I, along with other consumers of physical rehabilitation services, had completed. First, we heard an upbeat presentation on spinal-cord research. We learned about current studies, the process for drug trials, and the latest updates on nerve regeneration.

Then, we learned about how our muscles atrophy over time. A bone density lecture noted the fragile nature of bones no longer used for weight bearing. Then the group had a lengthy discussion on pain management issues, as many of us with paralysis told of pain we still felt in the limbs we can no longer use.

Finally, we heard about the secondary complications that can occur from being spinal cord–injured. Problems with the kidneys as a result of ongoing self-catheterization were once the most common complication. However, by now, renal failure and disease complications had been greatly reduced, they told us. In fact, with the advances in medications, procedures, and preventative care, complications of the kidney were no longer the leading cause of death in spinal cord–injured patients.

"The leading cause of death"—those words froze the pen in my hand, as I looked up at the speaker and tried to absorb what I had heard. I didn't need to know any more than what I had heard, but of course he had to give additional supporting data.

"In general, of course," the lecturer continued, "the spinal cord–injured population has a life expectancy less than the normal population."

Boom. There it was. The whole truth was out. The words kept repeating themselves in my head as the speaker moved on. Then reality began to sink in. I suppose it was obvious, the fact that I was a member of the spinal cord–injured population. It's funny, though. I'd never thought of myself that way. I always felt like I was Becky Galli without use of her legs. It'd never occurred to me that I'd joined a group.

But, I guess this happens all the time. We have a child and we become part of the parent category. We turn a certain age and become part of a generation segment. We learn a sport and become part of an athletic team. We obtain an e-mail address and password to join an online community. We acquire labels, some chosen, some not.

But, the statement still played in my mind, its cruel certainty blaring. The group I'd unwillingly joined had some serious fine print. We have "a life expectancy less than the normal population." It must be true; the speaker had clearly said it. But there was a looming question I had: If kidney problems were no longer my new group's leading cause of death, what was?

And, as if the speaker had heard my query, the next slide came up, and the lecturer announced, "The current leading causes of death in the spinal cord–injured population are:"

1) respiratory or pulmonary complications
2) suicide/accident.

My notes stopped there. I didn't even write down the third cause. The screen's images blurred. It was too much to take in. Yet, I couldn't help wondering as the speaker droned on, what will be the cause of my death? Respiratory complications, suicide, accident, or even kidney disease or failure? And, is it really more likely to happen to me solely because I sit in this ridiculous wheelchair?

When I got home, I made a vow to myself: life expectancy will not change my expectations in life. And I wrote down what my expectations were:

1) I expect to grow as a parent, nurturing my children and creating an environment for their success.
2) I expect to publish my writing.
3) I expect to become as independent as I can be from the wheelchair. I want to vacation, to travel, to experience as much of life as possible from this contraption I must use.
4) I expect to be ready for recovery, however small it may be.
5) I expect to become involved in at least one major philanthropic effort that would benefit the disabilities of my children or myself.

As I faced mortality's place in my life, as well as the limits of paralysis, I struggled to embrace the thought that things may never be the same. I needed to let go of the burden to somehow return things "to normal." I needed to accept my life as it was.

That day, I stopped trying to wiggle my left big toe.

EVEN THOUGH WE were divorced, Joe stuck by me through the crazed days of my paralysis. He visited me daily when I was in the hospital, even held my hand while we watched UNC play in their March Madness pursuit. One night he snuck a 1990 Brunello into my hospital room. And of course, there was the stunning heart-shaped necklace studded with sapphires and diamonds that he'd given me. The one I wore every day. I felt closer to him than ever before.

Once I was home, that familiar pounding—bam, bam, bam of the stamps on the envelopes—returned to my home when Joe visited long enough to sit at our office desk and pay my bills, writing checks from our joint checking account, still in place. When I was strong enough to leave the house, he would take me out to dinner to see how I was handling things. "I can take it, Beck," he told me more than once during our candle-lit dinners. "Let me know how you are really doing."

And I did. I looked forward to each outing and the chance to catch up and share my innermost hopes and fears about living with paralysis. He'd known me since I was eighteen and understood me well enough to realize that the many layers of Becky would be working hard to get through each difficult adjustment. On the outside, most would say I looked so strong. But Joe knew better. Underneath it all, I was churning, struggling with all the adjustments in private.

But during one candle-lit dinner in March, just after the two-year anniversary of my paralysis, Joe stunned me with news about his own private world: his plans to become engaged. I was shocked. I knew he had been dating, disappearing more frequently and without explanation. But he wanted to get married? What would happen to him, my rock, my confidante? What did that mean for me?

I swirled my cabernet, staring at the legs of its fineness in the candlelight and wondered: Had I let myself fall in love with him again? Had my magical thinking imagined the caring looks, the steadfast support, the engaging way he was in my life to be signs of love? Was that real? Was I going to have to lose him all over again?

We were silent on the car ride home. I made it inside in time to kiss the kids good night before the sitter took them upstairs for their bedtime routines. I wheeled into my bathroom, my only private room where I could lock the door, and cried.

He had been an ally in my battle between hope and acceptance after paralysis. And now he was giving me one more thing I needed to accept. The next day, I called Dr. Lucco to set up an appointment, invited my UNC girlfriends up for another party, and scheduled mani-pedis for that afternoon.

Paths in the friggin' wilderness. AGAIN. I could get through this; I was sure of it.

But I was also sure I could not do it alone.

⸙

AFTER JOE'S ENGAGEMENT, he still called and was heavily involved in all the children's issues, but he slowly pulled away from me and moved toward his new future with his fiancée. I knew we had divorced, and we should be living separate lives, but somehow I felt rejected again.

And now replaced.

My competitive and entitlement juices kicked in producing two maddening thoughts: first, what did she have that I didn't? And second, if he'd treated me then the way he treats me now, we'd still be married.

Even though I'd been the one to finalize the divorce, this future was not the one I had in mind. Paralysis had destroyed far more than my mobility; it crushed my plans for the closely knit family I wanted to create with another man, a man who wanted to be in the room with me and share my crazy life. Joe's remarriage put a glaring spotlight on our uneven starting-over points. His new beginnings cast a huge shadow on my stalled dreams. My life was not where it was supposed to be, where I wanted it to be. And Joe was moving ahead with his, full force.

Paralysis's rude intrusion had a cruel way of coloring the past that made acceptance of this remarriage beyond difficult, almost impossible. The "trophy wife" image kept flashing before my eyes. *I* was the one who had suffered through all of our family trials. *I* was the one who had managed to keep our home life stable enough to support Joe's career success. *I* was the one who had loved him so much that I convinced myself that his success was mine, too. Now she waltzes in and scoops up the cream off the top! How could I tolerate one more unwelcomed addition in my life?

I was angry and yet confused, too. I worried about how my feelings would affect our children. I did not like this woman whom I hadn't even met, or her role in Joe's life. I didn't know her, but I disliked both the idea of her and her apparent history with my husband. Yet, when I calmed down enough to consider the children, another voice tugged at my conscience.

How could I possibly openly dislike the woman whom my children's father was going to marry? How confusing would it be to Brittany to see her mother detest the person that her father loves? Should my daughter be loyal to me and dislike the woman? Or should she be loyal to her dad and embrace his new wife, and discount my opinion? Maybe she should just never talk to me about her father or his fiancée at all, shutting down all communication about that part of her life?

Did I really want that? At this very time in my young children's lives, when communication was so important, did I want to create an obstacle in my relationship with them?

Although Pete was only six years old, Brittany, soon to be twelve, was on the cusp of those challenging teenage years. Even the complex care Matthew and Madison needed would benefit from a positive relationship between our two households.

When I focused on my children, I could see beyond the immediate situation with a new but fragile spirit of resolve. I knew in my heart that my children would observe and respect my values and priorities, even with this unknown new role model in their lives.

I also knew it wasn't going to be easy.

Chapter 18

Dark Days

If you're going through hell, keep going.
—Winston Churchill

SHORTLY AFTER THE engagement, our family life would change forever—again.

The phone rang, piercing the mild hubbub of Madison's behavioral therapy session. The routine drills tapped into her language potential, teaching her to use her words that were often trapped in the minds of children with autism.

"Show me happy!" the therapist requested.

"Hurray!" Madison responded.

"Show me sad."

"Wah, wah!" Madison complied.

I wheeled my way over to the kitchen phone, answering quietly to avoid disturbing the session. "Hello?"

"Becky, it's Joe," he began. "I have some bad news." And after what seemed like eternity, he cleared his throat and said softly, "I am leaving Black and Decker."

"What?" I must have misunderstood. I inched my wheel-chair closer to the counter, wedging myself up against its edge as I strained to get closer to the wall phone, covered its matching wallpaper pattern of pink and blue flowers beginning to blur. I jammed the phone hard into my left ear. "What did you say?"

He repeated it.

It couldn't be. Black and Decker was his life—our life. It was the only company he'd ever worked for. His meteoric ascent to president of the worldwide tool group at the age of thirty-five made him the youngest president in the company's history. He loved B&D. It was his passion. How could he leave? "What happened?" I whispered.

More words, thick with emotion, blurred like static as I frantically tried to tune in to the important details. "We'll be fine," he assured me, giving me just enough specifics for my mind to absorb the reality of the situation.

"Show me surprise!" I heard the therapist prompt.

"Oh, Oh!" Madison replied.

"Show me angry."

"Grr, Grr," Madison answered.

At that moment, I envied my daughter's articulate display, for I had no words to express my feelings. My mind joined my body, immobilized by the unthinkable: Joe Galli, the hot-shot wonderkid who dedicated almost twenty years to the turnaround success of Black and Decker, had been fired.

Apparently he'd pushed too hard with his maverick ways, becoming a threat to senior executives. So they cut him loose.

Although no longer my husband, he was still one of my best friends and staunch supporters, despite the recent engagement. The career he built at Black and Decker was a mutually proclaimed joint venture, beginning with the recruiter's college campus offer. I was heavily invested in his success, in more ways than one.

"What do we tell the kids?"

"Tell them that Daddy's leaving Black and Decker. And everything is going to be all right."

The therapist's question interrupted my daze as I hung up the phone. "Who is it?" she asked Madison, showing her a photo of me.

"Mommy," Madison replied.

"Who is it?" the therapist drilled again, this time pointing to a picture of Joe beside the signature yellow DeWalt jeep.

"Daddy," Madison answered confidently.

I winced as I looked at that picture. DeWalt was the darling of Joe's collection of achievements at Black and Decker. Resurrecting the dormant brand name and incorporating a risky and flashy yellow color scheme, Joe launched the most highly successful product line in the history of the company. The thought of a tool-free focus for our family was incomprehensible; its imprint went so deep. I thought about our drill-bit Christmas tree; Brittany's presentations, playing Daddy with his DeWalt slides that were permanently parked in our living room; and Joe's own presentations to Brittany's classes. Every year since kindergarten, Joe would speak to her class at school, always giving the kids and teachers "goodie bags" of B&D products.

And now it was all over.

How could they do that to him? After all the sacrifices he made? That we made? That our family made? Something inside me shifted. It was as if I no longer felt betrayed by Joe; I felt betrayed with him.

Unbelievably, the next day was "take your daughter to work day." The carefully crafted tour of B&D's executive offices for Brittany, now eleven, was brutally canceled. With a put-on happy face, I pinched-hit for Joe, spending time with Brittany, showing her my book proposal drafts.

I needn't have worried, though. Three years and three career moves later, he would stride confidently across the cover of *Forbes* magazine as the "Sultan of Sizzle," Newell Rubbermaid's new CEO and the youngest CEO in the Fortune 200.

~⚭~

MEANWHILE, LIFE AT home moved on, bumps and all. I was home alone on Labor Day weekend, 1999, the twenty-first anniversary of my brother's death. The children were with Joe and apparently I had too much time on my hands. I had listened to my funky music, taken a shower, and jump-started my body with caffeine. But after three sets of arm curls, two doses of vitamins, and a can of tuna, I was still sad.

The tears just seemed to flow. One fleeting thought after another stuck helplessly in my mind like a spider's victims in its web. I'm not sure why my web was so sticky that day. Yes, it was the anniversary of the death of my brother. Yes, I was alone on a holiday weekend when my children were with another family, THE other family, Cindy's family. That was Joe's fiancée's name, I'd learned, the same name of the danged college cheerleader who caught the eye of my then boyfriend.

What is it with my men and Cindys? Ugh. My mind wandered. I couldn't focus.

My local friends had plans or were traveling. My sister was entertaining houseguests. My parents were in transit. Even my cyber-buddies were at rest. I was all by myself.

Usually, being alone energized me. I could relax the pace of my hectic schedule, focus on my writing, read, or catch up on paperwork. But sometimes it created an unwelcomed solitude and an unwanted perspective. It invited time to sit at my doorstep, hanging out, waiting.

My children were so much to manage, but they did put me in gear; I couldn't idle long around three active children. When I was alone, though, time begged to be managed. All the mindless routines done so automatically were suddenly subject to scrutiny. There was no rush to dress, eat, or prepare for the day. The extra time could truly allow me to be—all by myself.

All by myself. I thought about that phrase. How can you be all "by" yourself? I looked it up. Webster's said "by" can mean "close at hand." Perhaps when I'm "by" myself, there are two people, two selves, next to each other who are close at hand? Maybe there is a self-one "by" a self-two?

That day, time hovered above all the routines. Self-one, Becky before paralysis, checked out the new self-two in slow motion. Self-one did not like what she saw. "I hate it," she said as she watched self-two move through the motions of the day. Getting up. Stretching out those tight legs, knotted with useless tone and unpredictable spasms. Getting out of bed. "I hate it," Self-one kept repeating as the daily living pattern unfurled before her. "This is not me," she uttered with anguish. "This can't be my life!"

Then she watched self-two wheel into the bathroom, square up to face the toilet, and stop in front of it. She noted the precise way that self-two inched her wheelchair up to the toilet seat, braked, and carefully lifted each leg up on top of the tank, frogging them as she reached for the catheter and the gel. Every four hours, self-two empties her bladder that no longer works because of the paralysis.

Next, self-two moved the potty chair over the toilet bowl. She positioned her wheelchair next to it, creating a perfect forty-five-degree angle. She moved up to the front of the wheelchair, steadying herself between the two seats' surfaces. In one motion, she moved up and over to the new seat where rubber gloves and gel helped her empty her bowels. After a quick transfer back to the wheelchair, she rolled up to the shower bench placed midway in the roll-in shower stall. Again, the angles. Again, the balancing. Again, the transfer.

Self-one looked on with amazement. Self-two prepared for her shower, undressing with one hand while the other clung to the grab bar for support. Soap. Shampoo. Rinse. Then, she checked her body carefully for skin breakdown and massaged her feet to increase their circulation. After one final transfer, self-two buckled her seat belt in the wheelchair and moved to the sink area to dry and dress.

It is then that self-two paused and looked up. Self-one saw self-two's blue eyes filled with a distorted hope, glazed over with a quiet resignation. Self-one bristled with anger, noting the trappings of paralysis that now cluttered a once-simple routine. "Why?" she screamed, more at God than herself. She closed her eyes and remembered the pre-paralysis split-second routines. It was a high-volume, high-energy life, spent accomplishing so much, so well. "Where did it go? Why did it go?"

I shook my head and the twins disappeared. I was left with a haze of loss and anger, but mostly a raw sadness.

Every adaptation reminded me of what life was now compared to what it used to be. I'd willed my mind to accept them as "routine nuisances" or "necessary accommodations." But underneath the veneer of adjustments, I was mourning the premature death of a life so full of promise, a loss that made no sense. It seemed to never end, these life-after-loss adjustments.

It was hard, but in my better moments, I could widen and lift my thoughts to free them from the tangled web. Sadness was natural, I kept telling myself. I can't deny the loss. But I do have the power to manage it and the ability to learn from it. I have the capacity to cope, to shift my perspective.

At least I once had a brother; some never do.

At least I was married once; some never will.

At least I once walked; some never have.

⤙⧜⤚

I FINALLY SUCCUMBED. Almost two and a half years post-paralysis, I purchased a converted minivan for the purpose of learning how to drive it. Although I was never a van person

(I'd owned four Taurus station wagons), I must admit it was one cool van. With the flick of a switch, the floor lowered six inches and a ramp unfolded to the ground so I could wheel myself in unassisted. The driver, passenger, and middle seats could be removed so I could remain in the wheelchair and sit in any of those four locations. Hand controls were installed that gave the driver the option of using foot pedals or hand levers to drive. Eventually, I hoped to drive.

When Mom and Dad came for their Thanksgiving visit, Dad wanted to check out my new wheels. We avoided the stores on Friday after Thanksgiving, but braved a trip to a small mall on Saturday morning. I wheeled into the van and parked. Mom used the convenient driver-side sliding door to access her place right beside me. She buckled in and I put on my shoulder strap that would prevent me from falling forward. I didn't use the four straps that anchor the wheels to the floor; the belts were cumbersome and difficult to maneuver. Instead, I opted to use the handle on the back of the passenger seat to stabilize myself. It would be no different, I reasoned, than passengers on a bus, hanging onto the rails.

Dad shut his door and settled into the driver seat. He adjusted mirrors, seat height, radio station, and the heat. Mom and I chatted as I put some lotion on my chapped hands.

"Are we ready?" Dad asked.

Before we could answer, the van lurched forward, jolting Mom and me backward. I lunged for the handle on the back of the passenger seat, but my lotioned hands slipped and I fell, landing on my back. My lifeless legs sprawled above me leaving me staring at the ceiling, turtle-style.

"Oh, Becky," gasped Mom. "Are you all right?"

"Honey, are you okay?" Dad exclaimed.

"Yes, I'm okay." I replied, pausing to gather myself. Mentally, anyway. "Dang it all," I said in disgust. "Being paralyzed is such a pain!"

Then Mom looked at me and she began to shake. She quickly turned away and looked down toward her passenger door, but the shaking continued.

"Mom?"

She could not answer.

"Mom!"

Then she turned to look at me again.

"You're laughing!" I cried.

Then Dad joined in. "BB, your Mom's tickled. You know how she gets when she gets tickled." I looked at Dad through my airborne legs and the hilarity of the situation struck me, too. Mom's bout of tickle-box turnover was in full force. She was already at the nonverbal stage. Tears soon followed.

"What did you do to make the van start off like that?" I asked Dad, allowing Mom a moment to regain her composure.

"Well, I thought I'd check out these hand-controls," he said with a hint of a crooked smile. "I'd say they're a tad sensitive."

"Dad! I told you not to touch those!" Right, like I could ever manage my father. For the next ten minutes my parents worked to pull me up to a sitting position. Mom kept relapsing into tickle-town and I didn't want Dad to hurt his back, so I suggested he go inside and ask my sitter for help. Gratefully, I was uprighted without further incident. After I figured out a new wheelchair buckle-up routine that included floor straps to the front wheels, we were off to the mall.

"What would we have done if we couldn't have pulled you up?" Dad asked me.

"Maybe asked for help from my neighbors?"

"We could have driven you up to the fire station," he said, still fiddling with the steering wheel's knob, intended for my use only. "It's just up the road a bit and I'm sure they could have helped us."

I paused to create the mental picture of that scene. The van driving up to a fire station, a distinguished-looking gentleman in the driver seat, an attractive but tear-stained lady shaking with laughter behind him in the second seat, and my two feet adorned with black patent-leather Doc Martens waving in the wind.

From that moment on, I used the story of what happened with my parents as a cautionary tale and subtle way to train each new caregiver, warning them about the hand controls as well as reminding them to check for my "road-readiness" before stepping on the gas.

"We often let grief overcome us. And pain overcome us," I wrote to Gibson that night. "What a beautiful addition it can be to let humor overcome us."

Chapter 19

Acceptance Changes Everything

You may have to fight a battle more than once to win it.
—Margaret Thatcher

STRUGGLING TO ACCEPT the idea of Joe's remarriage was one thing. Surviving his wedding day when my children were included in the ceremony was an entirely different challenge.

> *The impending wedding and my kids involvement in it is, quite frankly, a bitch to handle.*

My fingers pounded into the keyboard to a new but suddenly steadfast e-mail buddy, Frank. The blinking cursor winked back at me. I knew my wise friend would hear me out patiently, as only he could, since, well, he'd been divorced three times.

> *This young, twenty-something exudes a casual familiarity with me on the telephone that is unearned and unwanted on my part. I can just feel my fingernails*

grow and sharpen with each conversation! I'm not one
of her girlfriends. I tend to see her at best as a colleague
in the co-parenting business, and a rookie at that, mind
you. I will attempt respectful, purposeful exchanges on
the phone about my children, and that's all.

As I stopped my written rant, tears welled up in my eyes. I
paused to catch my breath and slow my racing thoughts. Frank's
responses were thoughtful and caring, encouraging me to focus
on my role with the children.

"Others may have an influence on them," my insightful friend
reminded me, *"but only you are their mother."*

Still, when the wedding date was set for midsummer 2000, I
began to make plans to be elsewhere that day. I brainstormed trip
ideas with my girlfriends. Then the details began to hit home—
my home. Brittany was asked to be a junior bridesmaid. Peter was
going to be the ring bearer. And they wanted to include Madison
as the flower girl—a lovely thought, but one that required more
of me than I'm sure they realized.

Since my paralysis, I'd hired additional caregivers for
Madison to help her with her daily living needs and to manage her increasingly aggressive behaviors. Like most children
with autism, she needed a structured environment with planned
activities, a visual schedule to follow, and a consistent daily routine. She did not react well to change and had trouble with transitions. If pressed into a new situation without a plan or detailed
schedule, she could tantrum—cry, throw herself on the floor,
strike others or herself.

A few months before the wedding, the behaviors escalated
at home and at school. In fact, Madison's school had threatened
to suspend her—an errant but nonetheless alarming action—for
throwing a chair in the classroom. So, to honor the flower-girl
request, I had to find someone who could not only handle Madison in an unfamiliar setting, but who would also be willing to

attend Joe and Cindy's wedding—an awkward request that I eventually made of my dear caregiver, Pat.

News of the festivities continued to trickle into my world. The beautifully coordinated wedding attire for my three children was ordered, fitted, and neatly hung in their closets. I could sense their growing excitement. But when I told Brittany and Peter of my plans to be away for that weekend, they were upset, especially Pete. "No, Mom, I want you to be here at home. Don't leave, please," he pleaded with me. His soft, brown, six-year-old eyes looked right through me.

Pete was nine months old when Joe and I separated. He had no other framework for life other than that of a divorced household. One day when he was four, he came rushing into the house after visiting a neighborhood friend announcing, as if he'd made a breakthrough discovery. "Mommy, guess what? Jack's mommy and daddy live in the same house!"

And my heart broke a little more as I tried to explain marriage in the context of divorce.

So when those penetrating eyes looked at me once more for explanation, I had to examine my motives for leaving on the wedding weekend. What am I doing? Why am I doing it? And the biggest question, what message does it send to my children?

Does it say that Daddy hurt Mommy by marrying this woman? Does it say that Mommy must not like the fact that Daddy is marrying her? Does it say that Mommy is scared?

Am I abandoning my motherly duties if I leave? Am I running from a difficult situation—the very flaw that I criticized in Joe? Am I letting them influence who I'm becoming?

The answer became clear. I wanted to be there for my kids. This must be a terribly confusing time for them. I wanted to be available if they had questions. *Somehow, I can do this,* I told myself. So I canceled travel plans and stayed home.

⤳⧓⤳

AT LEAST I had a distraction. I had an event to plan.

In the spring of 1997, several months after my paralysis, Madison brought home from school a yellow scrunched-up flyer in her Barney backpack. It was an invitation to come learn about a specific therapy that "helped Mason learn." While I did not know her classmate Mason, I knew his mom, Polly, and his father. B. J. Surhoff, a Baltimore Oriole MVP contender and teammate of Cal Ripken, Jr. UNC alumni, Polly and B. J. had participated in a few events I'd chaired in my pre-paralysis days as president of the Baltimore Carolina Club. I'd heard a bit about their successful therapy with Mason and was eager to learn more. Their home was wheelchair accessible, and I was happy to be invited to the meeting. Brittany, a huge Oriole fan, was ecstatic to come along with me.

Like most children with autism, Madison had very limited communication skills. At age five, she did not speak. My job as her mom was to be the master interpreter of her gestures, cries, tantrums, and moods. It was exhausting. At the Surhoff meeting, we learned about a therapy, Applied Behavior Analysis (ABA), that used repetitive drills to teach words. We tried it with Madison. Unbelievably, she responded and started to speak, mastering her name, address, phone number, colors, and shapes within weeks.

Oddly enough, although Madison had both an early diagnosis and early interventions, I did not learn about this therapy from a physician or a teacher, even though she was getting excellent care from both. Instead, I learned about it from Polly, another parent who was willing to share her discovery.

I wasn't the only parent to have these happenstance stories. Because autism was a spectrum disorder, there was no one protocol for treating our kids. Soon a small group of parents met regularly. Beyond teachers and physicians, we felt we needed a parent group to foster the exchange of information. We wanted to help parents learn what other parents had discovered, but we struggled with our next steps.

I thought about what mattered in the frustrating search for help and information. What was it that we needed to be good parents?

One night, seated at my kitchen table, I took three coffee cans and traced their circles on a big piece of construction paper, interlocking each one. I named each circle's element, Resources, Referrals, and Research, and intersected them with Pathfinders in the middle. That's what we all needed, I thought—paths to find our way through the maze of information—not unlike the paths in the wilderness I'd experienced so many times before.

That theme and coffee-can creation resonated with the other parents and became the beginning of our logo and the start of our parent-crafted tagline: "Our mission is to find a path for our children." Within three years, in February 2000, our small group founded Pathfinders for Autism, a nonprofit organization directed at improving the lives of individuals with autism and their families. We took our first steps to fund-raise for our cause three months later, the same timeframe of Joe and Cindy's wedding.

Annually, the Baltimore Orioles wives chose a charity to be the beneficiary of their fundraising efforts. We presented our proposal for early-detection research and were selected. Within the same week, a Center Club colleague asked me if I knew of any charity that would like to participate in the traditional fall Casino Gala fundraiser. They were looking for someone to chair the event. Polly and I agreed to chair the event scheduled for July 29, twenty-one days after Joe and Cindy's wedding, the perfect distraction to keep my mind busy and forward-thinking. And the results were even more energizing. After the event, pictures splashed across the Arts & Society page of the *Baltimore Sun*. The Orioles wives sparkled with sequins and smiles over the captions that noted their famous husbands. *Orioles wives rally with the Center Club to raise $100,000 for Pathfinders for Autism.* The event, "A Midsummer Night's Field of Dreams," was a smashing success with record-breaking paid attendance and proceeds, the most money raised in the twenty-five-year history of the wives' charity events at that time.

⚭

DESPITE THE EVENT-planning distraction, the wedding day was hard, even though most of it is a blur to me now. I do recall that Madison's aggressive behaviors increased to the point that she could not attend. I was thankful that I'd stayed home so I could be there for her. Oddly, Joe and a good mutual friend dropped by my home that morning, the Saturday morning before his afternoon wedding, and visited for over an hour. I can't recall a single word that Joe said, but he was upbeat, business as usual, and in a strange way, reassuring to me.

After he left, Pat and I must have moved through our Saturday routines. I think I chatted with family and friends, wrote a few e-mails, and then watched some television before making my only mistake of the day. That memory is quite clear.

I called Peter.

The reception at Joe's home should be over, I thought. The kids would soon be heading to bed. I wasn't worried about Brittany; she had seemed enamored with all the wedding plans, as any young teenaged girl would be. However, I had fretted all day about my little guy, wondering how he was doing. I thought I'd say good night to him and reassure him that his mom was still here, just as he'd requested.

"Hi, it's Becky," I said to the guest who answered the phone. "Could I please speak to Peter?" I asked all in one breath.

"Oh, hi!" the guest replied above the music blaring in the background. "Pete's out there dancing right now. Do you want me to get him?"

"Oh, no," I said quickly. "Just tell him his mom called to say good night." As I hung up the phone, the tears began to fall. Although it was what I wanted—Pete to be engaged and happy—that independence brought with it another realization. The long fingers of divorce reached beyond my loss to include the loss of a part of my children. With one set of "I do's," they quickly became part of a new family that did not include me.

ALTHOUGH I MADE it through the wedding day, simple daily living in my expanded life with a stepmom was difficult. I had tolerated, not accepted the situation. I had only met her once—an odd, intense, and random encounter soon after their engagement. I scarcely remember the details, but I remember the feeling quite well.

Pat had dropped me at a stationery store where I must have been looking for invitations or greeting cards—I don't remember what exactly. I was sitting at a table with a store clerk looking through a large book of sample cards when I heard a voice behind me.

"Becky?"

I wheeled out from under the table and turned around to see who it was. I didn't recognize the young blonde woman, but was polite and said, "Hello." I'm sure my confused expression gave me away as I kept searching her face for something familiar.

"It's Cindy," she said simply as if I should know, instead of introducing herself. It still didn't register, but she kept looking at me like I should recognize her even though we'd never met.

"Cindy," she said again.

Cindy. Cindy, *Cindy*! It finally sunk in. I'm sure my mouth must have dropped open, and I probably blurted out, "Oh, hi," or "hello" or some appropriate greeting with a big plastic smile.

I don't remember anything more after that. We may have had a few more exchanges about the kids, or the store, or the friggin' weather. I do remember my face burning after she left and the store clerk's question: "Oh, you know Cindy? Isn't she *lovely?*"

"Actually, I don't know her at all," I said, staring a hole into the book of greeting cards. "Let's just say her role in my life has not been a good one."

After the wedding, I managed to be cordial to Cindy on the phone most of the time. However, when she started attending Peter's soccer games, venturing into *my* physical territory, I involuntarily shut down. I would arrive early at the games with my entourage of kids and a sitter to help me unload and navigate the rough terrain of the fields. Then *she* would breeze in, sporting the latest workout gear with her shiny blonde hair and skin aglow, and then plunk down beside me invading my space, *my family time* as if she belonged. I would sit stone-faced on the sideline, trying to fend off an earnest warmth I felt from her toward me and my kids, but was determined to ignore. I stared only at Pete darting down the field, even though she was right beside me.

It was hard to acknowledge her at these outings, much less look at her—her youth, her energy, and her promising future, the one that had originally been promised to me. "How dare you cheer for my son? Get your own family!" I wanted to shout. "You have my husband, isn't that enough? How much more of me and mine do you have to take?"

Yet after a while, being so self-righteous was exhausting. Although everything I felt and did was supremely justifiable in my mind, the process of maintaining a wall of anger was draining, the nonstop effort eating me up inside.

I knew I had to try another approach.

IN MY SEARCH for answers, I discovered a set of tapes by self-help author Earnie Larsen titled, *Unresolved Anger*. He contended that anger is always "justice-related." However, he took this a step further with the alarming thought that unresolved anger has an even more adverse effect on us. "Unresolved anger fixates us in our point of pain," he stated.

The thought horrified me; its truth was so obvious. Did I want to be trapped in this pain forever? How could I possibly move past it?

Larsen used the analogy of a science project in which pins are stuck into insects to mount them onto a Styrofoam board. Just as the pin affixes the insect to the board, so our anger fixates us to our pain. We must remove the pin to be free to move on, he advised. And until we do, we cannot be free to heal, to love, and to grow.

It made sense, my raw insides attesting to the truth of Larsen's statements. I had to figure out a way to let go of this anger before it destroyed me.

Then another bit of advice my father once gave me came to mind. When I struggled with attitude adjustments, he'd suggest, "BB, you need to act your way into a new way of thinking."

So I tried. I got down off my holier-than-thou pedestal and questioned myself for a change. Who was I to judge her anyway? I chose to divorce him, after all. Did I know the whole story? Did I want to know the whole story? Did it really matter? I knew the anger was starting to harden a piece of my heart that affected the way I lived, the way I behaved, and the way I loved.

And, I knew I deserved better. It was time to let Joe go, again, and make room for this new configuration in my life, if I could. I began acting my way into a new way of thinking, ratcheting up my phone voice to include a smile as I watched myself in my bathroom mirror while speaking to her. I practiced small talk on neutral subjects and rehearsed before each soccer game when I knew I would see her. I even invited her into my home, my only remaining "safe haven" from her "clutches."

I was taking the pin out, a little at the time. Maybe what mattered was what I knew. I knew that she cared sincerely for my children—all four of them. I knew that she seemed to be a positive and stabilizing force in Joe's life. I knew that she was always gracious and kind to me.

I slowly came to realize that accepting her would help my kids, my family, and maybe give me a taste of that illusive family feeling I was longing for. Suddenly, Richard Bach's book, *Running from Safety*, came to mind. I'd never forgotten his idea of flying up high enough to see the patterns of life. Maybe somehow all of this would make sense if only I could get up high enough to see it from a different perspective. I struggled to soar, but realized that gaining altitude takes time.

Gradually, my relationship with Cindy improved. As our interactions increased, I discovered that she was indeed a lovely person, who cared deeply for my kids, never hesitating to offer assistance. Yet, she did not try to be their mom and gently told me that she did not see that as a role she felt comfortable playing— because it was mine.

I'm sure dealing with me was no picnic for her either. My Southern charm can have an edge to it if I feel threatened or uncomfortable. We skated through some trying times as we learned more about each other, choosing to focus on the future instead of the pain of the past. We were respectful of and polite to one another, a posture that I'm sure challenged both of us. Sharing your husband is difficult, I'd learned. I am sure Cindy felt the same.

"Anger is like gunpowder," Larson contended. "It is neutral. It is what you do with it that can be explosive." Sometimes that was hard for me to remember, much less do. Yet as a parent, I reminded myself, we're supposed to be the professionals when it comes to doing the right thing for the kids. But it's hard, so hard to suck it up, tough it out, get a game face on, and all those other cliché things we know we should do when the truth is, it *hurts*. And it's difficult to hide that pain.

Yet, I'd seen the damage it had done in some of my friends' divorces. Some used their kids to accomplish their unfinished business with their former spouses. They filled their kids' minds with skewed stories of half-truths, provoking mistrust of the other parent. Others sabotaged weekend plans by purposefully being late or forgetful. Still others would pick a fight in front of the kids just to prove their point that the child's mother or father really was, fill in the blank for whatever uncomplimentary adjective they had chosen to teach their child that week.

I wondered if instead of teaching our children what is wrong with our ex-spouse, maybe, just maybe, we could try to teach them what is right about him or her. After all, we married that person and loved him or her enough to have a family. From a child's view, we could be the one that's looking stupid. "If he's so bad, then why did you marry him?" they could ask.

But they don't.

Kids need to find a way to love their parents—both of them. I knew that. And if I really wanted what was best for my children, maybe I should help them see it.

Dad often told a story about a boy he knew during his first pastorate at the orphanage in North Carolina. Many of the children had only one parent, some no family at all. One evening, Dad needed to reprimand a group of boys for leaving their baseball equipment outside overnight. He noticed that "Johnny" clung to his glove and used him as an example of how to take care of the equipment. Later, Dad asked "Johnny" about the glove.

"My daddy gave it to me," he said quietly.

Johnny's dad was in prison, my father learned. Johnny clung to what his father had given him. He may be a criminal, but he was still this young boy's father.

That thought struck home as I reflected on my wonderful relationship with my father. I suddenly wanted my children to experience as much as possible of what I had with my father. I had a choice, I realized; I could either be a roadblock or a conduit in the special relationship.

Yet my mom's story was the one that I found a way to use daily. She was impressed with what she'd read about one of her favorite actress's ability to be sincere in her love scenes with different leading men. The actress had shared the secret of her success—finding something in each man to love—his eyes, his hands, or his hair. She would then focus on that, and gear her lines with that motivation.

I could do that. I could find something to love about Joe, despite my hurt, and share it with my kids. "Your dad is a very smart man," I would remind them on occasion. "Look how hard he worked to come from a junkyard to run a company." And if they were impatient because he was late to pick them up, I'd say, "He may be late, guys, but he always comes. You can count on him."

And they could.

⁓⚭⤚

TWO YEARS AFTER Joe and Cindy's wedding, another change came tumbling into our family. Brittany, then fifteen, was tying the last Carolina blue bow around a size-one crescent-rolled Pampers. "That's 118, Mom," she announced as she surveyed my bedroom, now littered with ribboned disposable diapers, pacifiers, and bootees. "Let's start with the top layer."

Next we began to assemble a baby-shower diaper cake to celebrate the coming of Brittany's new half-brother. We were giving a shower for Cindy, Brittany's stepmother and my newly accepted colleague in the parenting business. I had finally acknowledged my membership in the ex-wife, former-wife, first-wife, or whatever-past-tense-you-please club.

Beautiful baby Alexander soon joined both families along with our complicated histories. Who was I to this child? I wondered. Cindy soon provided the answer. "Zander," she cooed to her precious son when she first introduced him to me, "this is your Aunt Becky."

Chapter 20

Farewell to My Father

There is hurt and there is love. They roll us through the
days like a turtle down the hill. All we can do when on our
back is roll one more time and head for the sea.
—Mark Nepo

THE PHONE RANG at 12:15 on a Saturday afternoon in fall 2003. My father's surgeon patiently tried to explain what my mind refused to comprehend.

Cancer, I had accepted. Cancer recurrence, I feared with all my being.

Dad had made it four years and seven months, just shy of the magical five-year marker, the one his doctors said could indicate a full remission. But the cancer had now returned, spreading to his lungs, where fluid was accumulating. The surgeon, a longtime family friend, called to explain the procedure that would drain the fluid and help keep the lungs inflated. When I asked what this could mean, he told me in his quiet, gentle way that Dad might only have weeks to live.

He might as well have taken the scalpel directly to my heart.

Overwhelmed, I immediately called Joe as I tried to absorb the news and figure out what to do next. During the last six years following my paralysis, I'd made the eight-hour trip from Baltimore to my parents' Huntington home only twice, after weeks of detailed advance work and scheduling. But by 2 P.M. that day, I'd made plans to be with them by dinnertime the next evening. Cindy, my newfound ally in all things family, graciously offered to drive me to Huntington the next morning, leave my van there, and fly back to Baltimore later that same day.

Rachel, now married with two children ages seven and nine, immediately began her nine-hour trip up from Georgia where she and her family had relocated. We decided not to announce our respective arrivals to Mom and Dad until minutes before each of us pulled in the driveway, as we weren't sure if they understood the seriousness of the recurrence. We knew they had been told the facts, but were concerned that our travel, so rare for Rachel and even more difficult and highly orchestrated for me, would intensify their worry.

Rachel arrived the day before I left from Baltimore. We agreed I would call her from the van and let her know when Cindy and I were almost there.

"We're pulling in the driveway, Sissy."

"Okay, I'll let him know," Rachel said in a loud business-like voice, just as we had planned. "Dad, there's a special delivery that's arrived," I heard her say before she hung up.

Cindy pushed the button to open the van door as Dad was coming out of the house. I glanced up to see him, but then quickly shifted my focus to wheeling carefully down my van's ramp, gathering my courage as I was about to meet my father's outstretched arms. Dad said nothing as he walked toward me; his smile was tight, trembling; his eyes were glazed with—was it joy or anguish? I couldn't tell, but I knew I had to break the thundering silence that was suffocating us.

"Hey, Pop!" I boomed in the most energetic voice I could muster. "Couldn't miss your big adventure, could I?"

After all we'd been through, adventure had become our family's euphemism for plans with uncertain outcomes. Forget plans; we mostly clung to possibility. Our lives had become one steady stream of rethinking possible.

Still, determined to be strong for my father, I'd rehearsed those lines in my mind and knew I'd nailed them, delivering them with every ounce of positive force I could find. Maybe my will, my grit, could somehow shore up his.

But when my father squatted down gingerly to hug me in my wheelchair, I felt each part of a strong, but now prominent, backbone. I hugged him tightly, horrified at what the cancer had done to this big, strapping six-foot-three giant of a man. He was so thin and pale.

He held me tight, too, and began to sob. "BB," he finally whispered. "You came!"

"Wouldn't miss it, Pop," I belted back. I fought off the tears, refusing to give cancer the upper hand in that precious moment with my father. Deep in my heart, I thought he could still beat it. Surely, our family was due a break. Surely, it was our turn to triumph over tragedy.

My own magical thinking prevented me from entertaining any other option but that my dad was going to make it. "You think the negative thought, and it could happen," my whimsical logic reasoned. Therefore, letting cancer win was not an option. I needed to believe it *and* show it with strong words and a confident attitude.

Still, I could not look at my father's troubled eyes—cancer's clutch was just too real. I focused on the sidewalk leading to the house, the leaves cackling as my wheels crushed the fragile remnants once alive with color.

Mom, Dad, and Rachel welcomed Cindy like family. They were proud of and amazed at the way we had worked through our relationship.

"How's little Zander?" Dad asked about the latest family addition, soon to have his first birthday.

"He's great," she replied, and we chatted easily about our families for a while. "Let me take a picture of you all before I leave."

ONCE WE HAD him settled in his hospital bed, a parade of specialists began to enter the room. The four of us sat still, barely breathing as the last physician came through the door. Although we knew the surgery was necessary to drain the fluid from Dad's lungs, the options for treating the recurred cancer were far less clear. We studied the young oncologist's slender hands as he used them to convey his points. He counted the treatment options, pausing at each of his five fingers to describe success-rate percentages so low that we wondered why they were considered options at all. As he reached the final alternative on his last pinky finger, we desperately hoped he would continue to count with five fresh options on his other hand.

But he didn't.

As he reviewed my father's age and health conditions, he told us what we did not want to hear: when kidney cancer returns, there is simply no good cure.

After the young doctor left us to discuss our choices, we immediately knew the magnitude of what had been said. The surgery would not treat the cancer itself, only relieve its encroaching effect on Dad's breathing. Low-percentage treatment options were not really viable in our family. We'd had that discussion many times, including our decision about Forest. Dad had seen such a range of suffering when his parishioners battled a terminal illness that he openly talked about wanting a quick death. "No heroics," he would often say. "I've lived a full life, a good life. And when it's my time, I will be ready. There are things worse than death."

Rachel and I would always "shush" him, telling him we hated to talk about those kinds of topics. But we did talk about them. We just never expected to have that conversation now, only five months short of that elusive five-year marker that may have given us many more years with our father.

"You girls know how we feel about these kinds of options, right?" he said to us, breaking the heavy silence smothering the room. It was obvious he and Mom were on the same page already.

Rachel and I replied that we knew, and that we understood. It seemed terribly important to Dad that we understood why he was choosing no treatment beyond this operation that could only help his breathing and delay, not prevent, his death. It seemed to me that our acknowledgement would give him permission—the accepting freedom—to die whenever his time came.

"How much time do you think I have left?" Dad had asked. The vague answer was positive enough that we all figured Dad would at least come home after he had recovered from the surgery. "Do you think I could make one last trip to my home place in North Carolina?" he pressed. Rachel and I marveled at his will, that persistent strength he had to keep including those things in his life that mattered and to keep pursuing the possible, despite the hard reality.

Though we were told he would probably be able to go to Lenoir, some six hours away, we were also cautioned that he might require special transportation, maybe even an ambulance.

As we left the hospital that evening, the unknown haunted me. How long would we have with our father?

⌒⬥⌒

THE SURGERY WENT well. The next step was for the fluid to clear so the tubes could be removed. Then home. We waited.

Daily, I called my kids from the hospital to update them on

their "Andad's" progress. Dad was feeling perky during one of my conversations with Peter, ten years old by this time.

"Let me tell him a joke, BB."

I handed him the phone.

"Hey, Pete!" he began. "Andad here," he continued as he swung his legs to the side of the bed. He sat up tall to let the tubes drain the fluid still present in his lungs. The joke was a family favorite, one I'd heard since I was Pete's age. But Dad delivered it with a freshness that transcended all the beeps in that hospital room. He clinched his fist at the punch line and I snapped a photo of that burst of energy. Even then, he was still Dad, enjoying making his grandson laugh.

One of the biggest challenges we had to manage during the days following Dad's surgery was the flood of visitors. Several ministers checked in on him regularly; they were joined one day by my father's good friend, Coach Bob Pruett, head coach of Marshall University's nationally ranked football team.

That evening, as the room full of ministers, family, and the coach prepared to leave, we all joined hands for a parting prayer.

"Coach Pruett, will you lead us?" Dad asked of his longtime buddy.

Rachel and I shot looks at each other. With a room full of ministers, our father chose Coach Pruett, who was not much of a public pray-er. After everyone left, Dad lay back on his pillow, closed his eyes, and folded his hands across his chest. "Put Pruett on the spot, didn't I?" he said with his eyes still shut and a hint of a crooked smile.

"Dad!" Rachel and I both exclaimed. "You're a mess! Poor coach. Didn't know what hit him."

"Oh, I bet he did."

EACH MORNING, WE received an update about the fluid in Dad's lungs. Complications began to set in, and with them increasing pain.

Several weeks prior, Dad had called to tell me he wanted me to continue his newspaper column—whenever the time came that he could no longer write it.

"I don't want to talk about that!" I'd protested. "You have many more columns to write." But now, as he began to weaken and we were face-to-face in his hospital room, he asked me about it again. It was a tall order. Dad was a veteran writer. He not only wrote a sermon every week, but also penned his Pastor's Perspective piece in the church bulletin as well as a column in the Hickory newspaper and a Sunday op-ed piece in Huntington.

My story about playing soccer with Peter had been accepted three years earlier by the *Baltimore Sun,* in the fall of 2000. When it ran, Dad's reaction was an excited one. "You are above the fold!" he'd exclaimed. "Great job, BB. You are on your way, honey."

A few months after that, during their Thanksgiving visit, Dad brought me coffee and my raspberry Nutri-Grain bar in the early-morning hours before the rest of the household had come to life. He came through my office, paused to look at a few of my column drafts, and then came into my bedroom. "BB," he said quietly, "I am so proud of you, sweetie."

"Thanks, Dad," I said, sitting up a bit in bed to take the coffee and breakfast treat.

"You know. BB, I always thought it would be Forest carrying on the family name and with it, our legacy." He pulled his chair closer to my bed to sit down beside me and looked square into my eyes, those blue eyes locking onto mine. "I thought I'd lost that dream forever with your brother's death," he said, swallowing hard and pausing, as if to give that moment to Forest as an honor. "But not so, honey. Not so. You," he paused again to gather himself, "you are touching people with your words. You're strong, BB, so strong. Stronger than you know."

I recalled the power of that moment now as I wheeled myself closer to Dad's bedside in the hospital room. Could I write his column? Was that the legacy he had envisioned for me? After several more freelance pieces for the *Sun*, I'd written about Pete's first wrestling match, at age seven, for a local weekly and began a monthly column I called "From Where I Sit." Yet, I still didn't feel qualified to take over his signature "Looking Homeward" column.

But I was accustomed to tall orders from my father and his "why-not" attitude. That steadfast philosophy of "to whom much is given, much is required" was applied liberally to himself, and in a loving but challenging way to others, especially his children.

So, in his hospital bed, in his classic connect-the-dots mode of operation, he picked up the phone and called Jim Casto, the associate editor of Huntington's *Herald-Dispatch*. "I'd like you to give Becky a shot at this, Jim," he said with as much energy as the cancer would allow. He nodded his head a couple of times, pressed his lips together with an air of satisfaction, and quietly hung up the phone. "You're set, BB," he whispered. "Go get 'em."

⚘

TERRI'S POEM ABOUT cancer was right. Cancer could not conquer my father's spirit. But, with the healing failing to come that week in the hospital, we realized his time with us was rapidly running out.

Dad sat up in bed, asking Rachel, Mom, and me to hug him. He told us how much he loved us, and that he would miss us. And he cried. Then, he quieted himself and said very clearly, "Please take care of yourselves."

I paused, as those words were not the ones I expected. He did not tell us to take care of each other, as I thought he would. He said to take care of ourselves. Take care of *ourselves*. The words spun outside my ears, whispering, as I remembered losing Forest. Is that what Dad had done? And Mom? Were they taking care of themselves? Dad's chaplain role. Mom's support group involvement. Their distance, preoccupation. Huntington, now our beloved Huntington! Was what felt like abandonment actually self-care?

The spinning continued, the losses swirling together, this time with my marriage, our children. What about Joe? Was he taking care of himself—and our family's best interests—by throwing himself into work? Was his detachment not about me at all, but simple self-care?

Had I demanded something of my loved ones that was impossible for them to give? Is self-care the first step in getting through loss? And looking outside the family for support a healthy way to begin?

⋰⋱

ABOUT A WEEK after the surgery, Dad started to deteriorate. His pain increased as did complications from the cancer's presence in his lungs. Mom, Rachel, and I agreed with the doctor's recommendation that it was time to bring in hospice care.

Mom seemed stable, possibly in shock, but amazingly calm and steady. But Rachel and I struggled with what to do. Stay in Huntington? Go home? We had no idea how long we had with Dad, but also knew he was leaving us a little each day. We were exhausted from long hours at the hospital, little sleep, and concerns about both Mom and our kids back home. We knew there would be a large funeral in West Virginia, then a six-hour trip to North Carolina for another service where he would be buried beside Forest in the cemetery near his beloved home place.

We considered Dad's words—*"Please take care of yourselves"*—and decided we each should go home, see our families, and try to rest up and regroup for whatever was next. But before we left, we each had special time with Dad, emptying our hearts of all the things we wanted our precious father to hear.

In the meantime, we brought in reinforcements. Rachel arranged round-the-clock care for Dad to supplement hospice so Mom could come and go as often as she liked. My wedding-warrior friend, Beth, drove in from Baltimore with her husband to help me before Rachel's departure and to eventually drive me back to my home. And then I arranged for Pat to fly in to Huntington before I left so she could stay with Mom until either Rachel or I could return.

⁕

FOR ELEVEN DAYS, each time I entered Dad's hospital room, I would zoom in, full speed in my wheelchair, and quickly screech to a halt by his side.

"BB!" he'd shout out, welcoming me with a big smile. We would talk as long as he could before pain or weariness would steal him from me. As the pain increased, he was often groggy from medication. But he would always greet me by my pet name and with whatever vigor he could find. But on the day before I was to leave for home, when I whirled into his room and stopped next to him, he glanced up, but did not call my name.

"Dad?" He looked at me, but did not hold my eyes.

"Sissy, Dad's different today," I told Rachel. "He barely greeted me."

"I know," was all she said. She'd said her good-bye to Dad as had I.

After the eight-hour trip with Beth, I opened the back door of my home in Baltimore at 9 P.M. on October 17, 2003. At 10 P.M., I received the call. My father had died.

My shoulders slumped, relieved. They felt strangely warmed

as if a soft blanket had been wrapped around them—a gentle tightness like a comforting hug. We lived those last twelve days with Dad much as we lived our lifetime with him—laughing, loving, and learning.

Dad was at peace. And so was I.

Chapter 21

Saying Good-bye to Mom

Life will crack your heart open again and again until it stays open.
—Rumi

"ARE YOU OKAY, Mom?" I asked, listening hard for more than her words were saying. After I returned home from Dad's funeral, I spoke to Mom at least twice a day. Although Mom doted on Dad throughout his battle with cancer, she had always minimized her own health issues, addressing each one in a no-nonsense fashion. She never complained.

"Oh sure, honey," she answered. "I just have a little frog in my throat this morning."

But I knew better. That quivering voice revealed the end of her morning crying time. She tried to mask the sadness, but I could hear the tears streaking her words. She was still parenting me, or trying.

"So, what are your plans for the day?" I knew her routine on most days by heart. But she loved to get out her little paintbrush and tell me the details. Somehow hearing each stroke made me feel better, too. Then she asked me about each of my kids and I gave a "full report," as she liked to get. Brittany was sixteen and heading into her junior year of high school. She'd moved from softball to volleyball and was on the cusp of an active dating life. Peter, ten, was small for his age, but wiry, strong, and fast—like Joe. Pete wrestled, but also played soccer and lacrosse, a huge sport in Maryland. Madison was doing well in a ten-month residential school and Matthew continued to be well cared for in his second specialized foster care home placement.

After the funeral, Rachel and I tried to think through small changes that could ease Mom's transition to living alone. She had become a shutterbug after Forest's death, keeping her camera in her purse at all times and snapping photos of just about everything. The walls were covered in family photographs—in some rooms from floor to ceiling. We wondered if those images would comfort Mom now—or torture her. But she wanted to keep everything in place. She declined offers of overnight support or live-in help. She wanted to alter very little about her home life with Dad, including the special morning routine they once shared.

"Tweetie, I've brought you your coffee," Dad would say, presenting her a steaming mug of Maxwell House as if she were a queen and he were her suitor. Both would awaken early, often at 5 A.M. Dad would slip into the kitchen to make the coffee and then bring it in to her while she was still in bed.

"Why thank you, kind sir," she would reply, her eyes twinkling with that never-failing love. Then they would sit and chat about their plans for the day as Mom got her knees "a-goin'," as she used to say. Her severe arthritis required her to use a cane and to perform a daily morning ritual that included heat, ointments, medication, and special exercises for her to move well enough to get dressed. Then they would move into the kitchen to enjoy the view of the valley below and the many birds in the yard. They loved hummingbirds. Each spring, Mom would prepare the red sugar water and Dad would hang it in just the right spot so they could view it from their table.

Rachel and I offered to put a coffeemaker in her bedroom, but she refused it, preferring to make the trek to the kitchen, brew her coffee there, and sit in her usual spot.

"What mug are you using today, Mom?" I asked, knowing my early-morning call would reach her at the kitchen table.

"Oh, my special one with you and Michael Phelps, BB. I love it!"

"Hard to believe I met the guy, isn't it?"

"Not for me, BB."

Prior to his multi–gold medal performance in the 2004 Olympics, Phelps had agreed to be an honorary member of Pathfinders for Autism. He knew of our work through Polly Surhoff; they trained at the same pool. He'd agreed to do a promo radio spot and I'd help write the copy. We met at the radio station and I had someone snap our picture. Mom may have had her wall of photos, but my new obsession was photo mugs. They gave a whole new meaning to the term "mug shot," which my kids teased me about. A double rack in my kitchen housed twenty-eight of them. Mom's mug was my effort to connect our worlds in a small but concrete way through our favorite time of the day—early morning, and our favorite morning-starting beverage—coffee.

"So are the trees still colorful?"

"Yes, they are beautiful. Simply beautiful."

"Wonderful! Enjoy it. I'll talk to you later today, Mom. I love you."

⚜

"I HAVEN'T SPOKEN a word all day," Mom confided to me in an afternoon call just before Christmas, the first Christmas after Dad's death.

"Oh Mom, I should have phoned earlier," I lamented. Rachel and I had done so well trying to make sure one of us called every morning during our carpools. Between the two of us, someone was always checking in. But sometimes the schedules with our children delayed us.

"No, no, honey," she quickly replied. "I'm not complaining. I've just noticed how fast the day has gone by and the fact that I haven't uttered a sound." Mom didn't have to say what was so clearly unspoken. She and Dad had talked all the time. About everything. About nothing. About plans. About plans to do nothing. She missed him terribly. And so did I. But somehow that didn't matter as much as making sure Mom was okay. I remembered what Dad told us about taking care of ourselves and not each other. I wondered if Mom *could* take care of herself.

⚜

I KNEW I had reached her in the middle of a crying time in another early-morning call. After several denials, she finally acknowledged what was bothering her.

"I can't believe the questions people ask me," she said.

Through the years, as we passed through our bouts of loss, we all had experienced insensitive queries and comments. If one more person told me that, "Everything happens for a reason," and "God doesn't give you more than you can handle," or "God brings these things into your life to make you strong," I was going to punch somebody in the nose!

I had vented regularly and often to Dad.

"First of all," I had said, sounding off during one of our analytical discussions, "when you tell someone, 'Everything happens for a reason,' who are you trying to comfort? Do you really think it is comforting for someone to hear that there is a *reason* for the death of a teenage sibling? Or for a child's seizures? Or even the necessary step of divorce? Or, is it actually comforting for *them* to say it, to quickly compartmentalize the horrific event in the, 'gotta-be-a- reason-for-that' department, so they can get on with their lives, confident that surely something that random must serve a greater purpose."

"I hear you, BB," Dad had said, encouraging me. "I hear you."

"Sure, there are reasons for bad things happening," I'd said, taking a breath. "Forest wasn't looking where he was going. Matthew's brain wasn't developing properly. And Joe and I couldn't maintain our focus on each other. And the paralysis? Well, I got the flu that kicked off a million-in-one inflammation and landed in the bottom third of the recovery category." I paused and took another breath. "But *why?* And why *me?* These are the real questions, Dad, the ones that are swept under the rug of those overused platitudes. Believe me, there is no comfort in hearing your latest tragedy has some kind of meaningful purpose, especially when your pain is raw and your will to keep going is vulnerable," I'd continued.

"How is that supposed to make you feel, Dad? About the nature of life? About what you have done to deserve this apparently purposeful random event? About what else could be in store for you? About what you can do to avoid being 'so blessed' yet again. They actually think that is helpful or in some way comforting? Really?" I shook my head. "To think there is a reason for tragedy," I slowed my cadence down, "and that we each have a tragedy threshold that God measures, choosing only those who can handle it, so it can make us stronger. Oh, yes, that is SO comforting to think I've been chosen for a tragedy, one designed especially for me, to make me strong."

"BB, you have some valid points, here. Ones that hold theological water, so to speak."

"We should write a book together, Dad," I'd told him, "I can see the title now, *Mean Things People Say to Those Who Are Hurting.*"

"Now, BB, you know they don't mean them to be hurtful."

"I know, Dad. But someone has to set them straight!"

We would laugh. It always felt good to laugh through my indignant rants that flared from time to time. Dad and I could ponder forever, analyzing life, people, purpose, or whatever topic either one of us wanted to throw in the ring at the moment.

But Mom was different. She could keep up with the ponderous conversations but didn't feel the need to jump in. Dad often admired her simple faith, so different from his own, and her steadfast prayer life. She did not need to ponder the great questions of the universe to be secure or content in her faith. Prayer was a way of living for her. In my college days, she wanted to know the time of my exams so she could pray for me—at that very moment. During my IBM career, she would pray for me during a sales pitch—at that very moment. And in the last few years, when I would be on deadline for a column, she would pray for me—at that very moment. Prayer was real time and interactive for Mom.

But today, she sounded wounded.

"I'm so sorry, Mom," I said, trying to comfort her. "It truly is astonishing what people can say when they are trying to help. What happened?"

"Well, people keep asking me, 'How are you?'" The emotion rose in her trembling voice as she raised it. "How do they think I am?" she said as tears thickened her words. "I am devastated. I am sad. I have lost my husband, and I miss him terribly. How do they think I am!" she sobbed.

"Oh, Mom." I whispered. I felt helpless. I listened and then joined her as we reminisced about Dad, how much we missed him, what a special man he was, and how it was tough to live without him. "You know, Mom," I said, taking some extra time to put as much tenderness as I could I my voice, "I am sure those folks did not mean to upset you by asking how you are."

Her breathing steadied.

"When you think about it, it's a greeting most of us use from time to time," I continued, choosing each word and tone with care. "I can see how it would be upsetting to you, but I think any hurt that you felt was unintentional, Mom. They just care about you."

Days later, I slipped and asked, "How are you?" in one of our own conversations. I cringed at the thought of what I may have inadvertently set off for my fragile Mom. But she surprised me.

"I'm a doin', BB," she said simply. "I'm a doin'."

And she was. She was not "fine," and did not want to say so. She was "a doin'," moving forward as best she could and did not want to misrepresent herself.

Go, Mom! I thought to myself, as I realized how she'd triumphed over one part of the victim-ness of grief, finding her own way to cope.

❧

SIXTEEN MONTHS AFTER Dad's death, during one of Mom's visits to my home, I noticed that she didn't come in for breakfast as she usually did. I ventured into her bedroom, where I found her peering out the window with her feet elevated on the ottoman and a heating pad on her knees.

"Hey there, BB," she greeted me. Her smile was bright, but she wore no lipstick. She always took the time to put on makeup, including her trademark lip shade—Sally Hansen's Cherry Berry Brew. If she didn't, we knew something was very wrong.

"Are you okay, Mom?"

"Oh, my knees are talking to me this morning," she said simply. She never complained, so I knew if she said her knees were "talking," that they hurt. She looked especially somber, her eyes missing their usual sparkle and her furrowed brow untouched by her welcoming smile. As we talked through the issue—the amount of pain, when the increase started, what had changed that might have caused it—we both realized its cause: she was no longer taking Vioxx, a drug recently found to have significant side effects and discontinued by her physician. Ever since, her pain had escalated.

Although she tried to rise above it, pain became its own ailment, just as real and pervasive as any other debilitative medical diagnosis. It changed Mom's life dramatically, stealing from her not only the finer touches that made Mom "Mom," but altering the very core of her comfort zone—what she could do in her daily life.

"Did you make it to water aerobics today," I'd asked in another check-in call, once she'd returned home.

"Well, yes. I did get there, but I didn't go in. I drove around for ten minutes trying to find a handicapped parking place near the entrance and then decided to come back home. I knew I couldn't walk that far."

"Oh no. I'm so sorry you weren't able to go. I know how you love your water aerobics. Maybe someone could drive you there, Mom."

"Oh, I hate to bother anyone."

And she'd soldier on, never complaining.

Rachel and I learned to listen for those lipstick-off moments, when her guard was down, but it was hard to be observant across the miles. So we solicited help from others. Her doctors agreed to e-mail us. Neighbors checked on her regularly as did her steadfast church family.

Pain management became the priority. I sent my spare wheelchair to her church, where it was stored for her weekly use. We explored getting a scooter for her and looked into other medical procedures. Yet, Mom wanted no drastic changes. No knee surgery. No driver. No full-time help. No house renovation or thought of moving to a nearby assisted-living complex.

Perhaps she was heeding Dad's sage advice, "Don't cut what you can unravel. She was a great unraveler, patient with life, and did not like to hurry; in fact, "hurry" was another outlawed word in our household. She didn't mind letting things unfold, hated to rush, and preferred to be early for any appointment.

After my illness, she would come to my hospital room and sit with me as we prayed for recovery, but prepared for a life of paralysis. The days in the hospital were long, but she found a pastime for us—she taught me how to watch my flowers bloom.

She was patient with herself, too, especially after Dad's death. She knew grief as a companion and respected its unwelcomed but necessary role in her life. For two years, she worked through the details of letting go of the love of her life, setting small goals for completing her "paperwork," the overwhelming business side of death that demanded constant attention. She addressed the hard issues, too: what to do with Dad's belongings and writings while balancing time with local friends and travel plans to visit Rachel and me.

Rachel and I had to let some issues unravel, too, as we sorted out how best to help our Mom under continually changing circumstances. We tried to balance the fact that some responsibilities could help keep her focused and moving forward, while too many could overwhelm her. We worked creatively to keep our three worlds connected. Her planned visits to our homes included time to watch her grandchildren in action— gymnastic meets, wrestling matches, volleyball games, and a Charlie Brown theater production.

When she was in her own home, we would occasionally send her rubrum lilies, her favorite flowers, just because. Then, I discovered I could order a pizza online in Baltimore and have it delivered in Huntington within an hour.

"Mom, get ready to answer the door," I would say when I called her on a Friday afternoon, pizza night at my house. "I have a surprise for you!"

She'd call me back a few minutes later, thrilled that we could share a meal across the miles.

Rachel and I laughed as we saw some of Mom's creative determination return, despite her increase in physical pain. "Well, I did one small load of laundry today," she confessed to me during a phone call.

"Mom! You know you're not supposed to go down the steps," I scolded her.

"I didn't, BB," she replied with a true smile in her voice this time. "I drove the car down the driveway to the downstairs entrance. How about that!" she gloated, so obviously proud of herself.

"Cool, Mom!" I said, practically cheering. "Dad's gotta be lovin' that one!" And we laughed until we cried, knowing just how far Mom had come in the midst of so many dramatic changes. She was making it, in her own way, on her own time. I could just imagine her smiling face, lipstick on, Cherry Berry Brew shining.

⚬⟋⟍⚬

JUST AFTER THE second anniversary of my father's death, my cell phone rang as I was coming into my home.

"Have you talked to Mom?" Rachel asked abruptly with no customary, "How are you?" or "What are you doing?" pleasantries. After so many years of life-altering phone calls, I immediately knew something was up.

"No, not yet today," I said. I'd been out all day and had not had a chance to call her.

"Something's wrong, Becky. I think I need to go up there."

"What do you mean?"

"She sounds disoriented, Sissy. Something's not right."

"Let me give her a call. Maybe we can get a neighbor to check in on her," I rattled on in partial denial, feeling guilty that I had not called her that morning as I usually did. We decided Rachel would call the neighbors and I would call Mom—I wanted to hear her voice. The phone rang several times before she answered. She sounded out of breath when she finally picked up.

"Mom?"

"BB?" she said. "Just a minute, honey."

I waited. "What are you doing?"

"Trying to reach the phone. Sorry. Hang on . . . ," she drifted out again.

I had sent her a dozen red roses for the anniversary of Dad's death. As she was settling herself, I asked her how her roses were doing. She said they were beautiful. I thought she sounded okay, but then began to wonder why she'd had trouble reaching the phone. We installed phones in every room so she would not have to rush to answer a call while walking with her cane. "Mom, where are you?"

"Oh honey, I'm just sitting here on the family-room floor, admiring those lovely flowers."

"Why are you on the floor?"

"I'm not sure," she murmured. "Just relaxing, I guess."

"Are you okay?" I asked, even though I knew that she was not. She said she felt fine. But when I told her Rachel had asked someone to come by to check on her, she didn't protest. Rachel was right. Something was terribly wrong. She never would have sat on the floor willingly.

Mom had fallen, our family friend discovered and immediately called an ambulance. Rachel was in her car heading to West Virginia before our mother even saw the first doctor.

In the hospital, the layers of mystery began to unfold. Mom's fall had resulted in severe bruising. When Rachel arrived, Mom was still confused as to what had happened to her, but appeared to be stable. Then Mom spiked a fever. They found a small wound that was not healing properly and needed a specialized surgical procedure, debridement, to cut away the damaged tissue so that healthy tissue could begin to grow.

My dear friend, Beth, agreed to drive me to Huntington, again. But before we left, the doctor told us that testing revealed a platelet disorder. It was terminal. At best, Mom had two to four years to live.

After all we had been through, Rachel and I were emotionally numb. We skipped grief's steps of denial, anger, bargaining, and depression, and went straight to acceptance. We were too weary to do otherwise. We had to fight whatever battle was ahead for our mom. We needed to save every ounce of emotional energy we had to help her.

FOR SIX WEEKS, Rachel and I tag-teamed our time with Mom, alternating trips back and forth to West Virginia as we struggled to understand what was happening to her. Based on her doctor's guidance, we expected her to recover from the fall and small wound, even with the terminal blood-disorder diagnosis. We thought we had two to four more years if we could just get her through this wound recovery.

But, despite multiple debridement surgeries, the wound was not healing. And, surprising to everyone, even the doctors, she was not regaining her strength and alertness. She weakened after each operation. She would stabilize, but not get any better. Her pain increased and she was frequently disoriented.

It became apparent that she could never live alone again. Those days tormented us as Rachel and I tried to find the right care for our mother, constantly analyzing what she needed and what we could provide. We were exhausted, still in grief for Dad, and stressed beyond clear thinking, much less long-term planning for Mom.

The future shut us down with all the variables and considerations. We longed for our father, his take-charge attitude and uncanny ability to know the right thing to do.

"We aren't Dad," I admitted to my sister during one of our tearful bouts of confusion as we tried to guess how Dad would have handled the situation. "We've got to break this down, Sissy. I think we need to look at today's situation as clearly as we can and then do the next right thing. That's all we can do. The next right thing." She agreed. And it seemed to simplify the magnitude of choices.

However, one well-meaning hospital visitor still managed to step on my last tired nerve. "So, you'll be taking your mom home with you?" she asked me in the hospital cafeteria.

I bit my lip hard to hold my tongue as I sat there in my wheelchair and wondered, *Just what part of my reality is she not seeing? Are you kidding me? I can barely take care of myself, lady, much less my sick and fragile mother!* I wanted to fire back.

But I didn't. "We're not sure what the next steps are right now," I said, measuring each word. "It's quite complicated," I added, widening my eyes a bit before looking down beyond my motionless legs to examine my wheelchair's wheel.

Don't hit that button of mine! I wanted to shout. Please don't hit the guilt button. Yes, I wanted to take care of my mom, but I held onto my dad's final words to us and reminded myself that the best thing I could do right now was to take care of myself.

※

IN EARLY DECEMBER 2005, five weeks after Mom's fall, Rachel and I started researching options to move her to Georgia or Maryland. To continue her healing process, the doctors had advised us, she needed to be moved to a subacute care unit. Rachel and I had chosen one and were making the arrangements for her transfer there when Mom suddenly deteriorated. We were told her recovery would be a long one, if, in fact, she would ever recover.

We both traveled to Huntington and met with the subacute care hospital administrator to review Mom's care and clarify our expectations. We then hired additional caregiving support to help monitor our mother's daily progress. To aid Mom's caregivers—hospital staff, friends, and additional paid help, I created a Ruby Faye Smith fact sheet complete with information on each of our family members, a brief update on her status, and a list of our daily goals to accomplish with and for Mom. "Write it all down if it's important," she taught us.

We were minding our mom.

From how many sugars she took in her coffee to her favorite CDs to the brand of soda she preferred (Sunkist) and how she liked it (on ice with a straw.) We also reviewed pain medication history, therapy schedules, and specific exercises to increase Mom's mental alertness.

Sometimes she was Mom; sometimes she was not. Again, Rachel and I struggled with what to do; even the next right thing was often unclear. The weeks of back and forth had depleted both of us. There was nothing more we could do for her in Huntington and she was not well enough to be transferred to a location near either one of us.

Confident we'd secured the best care possible for her, Rachel and I returned to our homes to gather our strength for whatever stage of life was next for our mom. We both knew there was a good possibility that we might not see our mother alive again.

But when the phone beside my nightstand rang early that cold Sunday morning, I was still surprised.

The doctor said Mom's body was beginning to shut down. I called Rachel, who'd just spoken to the doctor, too. We agreed we needed to find someone to be with Mom. I tried to reach Dot, Mom's neighbor, while Rachel tried to reach Susie, Mom's banker-friend. Dot wasn't home, but Rachel spoke to Susie. In the two years since Dad's death, Susie had become Mom's daughter-in-residence. She helped Mom with her "paperwork." But her visits were always more than that—often stretching into multiple-hour sessions that included sharing memories of Dad as well as tears. Susie had been there for Mom in a way we could not be, and I was so grateful to her for that.

Rachel asked her to go to visit Mom for us, one last time. Susie agreed. She called each of us from the hospital room and put the phone to Mom's ear.

I could hear Mom respond to each of my comments, although I could not understand her words. "I love you, Mom," I said through the tears. "I am so sorry I can't help you get better," I sobbed. "You are the best mother in the world," I blurted on. My breathing stifled. I could hear Mom responding, but could not understand her.

What else could I say? My heart was breaking. I could not believe I was telling my mother good-bye. And that I would never speak to her again. "I love you with all my heart!" I said one last time.

Deep pangs of longing ripped through my very soul and for a split second I wanted to be there, to hold her, to look one last time in those eyes, my mother's eyes, the first eyes I'd ever seen, that I'd ever loved, and that loved me back in a way I never understood until I held my own first child. Ah, the aching long-ing for what could no longer be!

But I knew I was where I was supposed to be. I'd watched her suffer so long that it'd become my own. I'd done my best. I had nothing left to give. I hoped and prayed to God that it was enough. That she felt it. That she knew it.

"I love you," she murmured.

She said it! I heard her. Susie took the phone. "Becky, she can understand you. She is crying, too."

And I dropped my weary head into my hand as I cradled the phone. "Thank you, Susie."

"I am glad I can be here, Becky. Your mother is so special to me, a sweet, dear woman," she paused. "We're going to call Rachel now."

Thirty minutes later, the hospital called. My mother had died—at the same age as my father, seventy-two.

I was at peace—emotionally spent and raw with loss—but at peace. Mom was no longer suffering. And Susie, dear angel Susie, had been by her side.

Chapter 22

Losing Matthew

There is a light that shines in the darkness, which is only visible there.
—Barbara Brown Taylor

A FEW DAYS before Mom's death, I received a call that Matthew had been admitted to the hospital. He was having trouble breathing, as he sometimes would, and needed to be monitored.

After Matthew's initial placement in a hospital for chronically ill children, Joe and I had moved him to the specialized foster home setting, where he received excellent care and services that met his medically fragile needs. Our goal was to provide comfort care for our son, where he could live as fully as his limitations would allow.

Matthew continued to be tube-fed and still seized almost daily, requiring medication and oxygen to relieve the episodes. He never regained his ability to sit or hold his head erect. He was still a beautiful child, with deep-brown eyes and thick eyelashes. His fair skin was almost like porcelain, it was so clear and pure.

His foster-care mom provided the constant and skilled

attention he needed with a tenderness that exceeded all of our expectations. Matthew lived a full life, attending school and participating in every activity available to him.

Before my paralysis, I would bring the kids to visit Matthew in his foster home when I could. Pat snapped some Christmas photos of us in our matching sweaters one year. But as the complexities of my life increased with the paralysis, our visits with Matthew were less frequent.

During the holidays, I would sometimes meet Matthew and his foster-care family at a nearby Chuck E. Cheese. Rachel and her family, Mom and Dad, and my kids would join us for shared pizza and games. One special visit included Cindy and Alexander. Matthew and I sat beside each other in our wheelchairs—I was able to hold him only once. I simply did not have the abdominal strength to keep him on my lap.

Through the years, Matthew would occasionally experience breathing difficulties and was admitted to the hospital for observation or for treatment. I had been called many times by medical staff members saying they thought he might be near death. But he always bounced back. He was a tough kid. So when they called me this time to let me know of his breathing difficulties, I felt sure this episode would resolve as all the others had; I told them to keep me updated on any changes.

Six hours after my mother died, the phone rang again. It was a call from Matthew's hospital; but it was not to report improvement. It was to let me know that my fifteen-year-old son had died.

I sat there holding the phone, reeling, trying to make sense of it all. Although Matthew had been chronically ill all of his life and close to death several times, the timing of his death—*on the same day as my mother*—stunned me into a muted shock.

I couldn't even cry.

Then the disbelief ebbed into guilt. Should I have gone to the hospital to see him when I received the call? What a terrible mother I was!

But honestly, I'm not sure I could have. I was so distraught about Mom that I was barely taking care of myself. The eight-hour trips back and forth to West Virginia had taken their toll; my paralyzed body was revolting. My bowels were a mess. I had a horrible urinary tract infection. My nerve pain seemed to escalate by the hour as those invisible rubber hammers pounded away at my body, sending it into reflexive spasms.

And, Matthew had always recovered.

But not this time.

⚮

PETER WAS AT Joe's for the weekend. I'd already talked to them once that morning to give the news about Mom. But before I called them again, I called Rachel, already en route to Huntington to make arrangements for Mom's funeral. When I told her, she grew silent and then quietly said, "Becky, she took him. Mom took Matthew."

The thought sounded so foreign, almost blasphemous to me. But as I turned it over and over in my numbed mind, it became a possibility. Mom had prayed daily for Matthew since his first seizure when he was three months old. "How is 'little Matthew?'" she would ask in that tender mothering voice. She knew the subject was fragile ground for me, yet she dared venture into it with her soft questions and caring handwritten notes. She often said she wished she could help more with Matthew or take the emotional pain of coping with his illness away from me.

We had both lost sons—in circumstances so different, but yet the same.

As I let Rachel's words sink in, the tears finally came and would not stop. I wept for the losses of my son and my mother. But when I thought about the concurrent timing, deep sobs racked my body.

I was simply overwhelmed to think that perhaps the last loving act of my beloved mother was to take care of my precious son.

⤚⧈⤙

AFTER I CALLED Joe and spoke to Peter—a conversation I barely remember—I had to prepare to talk to Brittany. A freshman at UNC, she was taking her final exams. Although she knew of Mom's hospitalization and the seriousness of her illness, I'd wanted to tell her about Mom's death after her last exam. But with Matthew's death, I felt I couldn't wait.

"Hey, Britty. Can you talk?"

"A little, Mom. I'm studying."

"Honey, I know. I'm so sorry to interrupt you but I wanted you to know that Nana died this morning."

"Oh, wow. I'm sorry. Was she in pain?"

"No, sweetie. No pain. She just couldn't get better, even though she was trying so hard." I paused to give her a moment. "Are you okay?"

"Yes, I'm fine. I'm sorry about Nana. I just have a lot going on here. I'm so stressed."

"I know, sweetie."

"I better study now. I'm so sorry about Nana, Mom."

"Thank you, but Britty, I need to tell you one more thing."

"What?"

"Well, honey, Matthew died today, too."

"What? Are you serious?"

"Yes. He had had some breathing issues like he's had before and was in the hospital. He took a turn for the worse very quickly."

"Oh my," she said, pausing, then taking in a sharp breath. "Wait, that happened today?"

"Yes, honey, today." I paused to give her another moment. "He was too sick to live," I told her, just like my Mom had told me about my brother. "Just too sick to live."

⚜

BY THE TIME Brittany and Peter could leave school for Mom's funeral, a terrible ice storm had blanketed the South, making the trek to West Virginia too treacherous for them to attempt. But they were home for Matthew's funeral. Peter joined Joe as a pallbearer.

I wheeled down to the front of the sanctuary, parked beside Matthew's casket, cleared my throat, and hoped the words I'd rehearsed would cooperate.

Five days ago, I sat beside my mother's casket and peered into a sea of faces as I tried to find the right words to pay tribute to her amazing life. Today, I sit before you with my son at my side and again I struggle to find the words to pay tribute to his amazing life.

My mother lived seventy-two years. My son lived fifteen. Yet, they both touched people profoundly, enriching their lives in their own unique ways. At my mother's funeral, I recounted the things that she had taught me. Her simple faith, her steadfast prayer life, her ability to nurture and sustain relationships, and the simple motto she lived by, 'Bloom where you are planted.'

Although the context of Mom's advice was in the partnership she felt with Dad and her role as the pastor's wife, I've learned and experienced that life often puts us in places we have not chosen, yet we can still bloom. We can still find ways to flourish in an unchosen circumstance.

But what about Matthew? In his short fifteen years, what has he taught me?

Matthew was born on February 28, 1990. A perfectly healthy little boy, he was a good baby, sleeping and eating well. He had an easy smile and a good-natured giggle that could melt your heart.

Then the seizures came at the age of three months. And with them the onslaught of an undiagnosed disease that tortured us all as we valiantly tried to find the answer and the cure. Doctors, nurses, specialists, blood work, biopsies, medications—none could slow the process of this undiagnosed disease.

Undiagnosed disease. I remember the first time I read that in a physician's report and recalled thinking—aha! I've got it! I just need a new physician. Surely there is someone who can diagnose my son!

But no one could.

And that is what Matthew has taught me— sometimes there are no answers to our questions. As hard as we press, as diligently as we pursue, sometimes there are no answers to our questions.

Matthew taught me to *live life with the questions.*

And I have so many. Why Matthew? Why my brother's death at age seventeen? Why my daughter's autism? Why my paralysis? Why my mother's and son's death on the same day?

I don't know the answers—but I will keep on living, and living as fully as I can even with the unanswered questions.

Although Matthew's life was short and complicated with many medical issues, he taught many of us things about ourselves. In a real sense, Matthew wasn't *abnormal*—Matthew was Matthew. He brought many people joy with his life. For those of you who cared for my son, I thank you. The nurses, teachers, friends, and amazing foster family—I know he touched and taught you, too. I thank you for giving him that opportunity.

And as for Matthew's Nana, my mother, Faye Smith? She loved little Matthew and prayed for him every single day. Sunday, December 11, 2005, was a hard day. I spoke to Mom at 7:40 A.M. and she died within thirty minutes. I must admit, when I received the call six hours later that Matthew had died, I struggled to find meaning. Although he had been chronically ill for most of his fifteen years of life and close to death several times, the timing was overwhelming.

Perhaps Mom convinced God that it was her turn to take care of my son. But I really don't know that answer. I will have to live with that question, too.

What I do know and believe is that they are both peaceful now. And celebrating a marvelous reunion with my father and my brother. I am grateful for the many lessons they all have taught me.

Chapter 23

The Wedding

Keep your dreams bigger than your memories.
—Dr. R. F. Smith Jr.

THEY'D BEEN DATING for over five years. Brittany and Brian met each other their freshman year in college only a few months before Mom's fall. Brian never had the chance to meet Mom, but had heard all the Nana stories from her tickle episodes to her small paintbrush details. Mom knew of Brittany's new "beau," and asked about him regularly, even from her hospital bed.

Brian called me one February morning in 2011 to ask if he could drop by my home for a few minutes. I scooted into the kitchen to greet him when he burst through the back door. Flushed from the brisk February cold, he rubbed his hands together, saying he wanted to talk to me about something. We moved into the sunroom where he pulled a chair from my breakfast table and sat down to face me. His hands quieted. His voice was steady.

"I love your daughter very much," he began. "I cannot imagine my life without her." The rest of his words melted, muted by his bright eyes so full of future and mine so full of joy. I remember nodding yes, and crying, and hugging—and oh yes, finally shutting my mouth.

He wanted to marry my daughter, my firstborn, The Brittany! I had dreamed of this day!

He had talked to Joe before coming to see me. He certainly didn't need my permission or blessing, but I was honored that he came.

Divorced for over twelve years by that point, Joe and I had a complex family life that spanned two households, closely intertwined by design. Brian had been on our family vacations—two Caribbean cruises and a trip to the Outer Banks with me, and similar vacations with Joe and Cindy. Then he went on our joint vacation—the whole eclectic blended group of us—to Cambridge, Maryland, an annual jaunt that had become a family tradition after Alexander's birth.

Brian asked all of three of us—Joe, Cindy, and me—before he approached our daughter. And we all gave him our blessing. Days later, a thoughtfully orchestrated engagement unfolded as planned.

"Mom," her voice blasted in my ear, a full octave higher than normal. "Brian and I went on a run and he was ahead of me and then he fell and didn't get up and then I rushed to see if he was hurt and he wasn't and, and, Mom," she took a quick breath and blurted, "Brian proposed to me!"

"Oh, Britty! What fabulous news!" I gushed in earnest but then artfully convinced her that she needed to come to my home right away to show me the ring—since Brian had secretly arranged a surprise brunch with his family and ours.

"Our family is thrilled to have Brian become part of our family," Joe would later announce at the engagement party in my backyard. "He's the complete package. Becky, Cindy, and I are so excited. We feel like we've won the lottery!" he boomed, his hands waving high. He went on to compliment Brian, his family, and Brittany's good taste in men. My nods matched his every word. Then he turned to me. "So Beck, you want to say a few words?"

"Oh sure," I said, thankful I'd had one strong margarita. I wheeled beside Joe and took the mike from him, looking out at the sea of loving faces on my deck. Most of my closure party girlfriends were there—Joy, Bing, Cynthia, Robin, Barbara, Kim, as well as Beth, Pat, and many of my sitters.

"What can I say? My heart is so full," I began. "He's marrying The Brittany," I paused. "Can you believe it?" And everyone laughed. "I wondered what I would feel like on this day, the day I knew my daughter would be married. I think the word is gratitude. Thank you all for your support and help through these years of adjustments. You helped me raise an amazing daughter and I am grateful. And I'm grateful for Brittany and her good fortune to find such a fine partner. Brian's smart, funny, but more importantly really loves my daughter—the one and only Brittany. What more could a mom hope for?"

WE WERE GOING to have a wedding! Mom would have been so excited. She loved weddings. When we sold their home in Huntington, we discovered a canvas sack stuffed with sheet music and annotated programs for weddings, including mine, from the last twenty years. She'd seen Dad preside over hundreds of weddings in their forty-six years together and could probably tell you the music from most of them.

Weddings were a special treat for another reason. Early in their marriage, Dad began the tradition of giving Mom the honorarium he received for weddings, her "wedding money," they called it. Her wedding money was to be used for special things not "in the budget," whatever that was. "I'll use my wedding money for that," she'd say when she wanted to splurge for a new pair of shoes or a fun gift for a grandchild or a surprise purchase for Dad. She would often hide her wedding-money treasures in the trunk of her car until just the right time to reveal them, a sneaky habit both Rachel and I adopted.

We set the wedding date sixteen months away, in late June 2012, but immediately began planning an engagement party in my new home. After Dad's death, I thought it was time to find a more suitable house for me, and for Mom's visits. I was tired of living in my living room and traipsing across the house each time I had to go to the bathroom. I sold my home, and bought and remodeled an older house near Pete's school that had two first-floor bedrooms and adjoining bathrooms. Mom visited the site once during the construction stage, but didn't live long enough to see it finished.

Although my new home had the convenience of downstairs bedrooms, it was still a two-story house so I put in an elevator, just as I had finally done in my previous home. Ever hopeful I would walk again, I'd initially struggled with the decision to put in an elevator. But after three years of paralysis with no improvement, I green-lighted the project. I'll never forget that first ride upstairs to visit the life I no longer lived, where my wheelchair and parenting collided in dramatic fashion.

I had not been upstairs since February 12, 1997, the day I woke up with those shooting pains in my legs. The last time I'd been up there, I could walk. I had prepared to be sad, even depressed. I'd mentally toured each bedroom and made sure I had a fresh Starbucks and some must-do monthly bills to write awaiting my descent.

The kids were at school. Pat met me at the top of the steps.

When the elevator door opened, I realized I'd prepared for the wrong thing. Nothing grounds you as quickly as the sight of a teenager's bedroom that has been un-mothered for three years. I couldn't have wheeled into Brittany's room if I wanted to.

Clothes were everywhere—clumped on the floor, spilling out of dresser drawers, and scattered across her unmade bed. Her large French provincial desk had no visible surface, stacked high with school papers, toiletries, odd dishes, and jewelry. An old Brownie uniform vest hung from her bedpost. The clock beside her bed blinked the wrong time. The smell of her hamster cage filled the musty room, even though she had promised me before she left for school that she had cleaned it.

"Oh my word."

"I've offered to help her," Pat said, as she surveyed the mess and my reaction. "Many times."

I'd told Pat that it was time to let Brittany take care of her own room several months prior, when she'd turned thirteen, something Mom had done with me during my teenage years. "I'm closing my eyes and closing your door," she used to tell me when the clutter was too much to bear. But I don't think my room ever was this bad—or was it?

"Oh, no worries, Pat," I paused, taking in more details. I spied my coffee mug, the one I'd bought in Florida at the Spa at PGA National the first weekend after Joe and I had separated. *The Best Is Yet to Be,* it read, now half filled with moldy hot chocolate. I shook my head and released a long slow sigh. "Okay, time to regroup," I muttered to myself. "Pat, would you mind getting a pad of paper and a pen please?" An hour later, a two-page list of action items rested patiently on Brittany's dinner plate.

That night, I took my second ride upstairs to complete a long-lapsed nightly routine. Brittany was finishing her homework while a sitter was giving Madison a bath.

"Can I ride with you, Mom?" Peter, then seven, asked as I wheeled into the elevator.

"Sure buddy. Hop on my lap and push the button."

As the elevator door opened upstairs, he slid off my lap, racing ahead to jump in his bed. I followed, but much slower, pushing my wheels down hard to move through the hall's carpet, its padding still intact. I entered his darkened room, the same room little Matthew had when he was a baby. But the crib had been replaced by a bunk bed. It was lit by Matthew's sailboat lamp atop his same chest of drawers—at a height I could no longer reach. I was barely able to see the lamp's blue-trimmed shade, much less its knob so I was grateful it was controlled by a wall switch.

Nestled between his soccer sheets, he asked me to come as close as I could to his bed. I pushed my wheelchair back and forth on the thick carpet, parallel parking it until my wheels touched the sideboard of his bed. I bent sideways across the gap as best I could to give him a hug.

"I'm glad you're here, Mom," he said softly as he scooted closer to narrow the space. And then with the briefest of pauses he said, "Mom, sometimes I wonder about my life."

Peter, ever the ponderer, even at an early age, had always had lengthy conversations with me prior to his nightly trips upstairs, stalling techniques, I surmised, designed to push the envelope on the bedtime curfew.

"Really?"

"Yes, like what my life is going to be like when I'm older. And where I am going to college."

I stroked his thick dark hair, just like Joe's, and smiled at the detail of his wonder. Basketball season had started and Carolina Blue had touched my downstairs life from my light-blue dishes to the UNC logo-ed blankets on the couch to the Tar Heel flag hanging outside the back door. But when I mentioned Chapel Hill, some seven hours away, he touched my hand to hold it. "But that's too far, Mom. I don't want to be away from you."

I squeezed his hand and found his bright eyes in the dark. "But, Pete, that's a long time from now. You'll be ready when it is time to go."

Then his little brain seemed to kick into overdrive. "I won-der what I am going to do when I am older," he said, propping up on his elbow. "What I am going to be like? Will I still like soccer? Still like playing with our cats? Still be in this same room? Still have the same friends?"

"Good questions, Pete. Won't it be fun to find out?"

"Yes, but now I can't go to sleep," he said, tossing the covers around him. "I have too much stuff in my head."

"Just think about one fun thing you want to do tomorrow. Focus on that and you can fall asleep," I said, tucking the comforter under his chin. "Let's face each day as it comes, buddy."

I smiled at that ten-year-old memory, so seared in my mind, as I reviewed the engagement party list. Now, more than ever, I needed to take my own advice.

In sixteen months, my daughter would be married.

And my son would be preparing to leave for his first year of college.

Life-changing events were ahead for us all.

⚭

ALTHOUGH BRITTANY HAD been planning her wedding since she was three and taking detailed notes for the last four years, we decided to use a professional—the same wedding planner that Joe and Cindy had used in their wedding ten years earlier. Elizabeth was a planning veteran with over thirty years in the business, just what this family of planners needed. She was warm, caring, and organized. But most importantly, she connected with Brittany and was open to her unique and creative ideas.

We divided up the research for the initial tasks. My job was to find a minister who, if possible, had at least met Dad or would be willing to include elements of his traditional wedding ceremony. Then I got an idea.

In 2007, Brittany's sophomore year at UNC, she called one Sunday afternoon with a strange question. "Mom, do you know Mike Queen?"

"Why, sure, honey. From Huntington, right?"

"Yes, he is. But now he's in Wilmington, and, well, I think he's Laura's pastor."

Laura was Brittany's first college friend. They met as freshmen in a mostly upper-class dorm. Laura had gone home for the weekend to Wilmington, a three-hour drive from Chapel Hill. At church that Sunday, she'd heard her pastor, Mike Queen, reference a column written by his Baltimore friend, Becky, a mother of four, who was paralyzed.

"Mom, you were in Mike's sermon!"

"Really? Oh my." I tried to piece it all together. Then I recalled a recent e-mail from Mike asking permission to share one of my wheelchair escapades in an upcoming sermon. Although we hadn't seen each other in years, we'd kept in touch via e-mail, where he regularly received my columns.

"Britty, now let me get this straight. Are you saying that Laura, the sweet gal that befriended you the first weeks of school, attends Mike Queen's church?"

"Since birth, Mom!"

"Holy cow," I breathed into the phone. Our family met Mike in North Carolina in 1978, months after Forest's death when Dad was being considered for the Huntington, West Virginia pastorate. Although Mike had moved to North Carolina to enroll in Southeastern Baptist Theological Seminary, he still served on the Huntington pastoral search committee since he'd been an active member there for years. As part of the selection process, he'd driven to a nearby North Carolina church to hear Dad preach. Afterwards, he took our family to lunch.

After Mike's report, Dad began his twenty-one-year pastorate in Huntington where he kept in close touch with Mike and mentored him throughout his seminary training and initial churches, including his pastorate in Wilmington.

"Mike's report on Andad's preaching changed our lives, Britty. He's a special person to our family."

During their last two years at UNC, Brittany and Laura were roommates. I became fast friends with Laura and her family and was included in Laura's wedding plans. Brittany was a bridesmaid; Brian her escort. Mike officiated. I flew in from Baltimore for the wedding on Saturday and stayed an extra day so I could hear Mike preach on Sunday. He reminded me so much of Dad—his style, his message, his humor, and that warm Southern charm.

As soon as Brittany put that ring on her finger, I thought of Mike and how special it would be if he could marry her. I had to ask, even though I knew firsthand the demands of the pastorate. Fully prepared to be turned down, I called Mike.

"Becky, your timing is amazing. Although it isn't public knowledge yet, I'm announcing my retirement next month. I will be available that summer and would be honored to do Brittany's wedding."

Words of gratitude stuck in my throat as my eyes filled. Mike would touch and shape my family's life again. He was going to marry The Brittany. Andad and Nana would be so happy.

DESPITE THE WEDDING planning hubbub, Pete and I maintained our morning routines as he finished up his junior year of high school. It was a Friday in late April and we were on schedule. I'd made his postseason Southern breakfast: bacon, eggs, grits, gravy, and two fresh hot buttermilk biscuits, Pillsbury, flash frozen, but at least not from a can. We had six minutes before we needed to grab the dog, get in the van, and head out for morning carpool.

"So Pete, I'm thinking about visiting our former neighbor, Cindi, who has moved to the Eastern Shore," I said, stirring my coffee. "She's remodeled and it's accessible."

"Cool, Mom," he said, layering the grits, gravy, and egg into the biscuit.

"I'll have to drive over the Bay Bridge."

"Really?" He paused, looked up at me wide-eyed and then gave me a half smile. "You'll be fine, Ma. You got it," he said and took a big bite.

I grinned back at his enthusiasm, so contagious—and inspiring, just like his father's. It took me twelve years to find the courage to drive. But when Peter learned how to drive a stick shift, my competitive juices finally fired up. I wanted to master the art of driving with only my hands.

Eighteen months after my paralysis, I'd taken driver's training and received my license, trading in my sunroofed station wagon for an accessible van. But for years, the van's hand controls just sat there, winking at me, taunting me with one thing I refused to do: drive.

The adaptation setup is simple. A spinner knob on the steering wheel allows the driver to steer the vehicle with one hand while the other hand uses a lever to the left of the steering column to control the gas and brake pedals. Push it to stop; pull it to go. No feet required.

I understood it. I knew how to do it. I just wouldn't.

Friends, family, and caregivers shuttled me around. No one ever complained or challenged me. Perhaps they understood my caution. I never was much of a risk-taker. Then I went to bed not feeling well and woke up paralyzed—that didn't help.

Through the years, I'd tried to motivate myself, betting one girlfriend I would drive before she learned how to send an e-mail, and teasing Brittany that I would drive before she would. Yet, I couldn't sustain my resolve.

But as I watched Pete hop into his Jeep Wrangler, eager to learn how to make that vehicle go, I marveled at his determination. Undaunted by stalls, jerky stops, and uneven starts, he soaked up every bit of his father's instructions on how to shift gears. And after only three weeks of experience, Joe asked him to drive to our annual joint vacation across the 4.3 mile-long Chesapeake Bay Bridge, suspended hundreds of feet above the water, a challenge Pete accomplished without hesitation.

His two-handed feat soon inspired mine. My first quest was driving morning carpools with Pete as my copilot. It was a quick route, one big loop of mostly right turns from my house to the school and back.

Left turns terrified me. With limited abdominal muscles, turning left forced me to lean hard into the steering wheel knob as I turned or I would tip over, face-planting in the passenger seat. Until I got the hang of it, Pete would hold my right shoulder to prevent my tipping.

After seven months of carpools, I was comfortable driving most places. I'd even braved taking the dog to a drive-through Starbucks that required three left turns and a narrow merge area. The Bay Bridge? Why not? I could use a break in the wedding planning.

We finished breakfast and I leashed Tripp, our puggle (pug and beagle mix), who loved carpool. With the press of my key ring button, the van door slid open and a ramp unfolded to the ground. I wheeled in with Tripp behind me, transferred into the driver seat, and closed the door with another touch of the button. I clutched the spinner knob with my right hand and pressed down on the lever to the left of the steering column to put on the brake. Down to stop; up to go. I pumped and pressed the van into place, waiting for Pete's split-second arrival.

He plopped in the passenger seat. Tripp snuggled between us. "Let's go, Mom."

⚜

PETE WAS HEADING into the final months of a fabulous junior year of high school. In middle school, soccer took a backseat to wrestling, where he excelled. The colleges were after him, including UNC, Harvard, Princeton, Cornell, and a dozen more. Stanford had offered him a rare early-admission invitation, extended to only thirty individuals within their thirty-five sports. He'd completed the application but would not know the decision until after July 1, the official first day of his senior year. Although his wrestling season was over, he would soon begin summer training. I'd planned to travel to Fargo, North Dakota, to watch him compete.

On the wedding front, sixty-five friends and family came to the engagement party in my home with forty-two returning for brunch the next day. We booked the church, the reception, caterer, and photographer, and then Cindy, Brittany, her maid of honor, Jill, and I headed to New York City for a three-day trip to find *the* dress. After two days, four stores, and eighteen dresses, we found the perfect gown at Kleinfeld, of *Say Yes to the Dress* fame.

The rest of the summer was packed with plans, including eighteen guests for a surprise birthday brunch for Brittany's twenty-fourth birthday, our annual joint vacation, and a short cruise to the Bahamas with Rachel and her family.

Yet not all the planning was so joyful.

Maybe it was the letdown after all the entertaining in my home and everyone's return to their full lives. Or maybe it was the engagement cards' sentiments or wedding ceremony review and all the absolute terminology that was being thrown around—forever, only one, meant for each other, etc.—but the next selection, the videographer, was hard for me.

The highly touted service not only included a video of the service and the reception, but also featured a new offering: The Love Story. The couple is interviewed about how they met and fell in love, creating a twenty-minute video to be shown at the reception. Bob, the videographer, brought samples. In each love story he played, we heard the bride and groom speak separately of their initial impressions of each other. Then they recounted their first date, their first kiss, and their first "I love you" exchanges all recorded in a setting special for them—a beach, a carnival, an orchard. And, of course, romantic music accented each poignant moment.

Elizabeth, Brittany, and Cindy were near tears, oohing and aahhing at every detail.

My eyes brimmed, too, but not from trying to remember. I kept trying to forget. The first embrace. The first kiss. The first time I saw love in his eyes. Joe, the man I married.

Joe, now Cindy's husband.

I wondered what tape was playing in Cindy's head, but I dared not imagine it. Instead I focused on the videographer's shoes. Were they brown? Worn? Crepe-bottomed or hard-soled? I don't remember other than they were not the film, the story set to music that captured the emotion that I'd come to value far more than the rest—love.

I shifted in my wheelchair, pressure relief. The others sat on the edge of their seats, too, but for different reasons. They leaned in to the video's story, drinking in each word.

"I can leave a sample DVD with you if you like," Bob offered.

"Oh, we'd love it!" Brittany and Cindy exclaimed in unison.

"No problem, I have several," he said as he smiled and handed them each one. "Would you like one, too?" he said to me, another DVD in his hand.

"Oh no," I said, waving it off as I shifted in my seat once more, my lips pressed in my tight smile. I glanced at his shoes once more. "But thank you."

Chapter 24

Facing Fear Again

You are imperfect, you are wired for struggle,
but you are worthy of love and belonging.
—Brené Brown

"YOU WERE RIGHT, Ms. Galli." Dr. Brown began. Dr. Lamos was unavailable, so I saw his colleague, Dr. Brown. During my drive to the Eastern Shore, my left leg had more spasms than normal. I thought it was because of the amount of time I'd sat in one position driving across the Bay Bridge, but the erratic jerks continued at home. Then I noticed an odd drainage during my self-care routines. I worried I had hurt myself. Although I didn't know Dr. Brown well, I wanted to be seen right away so I took the first available appointment.

"You have a small wound," Dr. Brown said.

"What?" I twisted around on the narrow exam table to face him. My hands clenched the thin paper beneath me as I started to shake all over.

"It's a good thing you came in. It is small and should respond well to treatment, but you should be seen by specialists at a wound center." His voice trailed on, the words jumbling.

"I'm sorry, Dr. Brown. I'm not getting all of this. I have a wound? I need to go to a wound center?"

"Yes." The voice began again, explaining all the things I knew. That even though the wound was small, I was at risk for it getting worse because of the paralysis. That since I could not feel pain, nor see it because of its location, I wouldn't be able to take care of it properly. He went on and on, but my thoughts ran over his words.

I can't have a wound. I am too careful. Yes, I am paralyzed, but I am not one of those careless people. I take good care of myself. I'm active. I do pressure relief. I stared back at his moving mouth, again not hearing what he was saying and finally blurted out the most pressing thought, the one that terrified me, "But Dr. Brown, my mother *died* from a wound—a wound that would not heal!"

He stopped, his face changing as compassion found its way into the professional facade. "I'm sorry," he said softly.

Then he let me talk. About Mom's fall, her injury, the blood disorder, the stubborn wound that refused to heal despite debridement, surgeries, a wound vac, stellar round-the-clock nursing care, and daughters who tried everything to help their mother recover. But couldn't.

"You are in a much different situation, Rebecca. You have caught this early. It should heal in six weeks. You will need specialized care, but you will be fine," he said. "We can make the appointment for you right now as you leave."

"Will I be able to travel? I've planned to go to Fargo to watch my son wrestle in three weeks."

"I don't know. The wound center can give you a better idea about that."

I gathered myself after he left, quickly wheeled to the lobby, and booked the next available wound center appointment.

When I arrived back home, Pete was hanging out on the deck, lounging in a chair with his shades on and his iPod blaring on some new Bose speakers. "How's the birthday boy?" I asked, smiling hard to stuff the wound report and keep the positive vibes going. I'd made his birthday breakfast, adding country ham and red-eye gravy to his Southern favorite, before heading out to see Dr. Brown.

"Awesome, Mom!" he said hopping up to give me a hug. "I just had the best birthday present ever!"

"Oh really? Did you get a call?"

"Yes I did," he paused for effect and gave me his half smile. "Mom, I got in to Stanford! They've offered me a scholarship!"

"Oh, Pete," I said, opening my arms wide as he squatted down to give me his wrestling bear hug. I wrapped my arms around his broad shoulders, burrowing my face in his neck as the tears released. His arms held me tight, squeezing me until I almost couldn't breathe. "I'm so proud of you, buddy," I whispered in his ear. *I am*, I kept reminding myself. *I am!*

Yet there was this sharp prick of pain, a lingering twinge in my heart—of loss, of longing, or was it of the unknown? Suddenly, I was transported back to another hug. Another conversation. Another set of dreams he'd shared with me when he was a little boy worrying about his future. To comfort his fears, I'd told him, "You'll be ready when it is time to go."

But now I wondered, was I?

❧

"YOU ARE GOING to be fine," the nurse assured me. People keep telling me that, I wanted to say to her. But instead, I watched her work. I could tell she knew what she was doing, clicking through the unimportant paperwork and zeroing in on the questions that mattered. She helped me transfer to the wide reclining examination chair, prepped me for the doctor exam, and then took a photo of the wound. "Dr. Mirza will be in shortly. Are you comfortable?"

"Yes, thanks." I stayed on my left side, staring out the exam-room window at the gray gravel atop of an adjoining building. I shut my eyes, tucked my hands under my chin, and tried to calm my thoughts. I couldn't believe I was there, at a wound care center. I heard a tap on the door. "Ms. Galli?" a voice said.

"Yes, come in."

Dr. Mirza came around to the window side of the bed to see me and shake my hand before he went through the wound exam procedure—measuring it, debriding it, dressing it, taping it. I transferred back into the wheelchair, telling him all about Mom. He gave detailed instructions for me and for the home-care nurse who would come daily to change the bandage.

"Let's see how you do in a week," he said when I asked him about Fargo travel.

"In fourteen years I have never, ever had any skin break-down, Dr. Mirza," I said, feeling the need to explain myself.

"I must say that is surprising, given the paralysis."

"I've been on nine Caribbean cruises, two eight-hour week-long trips to North Carolina, flown by myself, stayed in a hotel alone. I am active, very active, but also so very careful. In rehab, they showed us slides of wounds so large you could put your fist in them."

He nodded, unfazed, as he snapped off his rubber gloves and grabbed my chart. "But yours is very superficial, Ms. Galli."

"I'm not sure it's really a wound. I think it is an injury," I said. "A few months ago, my potty-chair seat had a small rip in it, so I taped over it with my son's wrestling mat tape. I fig-ured if kids' faces were smashed into it, it could certainly handle my bottom," I smiled. "But I wasn't counting on the wrinkles. I think when I lifted up and over, I must have scraped myself. I remember seeing a spot of blood on the seat, but thinking it was my menses," I said, pausing to let my case sink in. "So technically it's not a wound, right, Dr. Mirza?"

He looked up from the chart, his dark-brown eyes peering through the bottom half of his horn-rimmed glasses. "It's a wound, Rebecca," he said, unblinking. "It may have begun as an acute trauma, but now it is a wound. Because of the paralysis, it has failed to progress in the healing process. With good treatment, you will be fine."

Again, I'll be fine.

But I was not fine. I heard this man, but I still had a hard time believing, much less saying, that I had a "wound." Somehow I needed my situation to be different—not like Mom's and not like those careless folks who neglect good self-care. Plus, it was going to affect my daily life. I had to find a way to talk about it. Like so many times before, I needed to be able to explain the unexplainable, to share publicly the private pain of a personal loss.

I wheeled into the reception area and made a series of weekly appointments, tucking the reminder slips into my new floral file folder, crisply labeled, "Skin Issues." I waited for the hospital elevator, thinking about this next adventure. I have an injury, a booboo! There, I could say that without tuning beet red.

And it wasn't on my bottom, heaven forbid; it was under my leg.

⁓⟡⟡⤳

FOR THE NEXT week, Pete's Stanford offer trumped the "booboo under my leg" and Brittany's wedding planning. I always thought Pete would go to UNC, but realized this incredible opportunity—Stanford on a scholarship!—was something he couldn't pass up. It was also so strangely familiar—very much like the UNC/WFU quandary I faced at his age.

"So, are you going to accept, Pete?"

"Probably so, Mom. Probably so."

And he did. Joe and I supported his decision and prepped him for how to call the other coaches to let them know of his decision. "It's important to prepare for this conversation, Pete," Joe said as we sat around my sunroom table to talk through potential scenarios. "It's hard to predict reactions. No one takes rejection well."

I smiled at Joe and thought of the ultimate rejection I'd felt from him. How affirming to hear him state it so clearly. Then I watched him take Peter through a range of reactions, preparing him with responses for sour grapes, retribution, or an aggressive push to reconsider the decision or at least delay it. He reminded me of Dad, preparing by analyzing all the angles.

"Be polite. Be firm. Compliment their program and thank them for their time," I added, with Mom's graciousness coming to mind.

"The wrestling world is very small, Pete," Joe reminded him. "These are great coaches with fabulous programs. Never forget that as you speak with them."

⤙⚬⚬⚬⤚

"IT'S NO BETTER," the nurse stated flatly as I looked out the window and studied the two sparrows hopping around the gravel at my second wound-care visit.

"What! " I half-turned to see her. "Not at all?"

"Well, it is no worse, either," she replied, attempting encouragement as she wrote the measurements in the chart.

How could that be? A nurse came every day to change the dressing. I did my wheelchair push-ups for pressure relief every fifteen minutes and spent more time in bed. "I did everything you told me to do," I told Dr. Mirza after his exam. He turned to face me and looked me in the eyes. I think he could sense my impatience.

"I know you did, Ms. Galli, but this is not like a car repair—a one-time fix," he said, tilting his head back slightly, his brown eyes wide as he nodded with each word. "This is a dynamic process. There are often many adjustments we have to make in the healing process."

"Oh my," I sighed. *Can't anything ever be simple or even just linear?* "So should I cancel the Fargo trip? And our family Bahamas cruise?"

"I can't tell you what to do, Rebecca, but I will say that the most important part of healing in your situation is to offload the pressure."

"So I should stay in bed?"

"That is probably the best way to offload, but correct sitting posture, pressure relief, and special care in transferring will also help."

I cancelled both trips, stopped driving, and hired more help. I made progress in the next two weeks, but then the wound increased in sized from a tape tear during a dressing change.

After I pushed Mirza for answers and a swifter healing plan, he startled me, saying, "This will be a lifelong battle for you."

What isn't? I wanted to reply, but didn't. Devastated, I searched for more resources and ideas. My home-care service brought in a wound-care specialist, who recommended a wheelchair seating evaluation, a nutritional consult, and a new silicon tape to prevent tape tears. Another specialist pressure-mapped my wheelchair seat to make sure my weight was appropriately distributed during sitting. I limited my transfers, staying in bed for longer periods of time. I minimized my activities. I didn't go to Pete's last back-to-school night. We moved the wedding planning meetings to my bedroom so I could stay in bed.

The wound had almost closed when I apparently bumped it in a transfer; it reopened and unbelievably, I had a second wound.

Five hundred and thirty-one miles away, Rachel listened to each daily update for seventy-five days. But when she learned of the second injury, her tone changed. "I'm coming up, Sissy," she said in her matter-of-fact-already-made-up-my-mind voice.

"I'm fine, Sissy," I said. "I'm spending much more time

in bed. I'm getting 70 grams of protein, tons of vitamin C, and drinking plenty of water per the nutritional consult. The new cushion for my shower chair came in. My wheelchair seat was updated based on the pressure mapping. My girlfriends are bringing me meals for our 'boudoir dining' so I can stay in bed," I paused to take a breath. "I'm fine, Sissy. Really."

"I said I'm coming up." Her confident defiance edged the words.

"Well, alright. Don't have to get your panties in a wad," I teased her, secretly glad she was coming. I wanted my life back, dang it. I was missing my son's senior year and my daughter's wedding planning. Enough was enough.

Just before she flew up to see me, she attended an out-of-town wedding. Seated at her table at the reception was a doctor—a wound-care specialist. She picked his brain and came back with notes. "You will heal, Sissy," she said, reading her notes jotted on the wedding napkin. "This doctor says you must stay off of it, though. Pressure and friction are the enemy."

For seven days, she waited on me, serving me breakfast, lunch, and dinner in bed. She made sure I was in bed twenty-three hours a day. Life became a series of fifteen-minute intervals of elbow-propped segments. Upright sitting, even in bed, was limited, marked by a ticking kitchen timer.

Rachel talked to the nurses, questioned the doctors, Googled, texted, and e-mailed on my behalf. We scheduled a physical therapist to come in to assess my transfer technique to see if there were any adjustments I could make to reduce the friction. But mostly she sat on my bedroom couch and stayed with me as I slept, ate, rotated from side to side. Like Mom helping me watch the flowers bloom, my sissy helped me stay put and heal.

Three days after she left, I rang the bell at the wound care center. Both wounds had closed!

But not healed.

Within two weeks, one reopened.

"The injury site will always be your weakest link," Dr. Mirza told me.

This time, I got technical, taking a tutorial on wound healing, each stage and its duration. After six months, the site is only 10 percent as strong as the surrounding tissues. To fully heal requires eighteen months. And then, the healed area will only be 80 percent as strong as the tissue around it.

Scar tissue is never as strong as normal, uninjured skin, I learned.

And I always thought scars made us tougher.

⁓⚮⁓

LIFE BECAME A series of informed choices. I knew the stages of healing and what I was risking when I sat too long or transferred too often. I weighed each outing before deciding if it was worth it. There were no shortcuts to recovery; only setbacks and starting the process all over again.

In my research on how others with paralysis coped with wounds, I'd learned it could be tragic, even to those who had excellent care. Christopher Reeve's death was attributed to cardiac arrest, but it was prompted by a reaction to an antibiotic used to treat an infection his body was fighting—from a wound.

I was trying to live fully with what mobility I had left, but my world kept getting smaller and smaller. I missed my weekly trips to visit Madison, but made sure she came home for pizza and Mommy time during each trek to her periodic respite camp. I traveled to see Pete take third at National Preps his senior year, but missed flying to the Atlanta Prep Slam tournament that he won. I went once more to New York City with Brittany and Cindy for wedding-dress alterations, but missed the final fitting trip.

The wound was small but still open as we headed into the final stretch of wedding planning with Elizabeth. Eleven months after my first trip to the wound center, she e-mailed out the "Wedding Day Schedule." Midway down the second page my eyes stuck on one line:

3 P.M. Bride steps into gown.

My jaw dropped as my hands flew to my chest, crossing them over my heart. Had sixteen months passed already? My eyes filled as the memories flashed, paparazzi-style. A strange combination of joy and disbelief filled my heart.

My daughter was getting married.

Wasn't it only yesterday that I rocked her in the pink rocking chair? That she cut her first tooth? Took her first step?

Didn't I just stitch the sequins on her green frog recital outfit? Call out her spelling words? Book her summer camps? Watch her play dress up in Nana's old jewelry?

Hadn't I just survived logging those never-ending student-driver hours? Stayed up all night waiting for her to get home from the prom? Listened to her crying at 2 A.M. that freshman year of college when some idiot broke her heart?

And now, she'd found her love. The Brittany was getting married. For real. It was on the schedule.

Despite the smallness of my world, the hope for the future, the possible, warmed me.

⚮

A FEW DAYS later, Joe and Cindy hosted a little wine-and-cheese gathering for our final wedding-planning meeting with Elizabeth.

"You'll need an escort," Elizabeth said to me as we discussed the post-ceremony exit.

"Well, who normally would escort me?"

"Generally your husband," she said, checking her clipboard.

"Well, I don't have one of those," I said, and looked playfully at Cindy and smiled.

"Or your brother."

"Don't have one of those either—anymore," I said, still smiling, but a little softer.

Maybe it was that second glass of wine that colored that evening so beautifully, refusing to let loss overtake the mood of planning the most important day of my daughter's life. I was determined to stay upbeat; my escort mattered little.

"Could I just wheel back up the aisle by myself? I don't mind at all," I offered.

Apparently that was an idea, but not a good one, as Dad used to say, since there was a long silence and lots of puzzled looks flying around the room.

"How about David?" Brittany chimed in.

"But he's with Rachel," I said of my sister's husband.

"How about both?" Elizabeth suggested.

"Works for me." She jotted the note down and we moved on to the next agenda item.

I had an escort. I was no longer alone. At least on paper.

⚡

I TRIED, BUT I couldn't do it. I couldn't make it through the wedding without this conversation. I had to talk to Joe.

I had done such a good job of reining in the emotions, of focusing on the bride, the celebration, the thought of family and friends being together. But every time I envisioned her coming down the aisle with Joe escorting her, the tears began.

Forever. Until death do us part. In sickness and in health. How could I sit in the pew and listen to those vows, beside my ex-husband and his wife and stop the flow of tears?

I had to talk to him.

"I would change nothing," Forest had written. I couldn't get his words out of my mind. Would I change anything? I knew what I thought, but I wanted confirmation. I needed to talk to Joe and I needed to do it before the wedding.

Joe came over, frenzied with work and the wedding-reception plans that were morphing his home, the "farm" as we called the vast acreage once used for that purpose. The tent reception plans were changing by the minute with the impending weather. Storms and tornadoes were predicted, unprecedented for our part of the country, with triple-digit heat.

I asked him to come back to my room where I parked beside the couch. He paced back and forth, his cell phone off, but still connected to the earpiece. I clasped my hands on my lap, settling myself. I wanted my words to be just right, like I'd rehearsed.

"Thanks for coming over, Joe. I know it's crazy busy, but I need to talk to you. I am doing fine, really fine. My booboo is still here, but it's managed." I leaned forward and then straightened up, throwing my shoulders back, bracing myself for strength. "I need to make sure, though, that I make it through this wedding and not lose it."

His pace slowed and he turned to face me, taking out the earpiece and wrapping its cord around the phone three times before shoving it in his pocket. "Sure, Beck. What's up?"

"I have to know, Joe." I took a deep breath. "Were we a mistake?"

He sat down on the edge of the couch and looked me in the eyes. "No," he said quietly, his in-charge-at-all-times tone softening to a whisper.

I released the breath, still holding his eyes and asked what my heart had to know. "If you had to do it all over again, would you?"

"Yes," he said, not missing a beat, like he'd thought about it more than once before.

"Okay," I said, and let out a long, slow sigh. "Thank you. I needed to know that." I clasped my hands tighter. "So would I."

We sat there for a moment, the overhead fan stirring a gentle breeze.

"We just had too much, didn't we?"

He nodded, his head down before his dark eyes looked up again, their vacancy gone.

"Thank you for being there for me, Joe."

"I will be there for you, Beck, I will."

And we hugged. At first it was just a cursory hug, the dismissive one given when departing. But then it lingered and he hugged me tight, like the old days, the early days, like he was giving me his heart, his will, his word.

And the burden lifted; I had the proof I needed. The love I'd known had been real. We believed it was forever. And in a strange way, it still was, at least its memory. We were not a mistake. The joy I'd known was real. Gone, but real.

And now I could celebrate that moment with my daughter.

I had not lived a lie.

Chapter 25

The Greatest of These

One word frees us of all the weight and pain of life: that word is love.
—Sophocles

IT WAS BRITTANY'S idea. But it took a small army to pull it off.

"I want Madison to be here for the wedding, Mom," she told me soon after her engagement. "I have a plan."

She made it sound so simple. Get Madison from her residential school on the day of the wedding. Bring her into the bridal dressing area after Brittany had stepped into her gown. Take pictures.

"Then Madison could go back. It would be a quick visit, Mom, tightly scheduled so she shouldn't get upset," she said. "We could plan it down to the minute and create a special schedule just for her. It would be just the two of us for a few pictures," she told me, her eyes dancing at the thought of a professional photo of the two of them, something I'd been unable to accomplish since they were in elementary school.

Pictures were rated the number-one priority in Brittany's grand wedding plan—above the music, above the food, above the gown. These "captured moments" trumped every other wedding element.

"Okay, Britty, we'll try to make that happen."

The search for a bridesmaid-like dress for Madison was a challenge as we tried to find something the same color, but with a more comfortable fit in a material that would not irritate her sensitive skin. We knew she could not wear the matching spiked-heeled shoes, so we ordered three flats of the same color that sported the signature peony, Brittany's bridal bouquet flower and the focal design of her gown.

We made special arrangements for doing Madison's hair and makeup, giving the stylists a short primer on autism, while instructing them to keep their efforts simple, flexible, and to use short phrases when speaking to her.

Then there was the special bouquet. Since each of Brittany's bridesmaids had a different white-flowered bouquet, we decided to take flowers from each to create a composite one, just for Madison. Holding it, we thought, could help keep her hands settled, redirecting her tendency to hand-flap.

At Madison's school, her teachers created a social story around the unusual schedule of the day and practiced it. We had extra help, extra meds, extra plans, and extra attention to every detail as well as lots of extra prayers, "Please Madison, don't have an upset."

But if she did, we had a plan for that, too.

Madison was in her second residential placement. After Joe and Cindy's wedding, her erratic and disruptive behaviors increased dramatically. Despite additional school staffing and my efforts at home, hiring over fifty caregivers to support Madison's therapies, she was no longer progressing academically. The school agreed that a nonpublic placement with a structured and managed environment that spanned both school and home would be in Madison's best educational interests. So, at age seven, she moved to a ten-month residential program. She excelled academically for seven years until the behaviors escalated again. So at age fifteen, she moved to a twelve-month program that included behavior-management specialists and twenty-four/seven care.

Although each move was a difficult decision, I knew Madison benefitted from care I could not provide. I'd finally learned that lesson—after Forest, Matthew, Mom, Dad, and even accepting the limits of my own care—but that didn't make those choices easy. I visited Madison each Tuesday, physically when possible, or via FaceTime after the wound hit. About a year before Brittany's wedding, I was asked to chronicle our adventures in a monthly column, *Tuesdays with Madison*, for an autism website.

At age twenty, Madison still had limited words, but had learned to use a few functional phrases. Although still prone to occasional upsets, she had adjusted well to the consistent and structured care. I hoped she would be a willing participant in her sister's wedding plans.

⚬⚭⚬

SO FAR, THE sixteen months of wedding preparations were shaping up to be everything we'd hoped for—elegant, sophisticated, and fun. The only thing that wasn't cooperating was Mother Nature. On June 29, 2012, the day before the wedding, a *derecho,* now considered one of the most destructive thunderstorm complexes in North American history, ushered in 109-degree weather on Friday night's rehearsal dinner. At midnight, massive thunderstorms left more than 427,000 in the Baltimore area without power, including me, and Joe and Cindy, who were hosting the reception in their home.

Joe called me a little past midnight. "You know we are prepared for power outage with a generator. And we can handle the rain with the tent and the heat with the air conditioning. But I can't do anything about the wind, Beck." He paused. I could hear his breath match his pacing back and forth. "If the tent blows over, I'm not sure what we are going to do."

The tent stayed up, but it flooded. Cindy and Brittany were up at 5 A.M. to hand-dry the dance floor with beach towels. Power was restored early Saturday morning to Joe and Cindy's home, but my power was still out. I had to wash my hair in cold water and dress in the window light of my bathroom. Thank goodness hair and makeup was scheduled to be done at the farm.

Madison arrived on time and in a good mood. Although the entire morning had been preoccupied with the cleanup from the storm, we were still on schedule. She was dressed and coifed in a surprising flash. We didn't take the mirrors into consideration, forgetting how happy she could get just by looking into the mirror and giggling, hand-flapping, and "EEEEeee"-ing at her reflection. We'd also forgotten the calm that comes over her when someone brushes her skin (makeup brushes instead of her therapy brush) or touches her hair. She seemed to enjoy the process and the attention.

Then it was time for her to see her sister. I held my breath as Brittany entered the room.

"Madison, give Mommy a kiss," I said, hoping to ground her with our customary greeting. Now I needed to orient her to the new situation. This time, I was winging it. How could I have ever prepared her for the scene that was about to unfold when I wasn't prepared myself?

Brittany was stunning; Madison angelic. But it was the loving care between my daughters that sparkled the most, lighting up the room with a special moment. Brittany was right—it had to be captured. I gave it my best shot. "Madison, who is it?" I said, pointing to Brittany.

"Burtney," she said quietly, using her pet name for her sister.

"Go see Brittany, Madison," I said, gently directing her to the other side of the room.

Brittany greeted her. Then Madison turned around and began to look around at the bridesmaids, the photographer, the mothers, and other friends—fifteen of us in total, who seemed to distract her as the photographer tried to get a good angle.

Madison started to look uneasy, a little overwhelmed. Then Brittany handed her the special bouquet.

"Madison," she said, "What is it?" Brittany knew that simple questions were effective, and this was a standby we knew from Madison's therapy drills.

The phrase grabbed Madison's attention. She looked straight into Brittany's eyes and then down at the bouquet. She took her finger and gently touched a petal, and said, "It's a flower!" in her best Barney-the-purple-dinosaur voice.

The tension was broken. We all laughed with her and relaxed. The photographer went to work. An hour later, Madison was on her way back to school. Mission accomplished.

Everything else went off without a hitch. Peter escorted me into the church. Dry-eyed and calm, I watched Joe escort Brittany down the aisle, give our daughter to Brian, and then come back to sit on the pew with Cindy and me.

Mike paid a special tribute to Dad and The Brittany. I saw Mike, but heard my father's voice. Brittany's bouquet was wrapped with Mom's handkerchief, trimmed in tatting from her mom. In my purse, I carried the small bride-and-groom statue that once topped Mom and Dad's wedding cake. Rachel and David escorted me out.

Although we felt the heat and intense humidity, and anticipated rain given the 90 percent chance of showers, not one drop fell on the wedding day or evening. The band was fabulous—I think they stole my funky music tape from my Closure Party. The only Plan B of the evening was the quaint bed and breakfast we'd reserved for Brittany and Brian's wedding night. They still had no power. Thankfully, we'd booked an extra room at the guests' hotel.

⌘

"AREN'T YOU GOING to speak?" one of my college buddies asked me at the reception.

"No," I said, "I'm not allowed."

"Really? How strange."

But it was true. The wedding planner was quite clear about that. The mother of the bride is silent. But, I had so much to say! With music, peonies, sparklers, lights, and a warm feeling from a good red wine, what would I tell them? What would I say to them if I had the chance? What had I learned?

My mind zinged with the rapid thoughts as I watched them dance. My heartbreaks had taught me so much. How could I tell her that we have to take charge of our own happiness and not rely on any one person, especially our spouse, to be the

happiness-maker in our lives? That just because we love differently doesn't mean we don't love. That just because we handle
hard things differently doesn't mean we don't hurt. That just
because we don't express ourselves the same way doesn't mean
we don't feel.

They smiled as they danced. Brian whispered something in
Brittany's ear. She smiled brighter and lowered her eyelids, nuz-
zling into his neck. Their connection was so intense, so natural,
so effortlessly in sync.

How did Joe and I get so out of sync? We'd had so many
hard things, life-changing issues, marriage-changing issues.

I watched the couple move in unison, mastering the music
together.

Ah, maybe that's where I'd failed. I'd let the issues become
larger than our relationship. We stopped facing them together. I
closed my eyes as a tear slipped out. The memories seeped into
the moment with that complex pang of love tinged by loss. I'd

had the best of intentions, I know I did. I thought I was being a good wife by being a good mother.

Maybe not.

As kids, my siblings and I would ask Mom, "Who do you love more, Dad or me?" Then ask Dad, "Who do you love more, Mom or me?"

Their answers were always the same, artful, yet so wise.

"You are a result of our love," they'd tell us.

They lived their lives that way. Yes, they made sacrifices for us, but not at the expense of their marriage. I could see it now, but I didn't as a child. Somehow they always made us feel like number one, even though we weren't.

Then the conversation I'd had with Mom and Dad about Forest flooded back. When I'd asked Mom if she would have provided the daily care for Forest in our home if he had been able to survive, living on tubes and being medically fragile, like Matthew, she'd surprised me with her answer.

"I would have found good care for him," she'd said, "and done what's best for the family." Dad had agreed.

Then I remembered my question to him, the one I'd struggled with then and so many times since. "Am I supposed to give up hope, Dad?"

"Just remember, BB," he said, those steel-blue eyes full of compassion, "of faith, hope, and love, the greatest of these is love."

Brian twirled Brittany for one final dip. We clapped madly for them, but my mind was still working, kneading through the notion of the overriding power of love.

Suddenly, I knew what I wanted to say to my daughter and her husband. There was something I needed them both to know.

⚬⚬⚬

WHILE THEY WERE on their honeymoon, I wrote a letter to the newlyweds. They'd bought a puppy, Dudley, a puggle like his cousin, Tripp, who seemed to be more mischievous than most pups. He tested their patience often and intensely, far more than they had imagined.

For Brittany and Brian
June 30, 2012

First of all, I want you to know how happy I am for the two of you. My heart is bursting with joy for you now, the young couple so much in love, and for the couple of the future, sure to be filled with the deep, abiding care for one another that I see in you now.

The scripture reading selected for your wedding has it right. "Of faith, hope, love, the greatest of these is love."

Here is what I want to say to both of you on this, your wedding day—it is my daily hope and prayer for you.

Brittany and Brian, from this moment on, you will face life together as you have never faced it before. You are a couple, committed to one another for life. It is a special, sacred commitment.

I hope you can find guidance from this one simple thought: Let your love be larger.

Let your love be larger than adversity, than issues, than people or circumstances that threaten to pull you apart. Let it prevail, triumph, overcome.

Release the urge to be right, the urge to win, the urge to remember each time you have been right and won. And let your love be larger.

Love is all the things the Good Book tells us— patient, kind, understanding—but it is also the most powerful force we have. Use it wisely. Cherish it. Sustain it and nurture it.

Before you act, ask, is it kind? Is it necessary? Is it loving? And let your love be larger.

And as your circle of friends and family expand, let love teach you that it has more than one way to be expressed. That judging others' loving ways is a useless exercise. A more important action is to let your love be larger—and learn from it. What can a different expression of love teach you about others? Respect it, honor it, and open your heart a little wider to include it, even though it may be so foreign to you.

And with your children, remember that they are a result of your love for one another. Your love came first, then your shared love for them.

Let love overshadow the small stuff, embellish the large stuff, and wrap a layer of warmth around the cold realities that you may face.

Love is what we're meant to do, you know. Share our lives with another. Love can't fix all of life's hard times, but it sure can make whatever journey you are on, richer, fuller, and most importantly, shared.

And, just like your precious care for Dudley, love despite—because you can. ☺

Love (each other) despite—because you can.

And always let your love be larger.

Chapter 26

~⚬~

The Empty Nest

Don't let the perfect be the enemy of the good.
—Voltaire

I WOKE UP startled on the flight from Baltimore to San Francisco. "Did I snore?"

"No, not at all," Cindy said, her smile assuring me.

"Oh, I'm sorry," I said, shifting in my seat. "Looks like I took over the armrest."

"No worries. I'm glad you could sleep."

I was, too. I didn't sleep much the night before. I was up at 4 A.M. to be ready for the 6:40 A.M. flight to San Francisco.

We'd been preparing for months—booking flights, hotels, and specialized services. I found a delightful hotel manager in a small hotel near campus that was willing to let me call, e-mail, and text him my wheelchair concerns. I wanted to rent a power wheelchair to be able to get around campus. At over 8,000 acres, Stanford is one of the largest university campuses in the world. Cindy focused on logistics, securing accessible vans to transport us to and from the airport and to rent for our trips from the hotel into campus. Pete and Joe would be meeting us there after a much-anticipated fishing trip together. Cindy's father stayed with Zander since his school year had already started.

Despite all the planning, I was anxious. There were so many variables ahead. But Cindy was unflappable, confident, and assuring—her mantra, "no worries."

We were a team, I realized. The Moms. Yep, the Moms were coming.

I still had the wound. It was small, the size of the eye of a needle. But it was not closed, much less healed, so I knew the risk I was taking. I brought extra supplies in case the double bandage did not last the trip. I knew I could wind up in a doctor's office or emergency room if I missed a transfer or somehow dislodged the bandage.

My biggest challenge, however, was the mental preparation. I struggled to find that perfect zone where I could gracefully let go of my son, my youngest, without falling apart.

I'd sought the advice of other mothers. Some were practical: "Bring tissues." "Wear dark glasses." "Wait until you get into the car to cry," they'd advised. Others laid out the unvarnished truth: "It's awful," one said. "I cried every day for weeks." "I don't know how you are going to do it," another said. "It's so far away, Becky. How could you let him go that far away?"

But the best advice came from a twenty-five-year-old woman who was not a mother at all. "You will be fine," Brittany texted me the morning of the move-in day. "Just think of it as so exciting!"

It was strangely wonderful advice, far better than the stoic mantra I'd concocted, "He's ready. I'm ready," especially since I wasn't sure I believed my own words. Had I had prepared him enough for the transition? And was *I* ready? Besides, did I want to keep plucking at that tender thought as I struggled to keep my act together? Brittany's advice avoided that whole topic, focusing on what was true for both of us. Excitement was everywhere; I just had to focus on it.

It's so exciting! I thought as we had breakfast together before heading to campus, letting all the possibilities of what Pete would experience and learn here lighten my somber mood.

It's so exciting! I reminded myself as we emptied the car and filled half the dorm room with stuff, hypothesizing about the young man who would soon fill the other half. Unlike my daughter's all-day dorm move-in six years earlier, the unpacking of Pete's things went quickly. Soon he and his roommate gently dismissed us to wander the campus until convocation and the grand finale—a "welcome home" parent-student meeting back at the dorm.

The printed schedule left no doubt about the agenda: "The conclusion of this event is the traditional time for you to say good-bye to your family members."

But, it was a creative good-bye.

The dorm's ninety-seven students and their parents crammed into the sun-filled lounge where the resident-fellow family—parents, two kids, and a dog and cat who lived in the dorm's apartment—introduced us to the other resident advisors. After a slide show featuring each student, we were told the time had come for us to say good-bye.

Hugs and tears muffled our farewells until the students departed. Only the parents remained. "We know you've said good-bye, but here's one last chance for you to share your parting words," a voice said quietly above the emotional silence. "Take a marker and write a note to your child on the glass panes, if you like. Give it careful thought as it will be here all year."

Slowly the parents moved to the panes and began to craft their well wishes.

"It's so exciting," I whispered to myself as I took the pen in my hand. "Deep roots. Strong wings. Big heart. Show them what you've got, Pete."

And then I wheeled away from the windows and headed out the door. He belongs. He is well cared for. He is doing what he's supposed to do. All part of the plan. It's so exciting.

And I made it to the car.

DESPITE ALL THE precautions, the small wound doubled in size after the 2012 trip to Stanford and took another fifteen months to heal. The progress was maddening; it would close for a few days and then reopen if I bumped it during a transfer. Frustrated, I went to a plastic surgeon for another opinion.

"Yes, Ms. Galli, the wound is closed, but it has not healed properly," the young doctor explained. "You have an unstable scar."

"A what?"

"An unstable scar. It is closed for now, but it will reopen at some point because it has not healed with healthy tissue."

"I'm sorry. I'm just not getting this. So my scar tissue is not healthy?"

"Yes, I know it's confusing. When a wound heals, it needs to close with good, healthy tissue. When it doesn't, it becomes unstable and at risk for reopening. Your wound has technically closed, but it closed with fibrous tissue that's created this unstable scar. It will most likely reopen."

"Oh no." I let out a long, slow sigh. Here we go again. What *else* was I going to learn that I really had no interest in? "So what do we do with this unstable scar?"

"We have to start over and debride it, or cut out the fibrous tissue that's filled in the wound," he said. "Then healthy tissue can grow back in its place. We will monitor it closely to make sure the healing tissue is good tissue. Your nurse can check it with each dressing change."

"Wow. Okay."

"Do I have your permission to debride it?"

"Sure. Do what you gotta do." I sighed again, thinking about his terminology. Unstable scars—what we get when we don't heal properly.

Somehow that sounded more like a life challenge than a medical term.

⚬⚭⚬

I FELT LIKE Mom. I wheeled up to the sunny window in my kitchen, sipped my coffee, and took a peek at my calendar. Pete was coming home for his spring break of his sophomore year and the days were blank. It was hard to believe two years had passed already. I had nothing planned for his homecoming. How could that be? So, I picked up my phone and dialed Cindy.

"Hey, it's Becky. Is this a good time to chat?"

"Sure, sure. I'm home. Just dropped Zander off at school."

"I heard he had a great wrestling weekend. Loved the group texts from Joe. Great recap!"

"Yes, it was a good tournament—hard because he lost the first match. Made for a really long day of wrestling."

I remembered those days with Pete. When you lost your first match, taking third was so hard, Joe said the hardest. Besides having more matches in the consolation-round wrestle-backs, you had to deal with the emotional part of getting over the loss quickly to be ready for the next opponent. "How is Zan doing?" I asked. He was ten and already showing promise as a wrestler, following in his dad's and brother's footsteps.

"He popped up this morning. Didn't seem to be sore at all. He wrestled well even though he lost the last match to take fourth. It was so close," she paused. "I'm exhausted, though."

"I remember! Looking back, I do think in the long run they learn more from losing than winning. It's hard to watch as a parent, though. Really hard."

"Ugh, the worst!"

"So, I've been looking at my calendar, Cindy, and I was wondering if we could do a little planning so I can have something to look forward to?"

"Absolutely!"

"Do you think we could all have dinner at the Center Club during the week Pete's home? He missed our Christmas outing there since he was training. He said he'd like to go."

"Oh sure. Great idea."

"And Joe's birthday is that week, too, right? Maybe we could do something special for that—if you like?"

"Yes, I'll try to get a date from him before he leaves tonight."

"Oh, and Madison will be coming in on the 30th and I'll have a small birthday party for her here about 3 P.M. You guys are welcome to pop in for pizza. I'd love for you to see her."

"That may actually work! Zan has a wrestling camp but he should be finished."

"Great! Oh, and Cindy, I've got to update you on Brittany. I miss them so! I chatted with her this weekend. They love Seattle. Went to a LEGO exhibit and found a winery to tour. She said Joe called and said he may come out for a visit. She's so excited.

"Awesome! I will check with Joe about that visit, too. I know Britty is so busy there."

"She loves all the houseguests. I think she has at least one scheduled every month. I can't believe how quickly they have settled in and adjusted in three months."

"Yes, they are amazing!" she paused. "Let me try to catch Joe. Call you right back?"

"Sure. Thanks."

Twenty minutes later she called back. "Hey, Becky, real quick. We're set at the Center Club, and we can make Madison's party. But, instead of Joe going out to Seattle in June, would you want to go with me? We could celebrate Brittany's birthday with her. Think about it. We had so much fun when we went out to Stanford. I'd love to go with you."

I smiled until tears came. My life. My crazy life! Who'd have thought my global family could be so tight—with the help of the very woman I'd originally believed to have blown us apart.

Life was good. Not perfect, but pretty damn good.

Epilogue

Rethinking Possible

Life is not fair, but unending in its capacity to change us.
—Mark Nepo

IT WAS THAT time of year again. We'd been preparing for weeks. In fact, we'd booked the rooms a year in advance since herding this group of globe-trotting cats was always a challenge. It was almost time for our annual vacation, a weekend trip to Cambridge, Maryland.

Despite the challenges our family has faced, we still believe what's planned is possible. And we knew the plan by heart.

We knew getting there would be hectic. We knew Brittany and Brian would scrutinize their work schedule, arriving late and leaving early in order to maximize family time while minimizing time away from work. We knew that Cindy would pack her car and pick up Zander after school and hit the worst traffic, but never complain. We knew Peter would graciously load my van, lugging my potty chair, suitcases, and stacks of books and magazines I'd vow to read, but never found the time for. And that Joe would fly in from Hong Kong or Australia, "depending on the schedule" that year.

We knew there would be a backup on the Bay Bridge. We knew we would call each other to check our progress, betting on who would get there first. And we knew those who could, would stop at the outlets to hit Brooks Brothers and Under Armour, despite the increased traffic.

We knew that whenever we got there, the staff would greet us warmly and welcome us back, since we'd been going there over a decade. Even so, we knew there would probably be at least one mix-up on the rooms. We knew we could be booked on different floors. Or that my room may not be accessible. Or worse yet, some new hotel clerk would say they have no accessible rooms at all. But we also knew we would fix that and show them the e-mail with the name of the person who took the reservations, circled, Nana-style.

We knew we would have a late dinner the first night, pending everyone's safe arrival. We knew Brittany would get the shrimp entrée and Cindy would get a salad with extra beets on the side. And we knew when I ordered the Atlantic salmon that Joe would pull the waiter aside to tease him, asking him exactly where the *Atlantic* salmon came from.

"*Dad!*" we knew the kids would whisper, or try to kick him under the table. Then we knew Joe would smile his sneaky half smile.

We knew Peter would order a steak, maybe two, since he would be postseason. "Getting big, son," we knew Joe would say and squeeze Pete's bicep. "He may have to go up a weight class next year," we knew he'd announce to the table. And we all would smile and nod like we agreed, but the reality, we knew, was that decision would be a long way off—and not his dad's to make any longer.

We knew Joe and Brian would get a double espresso "to start." We knew all would get sparkling water, except Brittany, who would order still. We knew Cindy and I would order green tea with extra lemon, and then, if we mutually agreed, we would have a glass or two of wine.

We knew if we decided that we'd "been good," Cindy would order truffle fries for the table. We knew Zander would say that truffle oil "smells funny," but then we would ask him to take one and try it, and we knew he would forget. We also knew no one would complain if Cindy ordered another round.

We knew that Brittany wouldn't order dessert, but that Brian would order something that she'd have an interest in. We also knew she would eat at least half of whatever Brian ordered, "just a bite" at a time.

We knew we would skip dessert if the weather was nice so we could roast marshmallows in the poolside fireplace and make s'mores. We knew I would ask Zander to make "only one for Aunt Becky," even though I'd probably wind up eating three.

We knew at least one night would be game night, with cards, charades, or our new favorite board game, Tock. But if my dang wound resurfaced, we knew everyone would pile into my room for a marathon monopoly game so I could stay in bed but still take pictures.

We knew we would all meet at breakfast to review the plans for the day. We knew Brian, Peter, and Zander would play golf while the girls went to the spa. We knew Joe would say he'd loved to join the guys, but didn't "want to show them up" with his *Happy Gilmore* golf swing.

We knew everyone would hit the gym at least once a day. We knew Joe would run the steps and a few others may join him. We knew we would play miniature golf, go down the waterslide, and play oversized chess on the outdoor patio—depending on our mood. And we knew that if anyone was up for a game of pool or ping-pong, I would be a worthy opponent.

We knew I would take way too many pictures. Although some would go on Facebook, we knew most would land on photo mugs and be wrapped, adorned with hand-curled bows, and tucked under the Christmas tree.

Most of all, we knew we would have a great time.

"I WOULD CHANGE nothing." I still can't look at the life I've lived and say those words. I understand them. Admire those who can. And hope in my dying breath they'll be words I believe and the words I have lived.

But for now they are only a goal, a daily mantra I aim to own before my head hits the pillow each night. About the day. About the decisions I've made. About the way I've treated the people I care about and those whom I may have touched, but don't know.

I hope that day I'm able to say I would change nothing. That I have let my love be larger.

Though it hasn't always been so simple for me, this is what I know now. Life isn't about what you've lost, but about what you've learned—and what you do with what you have left.

Daily, I've learned, we have to accept what we know and rethink what's possible.

Acknowledgments

WHEN YOU WORK on a book for nearly twenty years, you have a lot of folks to thank! It all began in the fall of 1997, just months after my paralysis, with an email from an old high school friend, Scott Gibson. Our reconnection launched an email exchange that became the basis of my new career as a writer, op-ed columnist, and now author. Without Scott's curiosity, compassion, and steadfast presence in those early days of paralysis, this book would not exist.

As my father once wrote, "Writers write alone, but no one publishes alone." Amen. I am deeply grateful to my early mentors and editors, Jack Williams, Hal Piper, A. C. Snow, Charles Deal, Richard Gross, Jim Casto, Joel Davis, Paul Milton, Jim Joyner, Angela Bornemann, Elizabeth Eck, and Les Smith for their guidance and patience with me as this sales and marketing gal retooled her skills and learned how to write for their readers. To my online editors and fellow writers, Merope Pavlides, Teresa Kindred, Andrea Bateman, Sharon Greenthal, Susan Maccarelli, Megan Griffo, Liane Carter, Margaret Renkl, and Melissa Shultz, thank you for careful reviews and feedback. I am especially grateful to editor (and Phi Mu sorority sister) Debra Pickrel, who jumpstarted my publication pursuit after my parents' deaths, working tirelessly with me for over two years to create the backbone of this book.

Many thanks to my Stanford instructors, Anne Zimmerman, Faith Adele, Otis Haschemeyer, Caroline Goodwin, Peter Kline, and Gina Welch who put a foundation underneath my words and to the cohort who offered sustaining encouragement and thoughtful critique—Luanne Castle, Jane Saginaw, Kimberley Lovato, Ann Daugherty, Katy Grabel, Christina Matthews, Isabelle Cecils, Jody Solow, Barbara Shuster and Jennifer Lou, Kimberly Wohlford, and Kristine Mietzner. I'm also grateful for the perceptive coaching from Jenny Nash and Danielle Miller and for the inspiration from my Mastermind colleagues, Lisa Manterfield, Mary Jo Hazard, Jack Schaeffer, Larry Goldman, Dawn Downey, Maya Walker, Brian Joyner, Amanda Woodward, Anne DiCarlo, and C. V. Harquail, and to our indefatigable leader Dan Blank who taught us how to think of ourselves as creative professionals and to approach our writing as a job.

I am also indebted to the doctors, nurses, and therapists who have shared their invaluable skill sets and perspectives: Dr. Mark Lamos, Dr. Cristina Sadowsky, Dr. Kenneth Tellerman, Dr. Howard Moses, Phyllis Green, Susan Leiter, Dave Barringer, Downey Hinrichs, Barbara and Jeff Rozanski, Dr. Trish Amish, and especially the wise words of psychologist Dr. Al Lucco who still helps me sort out my life when it starts to slip sideways.

This book, the pages that you are holding in your hand, would not exist without my publisher, Brooke Warner. Brooke's experience and industry savvy have given me the opportunity to finally put this story out into the world. She pushed me to dig deeper to share not only the words, but also the insights, challenging me to "rethink possible" whenever my process stalled.

Beyond the professionals and those who have chosen to pursue writing as a career, I am tremendously grateful for Pathfinders For Autism, and for my other founding board member

colleagues Brian Mund, Rick Opfer, Brad Donovan, and especially the leadership and generosity of Polly and BJ Surhoff as
well as our current board members, Bruce Schindler, Mike Ford,
Alisa Rock, Matthew Birkelien, Linda Carter-Ferrier, Megan
DeGroat, John Kamauff, Carin Lazarus, Mike Shelah, Lori
Simpson, and Alicia Wopat who all join me in the belief that a
parent-sponsored organization could be a tremendous resource
for others who were struggling with an autism diagnosis. I did
not realize it at the time but the hard work of founding Pathfinders kept me focused outside of myself and helped quiet the
chaos after paralysis. A special thank you to the extraordinary
Pathfinders for Autism staff: Rebecca Rienzi, Jenn Hobbs, Trish
Kane, Neal Lichter, Shelly Allred, Kim Dennis, Emily Metelski,
and Quinn Lulie whose passion and expertise make them the
first place I call, even now, whenever I need help with managing
my Madison's care. This organization embodies the title of this
book, rethinking possible. You help parents in a very difficult
journey. I am awed and inspired by you daily and deeply honored
to contribute a portion of this book's proceeds to our cause.

I am also beyond grateful for my amazingly dedicated
friends. Thanks to the strong women in my life: my UNC Tarheel
buddies: Joy Ackley, Sharon McGuire, Cynthia Downs, Melinda
Hairfield, Robin Costello, Donna Maitz, and Donna Bunch; and
my Baltimore friends: Beth Behrle, Kim Zaharris, Cindi Mather,
and Skipper Singer, who tolerated this zig-zag writing journey
and my associated moods, yet always fortified me with sincere
interest and dogged encouragement. I am especially grateful for
my childhood friend, Barbara McManus, my steadfast IBM friend
Al Gigliotti, and nanny extraordinaire Pat Lorenz who helped
me live this life and encouraged me to write about it. I could not
have made it through the wildernesses without you and the other
Lorenz-trained caregivers: Krista Hunt, Krista Howell, Sarah
DeFelice, Jamie Novak, and sixty-three others.

We often don't realize what sustains us until we have the

chance to look back and reflect. After completing this book, I've discovered a newfound appreciation for my church families, the loving and ongoing support from Fifth Avenue Baptist Church, my parents' Camelot, and the good people of Huntington, West Virginia who, even now, help me keep my father's words alive through each *Looking Homeward* column. And to my Chestnut Grove Presbyterian Church family, thank you for wrapping your warm and loving arms around me during some of my darkest days after paralysis with visits, meals, and prayers for me—especially when I was too angry to pray for myself.

Finally, I'm grateful to my family who gave me this story. To my parents, who didn't live long enough to hold this book but colored every page with their unyielding optimism, humor, and love, thank you for showing me the value of family and how to live fully despite shattering loss. To my children—Brittany, Matthew, Madison, and Peter—and to Joe, Cindy, and Zander, I am grateful for what each of you has taught me about the expansive capacity of love. Thank you for your unwavering support and for allowing and encouraging me to write our story. I am especially grateful to my sister, Rachel, my sweet sissy, for her willingness to let me relive some of our most painful days as we compared memories and discoveries. Grief is a strange companion, we both learned, especially when you poke it and bring it back to life. I could not have written this book without her opened heart and faithful listening ear.

About the Author

REBECCA FAYE SMITH GALLI (Becky) is an author and columnist who writes about love, loss, and healing. Surviving significant losses—her seventeen-year-old brother's death; her son's degenerative disease and subsequent death; her daughter's autism; her divorce; and nine days later, her paralysis from transverse myelitis, a rare spinal cord inflammation that began as the flu—has fostered an unexpected but prolific writing career. In 2000, *The Baltimore Sun* published her first column about playing soccer with her son—from the wheelchair. 400 published columns later, she launched Thoughtful Thursdays—Lessons from a Resilient Heart, a weekly column that shares what's inspired her to stay positive. She also periodically contributes to

The Baltimore Sun's Op-Ed page, *Midlife Boulevard*, *Nanahood*, and *The Mighty.* Join her Thoughtful Thursdays family at www.beckygalli.com/signup and follow her on Twitter, Facebook, and Instagram at @Chairwriter.

Author photo credit: Rachel Rock Photography

Selected Titles from She Writes Press

She Writes Press is an independent publishing company founded to serve women writers everywhere. Visit us at www.shewritespress.com.

Four Funerals and a Wedding: Resilience in a Time of Grief by Jill Smolowe. $16.95, 978-1-938314-72-8. When journalist Jill Smolowe lost four family members in less than two years, she turned to modern bereavement research for answers—and made some surprising discoveries.

There Was a Fire Here: A Memoir by Risa Nye. $16.95, 978-1-63152-045-7. After a devastating firestorm destroys Risa Nye's Oakland, California home and neighborhood, she has to dig deep to discover her inner strength and resilience.

A Different Kind of Same: A Memoir by Kelley Clink. $16.95, 978-1-63152-999-3. Several years before Kelley Clink's brother hanged himself, she attempted suicide by overdose. In the aftermath of his death, she traces the evolution of both their illnesses, and wonders: If he couldn't make it, what hope is there for her?

Fire Season: A Memoir by Hollye Dexter. $16.95, 978-1-63152-974-0. After she loses everything in a fire, Hollye Dexter's life spirals downward and she begins to unravel—but when she finds herself at the brink of losing her husband, she is forced to dig within herself for the strength to keep her family together.

Secrets in Big Sky Country: A Memoir by Mandy Smith. $16.95, 978-1-63152-814-9. A bold and unvarnished memoir about the shattering consequences of familial sexual abuse—and the strength it takes to overcome them.

Not by Accident: Reconstructing a Careless Life by Samantha Dunn. $16.95, 978-1-63152-832-3. After suffering a nearly fatal riding accident, lifelong klutz Samantha Dunn felt compelled to examine just what it was inside herself—and other people—that invited carelessness and injury.